GCSE
CHEMISTRY

Jane Morris
Head of Science, The Mount School, York

Bell & Hyman

Published by
BELL & HYMAN
an imprint of UNWIN HYMAN LIMITED
Denmark House
37–39 Queen Elizabeth Street
London SE1 2QB

© Jane Morris, 1986
First published by Bell & Hyman 1986
Reprinted 1987

All rights reserved. No part of this publication
may be reproduced, stored in a retrieval system,
or transmitted in any form or by any means,
electronic, mechanical, photocopying, recording
or otherwise, without the prior permission of Bell
& Hyman.

British Library Cataloguing in Publication Data

Morris, Jane *1950* Chemistry: a complete
course for GCSE.
 1. Chemistry
 I. Title
 540 QD33

ISBN 0 7135 2672 6

Book design Geoffrey Wadsley
Drawings RDL Artset Ltd
Cartoons Jane Cope
Cover design Gillian Young
Typeset by MS Filmsetting Limited, Frome, Somerset
Printed and bound in Great Britain
by William Clowes Limited, Beccles and London

Preface

This textbook is written for all those preparing for GCSE or similar chemistry examinations, and includes the core content required by all Examination Board Groups.

GCSE Chemistry seeks to cover thoroughly the groundwork of the subject, but in such a way as to be accessible and enjoyable to a wide range of students. The text has been carefully written to cater for the language level of the less able. It provides a useful knowledge of basic chemistry to those who do not eventually sit the GCSE examination. At the same time, the comprehensive coverage given to chemical principles and calculations will fully prepare more able students for subsequent A-level chemistry courses.

Most pages are highly illustrated with a number of diagrams, cartoons and photographs, many of which were taken specially for this book. The integration of text and illustration presents ideas and facts visually as well as in words. Calculations are approached gently, and with a number of worked examples. Social and environmental issues are discussed throughout the book, and the economic and technological implications of chemistry in the world are also covered.

The sequence followed has been carefully planned to introduce new ideas in a logical way, and to reinforce and develop them at later stages. In its structure, the book seeks to integrate modern insights into teaching chemistry without losing the best of traditional approaches. Thus, after setting chemistry in its everyday context, Chapters 2–7 cover many of the simple ideas and facts used in an introduction to chemistry. Chapters 8–13 deal with some of the central ideas of the subject – states of matter, rates of reaction, atomic structure and bonding, and the mole. Acids, alkalis and salts are covered in Chapter 14. Chapters 15–20 puts the chemistry of a number of elements in the context of the periodic table. Finally, Chapters 21–29 cover a range of processes and products of industrial and economic importance. Processes include those that provide energy and metals; products include organic chemicals, sulphuric acid and fertilisers.

A number of graded questions follow most chapters, including many from various Examination Boards. Questions are classified according to the degree of difficulty, and the predominant skills being tested. A key to how these are marked on each question appears below.

GCSE Chemistry has been written in a simple, open and non-prescriptive style. It also seeks to counteract the impression given in many texts that chemistry is a largely male preserve. Bias has been omitted from the text, and both photographs and illustrations show a balance of men and women. It is hoped that teachers and students alike will use this book as a resource to develop and reinforce the basic principles of chemistry, and to appreciate its relevance in the world outside the classroom.

J.M.

Key to symbols used to classify questions

Level of difficulty   ● fairly easy
                           ■ average
                           ▶ fairly advanced

Main skill needed   **R** recall
                           U understanding
                           H handling ideas and data

Acknowledgements

The author would like to thank David Waddington for help and encouragement during the writing of this book. Thanks also go to Pippa Dennis for her help in typing the manuscript.

Examination Questions

The author and publisher thank the following examination bodies for permission to use selected examination questions at the end of chapters.

NEA	Northern Examining Association (Associated Lancashire Schools Examining Board, Joint Matriculation Board, North Regional Examinations Board, North West Regional Examinations Board, Yorkshire and Humberside Regional Examinations Board)
SEB	Scottish Examination Board
MEG	Midland Examining Group (Oxford and Cambridge Schools Examination Board: Salters' Chemistry Project specimen questions)
SEREB	The South-East Regional Examination Board
WMEB	The West Midlands Examination Board
NREB	North Regional Examinations Board
NWREB	North West Regional Examinations Board

Photo Credits

The author and publisher would like to thank the following for permission to reproduce photographs.

3 top: Shell Photographic Service
9 NASA/USIS
21 left: Charing Cross Hospital Medical School
   centre: National Coal Board
   right: British Oxygen Company
24 upper: Property Services Agency
   lower: Crown Copyright (Controller of Her Majesty's Stationery Office)
25 upper: Associated Press
32 British Aerospace Dynamics Division
33 upper: Associated Press
40 left: Mansell Collection
   lower: Water Authorities Association
41 right: CEGB
   lower: Thames Water Authority
48 top, centre and bottom: RTZ Services
52 British Antarctic Survey
57 left: Kodak (Bruce Gilbert)
   right: Mary Evans Picture Library
64 Shell Photographic Service
72 Shell Photographic Service
83 British Geological Survey
94 upper: British Aerospace Civil Aircraft Division
   lower: CEGB
136 Vitax Limited
138 Radcliffe Infirmary, Oxford (Slade Hospital)
150 left: BIPAC
   lower: ICI Mond Division
154 upper: ICI Mond Division
   lower: Lighting Industry Federation
   right: Pilkington Brothers
155 upper: BP International
   lower: British Geological Survey
   right: Mansell Collection (Alinari)
160 upper: British Geological Survey
   lower: Permutit Company

161 left: Greater London Council (Godfrey New)
164 ARDEA London
165 Imperial War Museum
170 upper left: Scottish Tourist Board
   upper right: Kodak
173 upper left: Goodyear Tyre and Rubber Co
   upper right: BP International
   lower right: Lighting Industry Federation
174 British Geological Survey
176 The British Library
178 upper: Charing Cross Hospital Medical School
   lower right: British Steel Corporation
179 upper centre: B W Pearce & Sons
   upper right: Wednesbury Tube
183 left: De Beers Consolidated Mines
   centre: British Geological Survey
   right: Shell Photographic Service
184 upper left: Eagle Alexander/Solid Fuel Advisory Service
   upper right: Electronics and Wireless World/Ferranti
   lower right: Wednesbury Tube
186 Thorn EMI Fire Appliances
187 Michael W Richards/RSPB
189 Camping Gaz (GB)
193 Charles Tait Photographic
197 upper right: Turbo
201 left: Charing Cross Hospital Medical School
202 top left: Angela Johnston
   top right: Allcord
   centre right: Tower Housewares
203 Part of DNA molecule: Nuffield-Chelsea Curriculum Trust (1970) Nuffield Advanced Science–

Chemistry Overhead Projection Originals. Longman
204 upper right: British Railways Board
   lower left: Trustee Savings Bank
   lower right: Central Office of Information
210 BP International
214 upper left: CEGB
   upper right: CEGB (NE Region)
   lower left: BP International/UKAEA
   lower right: UKAEA Culham Laboratory Photographic Services
215 upper: Documentation Française
   lower: Swedhouse
220 E L Pinder
224 right: British Airways (David Snelling)
230 Pains-Wessex Schermuly
232 ICI Agricultural Division
236 New Zealand High Commission
239 top: Barnaby's Picture Library
   bottom: ICI Mond Division
242 ICI Agricultural Division
243 Mary Evans Picture Library
246 ICI Agricultural Division
247 left: ICI Plant Protection Division
   upper right: Intervention Board for Agricultural Produce
   lower right: Oxfam
250 Mansell Collection
253 UKAEA
254 CEGB/UKAEA
255 left: Medical Illustration, St Bartholomew's Hospital
   right: Associated Press

Back cover: computer graphic image showing part of the molecular structure of a fungicide; ICI Pharmaceuticals Division

Contents

1	Chemistry in Today's World	2
2	Elements, Compounds and Mixtures	4
3	Chemical Shorthand	12
4	Gases in the Air	18
5	Metals and Non-metals	28
6	Hydrogen and Water	31
7	Competition among Metals	44
8	Solids, Liquids and Gases	52
9	Rates of Reaction	64
10	Atomic Structure	76
11	Ionic and Covalent Bonding	80
12	The Mole	100
13	Chemical Equations	122
14	Acids, Alkalis and Salts	132
15	Introduction to the Periodic Table	146
16	Group I and II Metals	150
17	Group VII Elements: the Halogens	164
18	Group VIII Elements: the Noble Gases	172
19	The Transition Metals	174
20	Group IV Elements	182
21	Organic Chemistry	186
22	Everyday Organic Chemicals	196
23	Energy	204
24	Electrolysis	218
25	Electricity from Chemical Reactions	228
26	Reversible Reactions	230
27	Sulphur and Sulphuric Acid	236
28	Ammonia, Fertilisers and Food	242
29	Radioactivity	250

Answers to Questions involving Calculations	258
Hazard Warning Symbols	259
The Periodic Table of the Elements	260
Properties of the Elements in Alphabetical Order	262
Chemical Words	264
Index	266

1 Chemistry in Today's World

Today's world without chemists working 'behind the scenes' would be a very different place.

Chemists ensure that foods we eat are safe and wholesome. The raw materials in your breakfast foods are tested by chemists to analyse the nutrients in them.

You may need to take a medicine when you are ill, and this has been prepared and studied by a chemist called a pharmacologist.

The plastics that are used to make pens and rulers, bowls and buckets and thousands of other everyday objects, have been invented and made with the help of chemists.

1 Chemistry in Today's World

There would be no petrol to run cars, motor bikes and other vehicles, unless chemists had helped make the petrol from crude oil.

Our houses would be very dull without the help of the chemists who make a range of coloured dyes for paints, wallpapers, fabrics and crockery.

You couldn't be sure some of your clothes wouldn't dissolve when you washed them, unless chemists had helped in making the fabric and the washing powder.

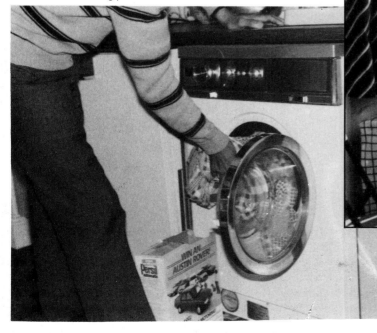

Chemists are 'behind the scenes' in almost every area of our life. Chemists look at the substances that surround us in the world. They try to understand how and why they behave as they do.

2 Elements, Compounds and Mixtures

Examples of some common elements

Name	Symbol	Description
Aluminium	Al	lightweight shiny metal

Bromine	Br	dense brown liquid

Carbon	C	black solid found in coal

Iron	Fe	dense strong metal

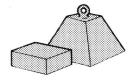

Oxygen	O	colourless gas found in the air

Lead	Pb	very dense grey metal

Chemistry involves finding out about the substances that make up the world around us. Every substance we know about is made from **atoms**. All living things – plants, animals and even you yourself – are made from atoms. All 'dead' things such as rocks, soil, water and air are also made from atoms.

What are atoms?

If you were very rich, and had a gold coin to spare, you might cut it in half. If you cut the half in half, and could go on cutting each piece in half, eventually you could go no further. You would have an atom of gold. An **atom** is the smallest particle that can be obtained by chemical means. Atoms are smaller than you can imagine. The ink in the full stop at the end of this sentence contains many millions of carbon atoms. Scientists have built machines that can split atoms into even smaller particles. Chemists do not usually study these particles.

At present, chemists know about 105 different sorts of atom. These make up the chemical elements. Carbon is an element because it contains only carbon atoms. Gold is an element because it contains only gold atoms. An **element** is a substance made of only one sort of atom. It cannot be broken down into simpler substances by chemical means. Each element is given a **symbol**. This is a kind of chemical shorthand to represent an atom of that element. Most symbols are similar to the name of the element. Eleven elements have symbols based on their old Latin or Greek names. Iron used to be called *ferrum* and it still has the symbol Fe. Lead used to be called *plumbum* and has the symbol Pb. When you next get a visit from the plumber, remember that the name came from fixing lead water pipes.

A glass of water contains an enormous number of atoms. Suppose the atoms in this glass of water could be shared out between all the people in the world today. If every person counted the atoms at the rate of 100 atoms a minute, it would take 82 million years to finish counting!

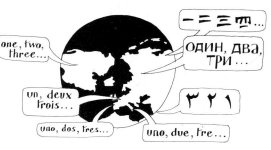

You yourself are made from about ten main elements. If the elements in your body could all be separated out from each other, you would have a list of elements that would form a 'Person' Recipe.

> **A 'PERSON' RECIPE**
>
> A person weighing 50 kg (just under 8 stone) could be split up into:
>
> | Element | Description |
> |---:|---|
> | 60 000 litres **hydrogen** | explosive colourless gas |
> | 24 000 litres **oxygen** | colourless gas found in the air |
> | 1300 litres **nitrogen** | unreactive colourless gas found in the air |
> | 25 litres **chlorine** | poisonous green gas |
> | 9 kg **carbon** | black solid in charcoal and coal |
> | 1 kg **calcium** | shiny reactive metal |
> | 500 g **phosphorus** | waxy white solid – burns easily in air |
> | 200 g **potassium** | dangerous soft metal – catches fire on contact with water |
> | 150 g **sulphur** | yellow solid – burns with blue flame giving poisonous fumes |
> | 75 g **sodium** | soft metal – reacts with water giving hydrogen |

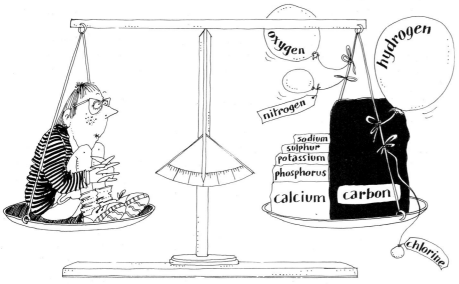

A person weighing 50 kg could be split up to make many elements.

Mixtures

When roads are icy in winter, **rock salt** is often spread. This is mined straight from the ground, and is a mixture of salt and sandy grit. The salt helps melt the ice, and the grit gives a grip to the road surface. The salt and sand are **a mixture**, and are quite easily separated. Salt dissolves in water and sand does not. They can be separated in the following way.

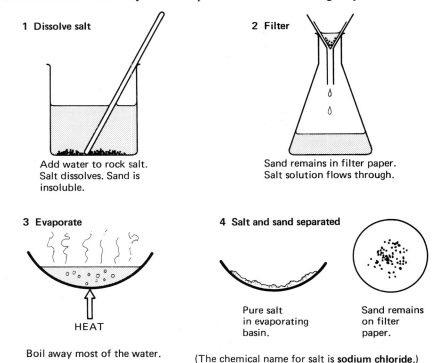

(The chemical name for salt is **sodium chloride**.)

The two substances have been separated because one is soluble in water and the other is not. Solubility is called a **physical property**. Other examples of physical properties are boiling point, melting point and density. **A mixture** can be separated easily using differences in physical properties.

When iron filings and powdered sulphur are stirred together, they form a mixture. One way of separating these is to use a magnet. Iron has the physical property of being magnetic.

Separating an iron and sulphur mixture

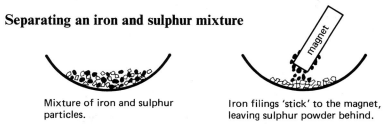

The ink you use in a fountain pen is a blue dye dissolved in water. Even a solution like this is still a mixture of water and the dye. This mixture is too fine to be separated by filtering. The filter paper is not a fine enough 'sieve'. When the ink is boiled, only the water evaporates, leaving the dye behind. The water vapour can be cooled in a condenser and collected. This process is called **simple distillation**.

2 Elements, Compounds and Mixtures

Simple distillation of ink

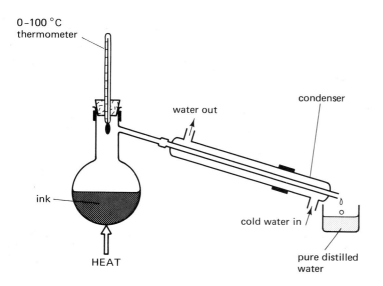

Ink is a mixture of a dye dissolved in water. Before distillation, the ink particles and water look like this:

Before distillation

After distillation

Pure water is distilled off.

Ink remains in flask.

water particle

ink particle

Fractional distillation of crude oil

Crude oil is a mixture of various liquids. Each liquid has a different boiling point. This difference in properties can be used to separate the mixture into 'fractions'. Each fraction contains liquids with similar boiling points. The process of separation is called **fractional distillation**. This involves boiling and condensing the liquid mixture many times in a **fractionating column**:

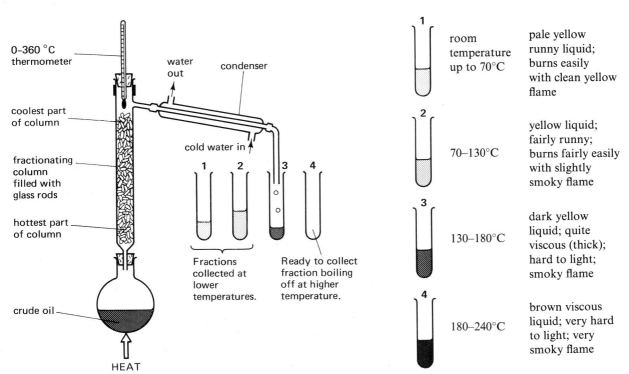

Liquid distils at: *Description*

1. room temperature up to 70°C — pale yellow runny liquid; burns easily with clean yellow flame

2. 70–130°C — yellow liquid; fairly runny; burns fairly easily with slightly smoky flame

3. 130–180°C — dark yellow liquid; quite viscous (thick); hard to light; smoky flame

4. 180–240°C — brown viscous liquid; very hard to light; very smoky flame

Chromatography

The ink in a black felt-tip pen is usually a mixture of coloured dyes. These can be separated by **chromatography**. A spot of the ink is absorbed onto some chromatography paper. The paper is stood in some ethanol, or other suitable liquid. As the ethanol rises up the paper, it dissolves the dyes and 'pulls' them up the paper. Each dye is pulled a different distance up the paper. A dye that is strongly absorbed onto the paper and is not very soluble in the ethanol hardly moves at all. Another dye that has not been strongly absorbed by the paper and is very soluble in the ethanol will travel further up the paper.

Chromatography used to investigate black ink

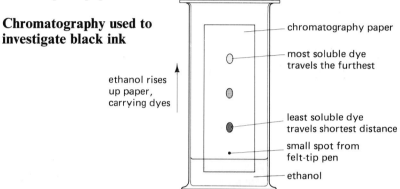

Separating a mixture of iodine and sodium chloride

A mixture of iodine and sodium chloride (common salt) can be separated by gentle heat. When iodine is gently warmed it melts to form a dark liquid, which quickly turns to a purple gas. When iodine vapour is cooled it turns straight from a gas to a solid. When a gas turns straight into a solid, or a solid turns into a gas, without forming a liquid 'in between', this process is called **sublimation**. Gentle warming has no effect on sodium chloride because it does not even melt until it is heated to 801°C. This difference in physical properties can be used to separate the mixture.

Separating a mixture of iodine and sodium chloride

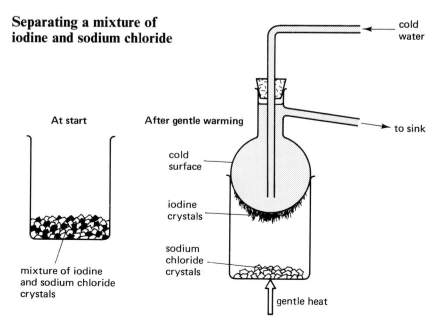

2 Elements, Compounds and Mixtures

Compounds

When iron and sulphur are mixed and heated together, you can see several changes. The mixture glows red-hot and then turns into a dull grey solid. A **chemical reaction** has taken place between the iron and sulphur. They are now chemically joined together. The grey solid is called iron sulphide. Iron sulphide is a compound of iron and sulphur. A **compound** contains two or more elements chemically joined together. It can only be broken down into its elements by using more chemical reactions.

The reaction between iron and sulphur

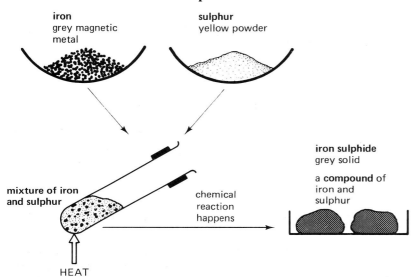

Another example of a compound being formed is when hydrogen and oxygen react together to make water.

The reaction between hydrogen and oxygen

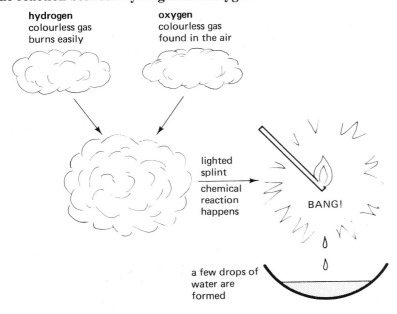

The reaction between hydrogen and oxygen is used to launch this space shuttle.

If you were small enough to see the atoms in the reaction between hydrogen and oxygen, they would look like this:

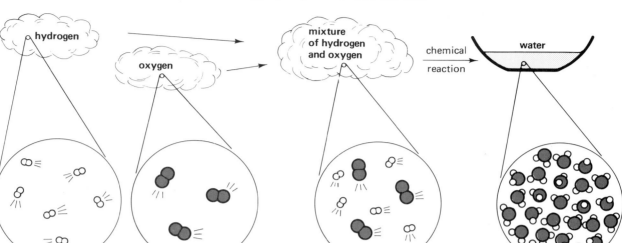

Water is a compound of hydrogen and oxygen. A compound can be very different from the elements from which it is made. Hydrogen is a colourless explosive gas. When it is chemically joined to oxygen, the compound water is produced. Water is not a mixture of these two gases, but a new substance. As you know, water is very common and is necessary for all living things.

Your own body is made from many different compounds. If you look back at the 'Person' Recipe at the beginning of this chapter, it is obvious that you cannot just be a mixture of all these elements! A large part of you is made from water – a compound of hydrogen and oxygen. Another compound in your body is fat. Fat contains carbon, hydrogen and oxygen, all chemically joined together.

Summary

1 **Atoms** are the smallest particles obtained by chemical means.

2 **Elements** are substances made from only one sort of atom. They cannot be broken down into simpler substances by chemical means.

3 Each element has a **symbol** to represent it, for example:
carbon = C   oxygen = O   iron = Fe

4 **Mixtures** can be easily separated, using differences in physical properties, for example solubility, magnetism, boiling point, absorption.

5 **Compounds** contain two or more elements, chemically joined together. The properties of a compound are often very different from those of its elements.

2 Elements, Compounds and Mixtures

Questions

1 ● (a) What is an atom? (b) What is an element? (c) Give examples of three elements and their symbols. **R**

2 ● Some sawdust has been accidentally dropped into a bowl of sugar. Explain how you could separate out this mixture and get samples of pure dry sawdust and sugar. (Remember that sugar 'burns' if it is heated to dry it.) **U**

3 ● You are given a mixture of the following liquids:

Liquid	Boiling point/°C
Methanol	64
Ethanol	78
Propan–1–ol	98
Butan–1–ol	118

Describe an experiment you could do to separate this mixture back into the four original liquids. Draw a diagram of the apparatus you would use. Which of these liquids would be (a) the first to be collected, (b) the last to be collected?
Give a reason for your choices. **H**

4 ● You are asked to investigate the coloured dyes present in a tube of Smarties. Suggest an experiment you could do to find out whether the dye used in brown Smarties is a single substance or a mixture of different dyes. **U**

5 ● (a) What is a compound?
(b) What is the difference between a compound and a mixture?
(c) Give an example of a compound and say how it is formed from its elements. **R**

6 ● Four common elements in the Earth's crust are:
aluminium (8% by weight)
iron (5% by weight)
oxygen (50% by weight)
silicon (25% by weight)

(a) Put the elements in order of abundance into the table, with the most common first and the least common last.

Element	
1	most common
2	
3	
4	least common

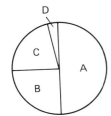

(b) Look at the pie chart. It shows the proportions by weight of some of the elements in the Earth's crust. Answer the questions which follow it.
(i) The oxygen is represented by the letter —.
(ii) The letter B represents ——. (SEB) **H**

7 ■ The following diagram represents an apparatus used to distil salt water.

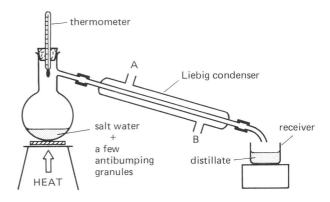

(a) State why the bulb of the thermometer should be placed just opposite the outlet to the condenser.
(b) State whether the water enters the condenser at A or B, and explain why.
(c) Explain the reason for the presence of the antibumping granules.
(d) State how you would know that the distillate was **pure** water.
(e) Why is it **not** possible to remove the salt from the water by simply filtering the solution? (NEA) **U**

8 ■ Paper chromatography can be used to investigate the dyes used in food colourings. The results of an experiment are shown below:

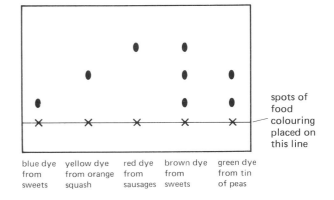

blue dye from sweets | yellow dye from orange squash | red dye from sausages | brown dye from sweets | green dye from tin of peas

(a) Which food colourings are made of only one coloured dye?
(b) How could you make the green dye?
(c) How could you make the brown dye?
(d) Suggest one reason why manufacturers add colouring to foods. **U**

3 Chemical Shorthand

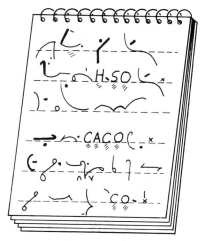

'Shorthand' is a quick and easy way to write down words. Once 'chemical shorthand' is understood, this too can be a quick and easy way to describe a reaction.

Elements and symbols

A secretary sometimes writes a letter in shorthand. The symbols used represent different letters and sounds. They provide a quick and easy way of writing something down. A chemist does not always have to write down a long description of a chemical reaction. 'Chemical shorthand' can often be used instead. This too, is a quick and easy way of describing a reaction.

A 'shorthand' way of writing down an element is to use its **symbol**. All 105 elements have their own symbol, which may be one or two letters. Remember that a few elements have unusual symbols. The symbol for lead, for example, is Pb.

Elements are sometimes listed in alphabetical order. There is an alphabetical list of elements at the back of this book. You will often see elements arranged in a table displayed in a chemistry laboratory. Its full name is the **periodic table of elements.**

Part of the periodic table is printed here. See how many of the elements you recognise. Notice that metals are on the left and bottom of the table. Non-metals are at the top right hand side of the table. They are divided by a 'staircase' that runs across the table. The periodic table is discussed in more detail in Chapter 15.

The periodic table of elements

key	atomic number / name / symbol

3 lithium Li	4 beryllium Be				METALS							5 boron B	6 carbon C	7 nitrogen N	8 oxygen O	9 fluorine F	10 neon Ne
11 sodium Na	12 magnesium Mg											13 aluminium Al	14 silicon Si	15 phosphorus P	16 sulphur S	17 chlorine Cl	18 argon Ar
19 potassium K	20 calcium Ca	21 scandium Sc	22 titanium Ti	23 vanadium V	24 chromium Cr	25 manganese Mn	26 iron Fe	27 cobalt Co	28 nickel Ni	29 copper Cu	30 zinc Zn	31 gallium Ga	32 germanium Ge	33 arsenic As	34 selenium Se	35 bromine Br	36 krypton Kr
37 rubidium Rb	38 strontium Sr	39 yttrium Y	40 zirconium Zr	41 niobium Nb	42 molybdenum Mo	43 technetium Tc	44 ruthenium Ru	45 rhodium Rh	46 palladium Pd	47 silver Ag	48 cadmium Cd	49 indium In	50 tin Sn	51 antimony Sb	52 tellurium Te	53 iodine I	54 xenon Xe
55 caesium Cs	56 barium Ba	57 lanthanum La	72 hafnium Hf	73 tantalum Ta	74 tungsten W	75 rhenium Re	76 osmium Os	77 iridium Ir	78 platinum Pt	79 gold Au	80 mercury Hg	81 thallium Tl	82 lead Pb	83 bismuth Bi	84 polonium Po	85 astatine At	86 radon Rn

(NON-METALS: 2 helium He)

Compounds and formulae

When two or more elements join together chemically, a **compound** is formed. The 'shorthand' way of writing a compound is to use its **formula**. Water, for example, is a compound of hydrogen and oxygen. The formula of water is H_2O. The formula of a compound shows two useful things:

which elements are present shown by their symbols.

how much of each element is present.

The H and the O show that water contains the elements hydrogen and oxygen, chemically joined together.

The figure 2 shows that there are twice as many hydrogen atoms as oxygen atoms in water

In water, the hydrogen and oxygen atoms are arranged like this:

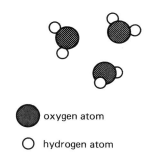

● oxygen atom

○ hydrogen atom

Another way of writing the formula of water might be like this:

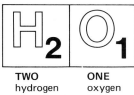 or

TWO hydrogen atoms — ONE oxygen atom

The small number after each symbol shows how many atoms of that element are present. The number 1 is always missed out in a formula. Where there is no small number written after a symbol, imagine a '1'.

Another compound is iron sulphide. Its formula is **FeS**. There are no small numbers at all in this formula so imagine iron sulphide to be like this:

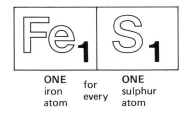

ONE iron atom — for every — ONE sulphur atom

Ammonia has the formula NH_3. The nitrogen and hydrogen atoms in ammonia are arranged like this:

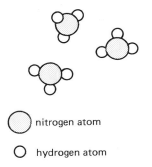

○ nitrogen atom

○ hydrogen atom

The plural of the word formula is the Latin word *formulae*. The table below shows the formulae of some common compounds.

Formulae of some common compounds

Name	Formula	Each compound contains:
Ammonia	NH_3	**one** nitrogen atom for every **three** hydrogen atoms
Carbon dioxide	CO_2	**one** carbon atom for every **two** oxygen atoms
Iron oxide	Fe_2O_3	**two** iron atoms for every **three** oxygen atoms
Sodium chloride	NaCl	**one** sodium atom for every **one** chlorine atom
Sulphuric acid	H_2SO_4	**two** hydrogen atoms for every **one** sulphur atom for every **four** oxygen atoms

3 Chemical Shorthand

Molecules

Most atoms prefer company! They often join together in groups to make molecules. A **molecule** contains two or more atoms chemically joined together. A hydrogen molecule contains two hydrogen atoms chemically joined together.

Molecules come in a great variety of shapes and sizes. The smallest molecules contain only two atoms, and are called diatomic molecules.

chlorine Cl_2 — Chlorine is a diatomic molecule.

Molecules in living things may contain many thousands of atoms joined together.

A hydrogen molecule

two hydrogen atoms joined together

written: H_2 — this small 2 means a hydrogen molecule contains two hydrogen atoms

Molecules can be:

Elements		or	Compounds	
Hydrogen	H_2		Carbon dioxide	CO_2
Nitrogen	N_2		Water	H_2O
Oxygen	O_2		Hydrogen chloride	HCl

Chemical reactions and equations

When elements react together to form a compound, a **chemical reaction** has happened. It is often possible to tell when a chemical reaction happens by observing various changes.

Evidence to show when a chemical reaction is happening

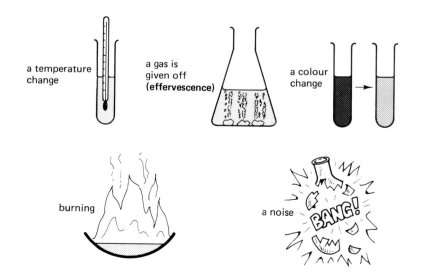

a temperature change

a gas is given off (**effervescence**)

a colour change

burning

a noise

3 Chemical Shorthand

When a chemical reaction happens, the substances that react together are always chemically changed, and new substances are formed.

The 'shorthand' way of describing a chemical reaction is to write an **equation**. Here is an equation for the reaction between iron and sulphur:

Word equation	iron	+	sulphur	→	iron sulphide
Symbol equation	Fe	+	S	→	FeS
	element	+	element	→	compound

Chemical reactions do not only involve elements reacting together. Compounds can react too. Sulphuric acid and copper oxide are two compounds that react together:

Word equation	sulphuric acid	+	copper oxide	→	copper sulphate	+	water
Symbol equation	H_2SO_4	+	CuO	→	$CuSO_4$	+	H_2O

Carbon burns in air to form carbon dioxide. This is a chemical reaction between carbon and the oxygen in the air:

Word equation	carbon	+	oxygen	→	carbon dioxide
Symbol equation	C	+	O_2	→	CO_2
Meaning	one carbon atom	reacts with	one oxygen molecule	to give	one carbon dioxide molecule

When hydrogen burns in air to form water, the following reaction takes place:

Word equation	hydrogen	+	oxygen	→	water
Symbol equation	$2H_2$	+	O_2	→	$2H_2O$
Meaning	two hydrogen molecules	react with	one oxygen molecule	to give	two water molecules

There is more useful information about writing chemical equations in Chapter 13.

How many molecules are reacting?

In an equation, when more than one particle is reacting, this is shown by a large number written before the symbol or formula:

one oxygen molecule   two oxygen molecules

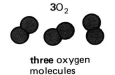

three oxygen molecules

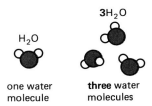

one water molecule   three water molecules

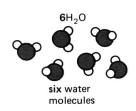

six water molecules

Note that when an equation shows one water molecule reacting, it does not show $1H_2O$. If there is no number before a formula, it means only one of those particles is involved.

3 Chemical Shorthand

State symbols

Another useful chemical shorthand included in some equations is the **state symbol**. There are four state symbols, and they show whether a substance is a solid (s), liquid (l), gas (g) or is dissolved in water (aq). The state symbol is written in brackets after each substance shown in the equation.

The four state symbols

Symbol	Meaning
s	solid
l	liquid
g	gas
aq	aqueous solution, i.e. dissolved in water

Here are some of the equations already described, showing state symbols.

Burning carbon in air:

Symbol equation $C(s) + O_2(g) \rightarrow CO_2(g)$

Meaning: carbon is a solid; oxygen is a gas; carbon dioxide is a gas

Reacting sulphuric acid with copper oxide:

Symbol equation $H_2SO_4(aq) + CuO(s) \rightarrow CuSO_4(aq) + H_2O(l)$

Meaning: the sulphuric acid is dissolved in water – it is dilute acid; copper oxide is a solid; copper sulphate is dissolved in water; water is a liquid

When a substance is dissolved in water the symbol (aq) is used. For example:

$$H_2SO_4(aq) \quad CuSO_4(aq)$$

When water itself is actually part of the chemical reaction, the symbol $H_2O(l)$ is used. '$H_2O(aq)$' is *never* used.

Reactants and products

The **reactants** in any chemical equation are the substances at the start of the reaction. They are shown on the left-hand side of the equation. The **products** are the substances formed at the end of the reaction. They are shown on the right-hand side of the equation.

$$\underbrace{H_2SO_4(aq) + CuO(s)}_{\textbf{reactants}} \rightarrow \underbrace{CuSO_4(aq) + H_2O(l)}_{\textbf{products}}$$

reactants are the substances reacting together at the start

products are the new substances formed

3 Chemical Shorthand

Summary

1. An element is represented by its **symbol**. For example:
   hydrogen H; iron Fe

2. Elements are classified in the **periodic table**.

3. A compound is represented by its **formula**. A formula shows which elements are present in a compound. It also shows the various proportions of each element present.

4. A chemical reaction is represented by an **equation**. Equations may be in words or symbols:

Word equation	sulphur	+	oxygen	→	sulphur dioxide
Symbol equation	S	+	O_2	→	SO_2

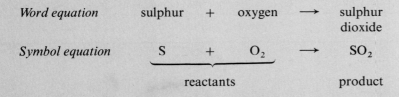

   reactants   product

5. The **state symbol** shows whether a substance is:
   - solid   (s)
   - liquid   (l)
   - gas   (g)
   - aqueous solution   (aq)

   Equation using state symbols $S(s) + O_2(g) \rightarrow SO_2(g)$

Questions

1. ● Study the periodic table on page 147. Write two tables showing the names and symbols of five metals and five non-metals. Under each table say whether you have found these elements on the right or the left hand side of the periodic table. **R**

2. ●(a) What is a chemical reaction?
   (b) List *three* observations you might make when a chemical reaction was happening.
   (c) Write word and symbol equations for two chemical reactions. Include state symbols. Show which are reactants and which products. **R**

3. ● What is a formula, and what does it tell you about a compound? Describe carefully what information each of these formulae tell you about the compound:

Compound	Formula
Silicon dioxide	SiO_2
Potassium iodide	KI
Sodium sulphide	Na_2S
Calcium carbonate	$CaCO_3$

   R

4 Gases in the Air

Every time you breathe in, about half a litre of air passes into your lungs. Every day, you breathe about 15 000 litres of air. Without air to breathe, you would be dead in minutes. We all take the air around us for granted! Air itself is a mixture of a number of gases.

Gases in the air

Gas	Formula	Model	% by volume in air
Nitrogen	N_2		78
Oxygen	O_2		20
Argon	Ar		1
Carbon dioxide	CO_2		0.03
Water vapour	H_2O		varies between 0.5–4
Sulphur dioxide	SO_2		traces occur in air in towns

Mixtures can easily be separated, using the physical properties of the substances involved. Air can be separated into the different gases it contains by **fractional distillation**. At room temperature, air is a mixture of gases. If air is cooled to about −200 °C, it condenses and forms a liquid. This would be the everyday temperature if you lived on the planet Neptune! Life as we know it is impossible on the outer planets. Nearly all the gases have condensed to form liquids or have frozen into solids.

Fractional distillation of liquid air

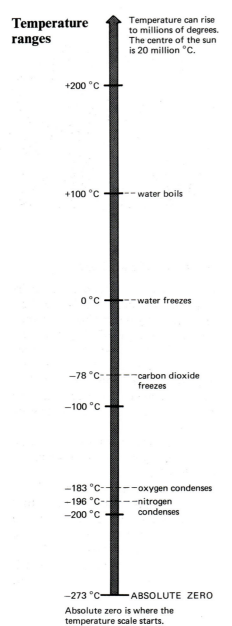

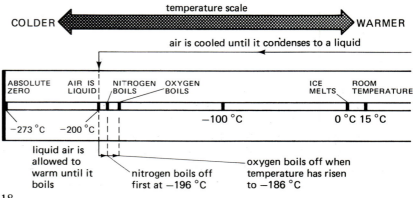

When very cold liquid air is boiled, it behaves like any other mixture of liquids. As the temperature is allowed to rise slowly, the various gases in the mixture boil off, one by one, by fractional distillation.

Nitrogen

Nitrogen makes up 78% of the air – so there is a lot of it around! The main thing to know about nitrogen is that it hardly reacts with anything. It is said to be **unreactive**.

Structure of nitrogen

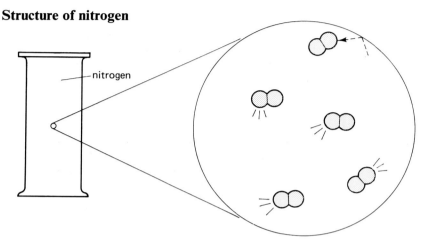

Nitrogen gas contains small, separate diatomic molecules. Formula: N_2

Properties of nitrogen

Physical properties   Colourless gas. Same density as air. No smell.

Chemical properties

Indicator	Does it burn?	Calcium hydroxide solution (limewater)
pH 7 (neutral)	Lighted splint put out	No effect

Nitrogen from the air can be made to react under extreme conditions. In the Haber process it is reacted with hydrogen gas to make ammonia. Very high pressure and a moderate temperature are needed before ammonia starts to form. Ammonia is useful to make fertilisers (see Chapter 28).

Properties of chemicals

Suppose you are asked to describe what one of your friends is like. You might start by describing what they looked like – how tall they were, the colour of their eyes and hair, whether they were fat or thin. You might then go on to say what sort of person they were – whether they were calm or excitable, whether they had a sense of humour.

In a similar way when you describe a chemical, you list its **properties** – what it is like.

Physical properties describe what a substance looks like, and other measurements that could be made like density, melting point, smell, etc.

Chemical properties describe how a substance reacts chemically – which substances it reacts with, and what happens.

Oxygen

Oxygen makes up about one fifth of the air. It is the important part of air that all animals need to breathe.

Where is oxygen found?

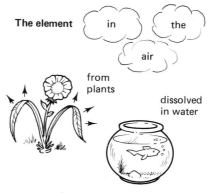

One fifth of the air is oxygen.
All plants and animals need oxygen for respiration.
Green plants produce oxygen in **photosynthesis**.
Fish need oxygen dissolved in water for **respiration**.

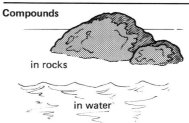

One half of the earth's crust is made from oxygen chemically joined to other elements.
For example, sand is mainly silicon dioxide, SiO_2.
89% by mass of water is oxygen, chemically joined to hydrogen.

Making oxygen in the laboratory

Getting pure oxygen from the air is difficult and expensive. In the laboratory, it is easier to use a simple chemical reaction which produces oxygen. A solution of **hydrogen peroxide** can be used to make oxygen. (It is also used to bleach hair.) This solution breaks down quite easily into water and oxygen. When a compound breaks down into smaller, simpler substances, it is said to **decompose**. A small amount of manganese dioxide powder is added as a catalyst, to help the reaction go faster. Catalysts are explained in more detail in Chapter 9.

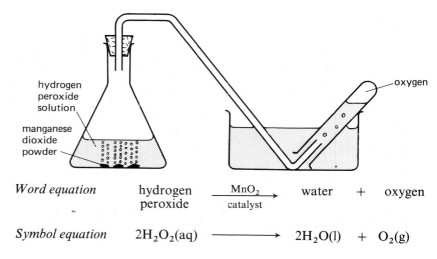

Word equation   hydrogen peroxide $\xrightarrow{\text{MnO}_2 \text{ catalyst}}$ water + oxygen

Symbol equation $2H_2O_2(aq) \longrightarrow 2H_2O(l) + O_2(g)$

4 Gases in the Air

Structure of oxygen

Oxygen gas contains small, separate diatomic molecules. Formula: **O₂**

Properties of oxygen

Physical properties   Colourless gas. No smell. Same density as air.

Chemical properties   Oxygen is very reactive. Any substance that burns in air will burn very brightly in oxygen.

Glowing splint	Metals	Non-metals
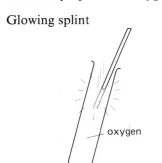	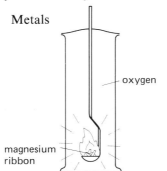	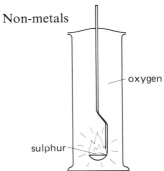
Relights and burns brightly.	Burns brilliantly – white ash of magnesium oxide is formed: $$2Mg(s) + O_2(g) \longrightarrow 2MgO(s)$$	Burns with bright blue flame; colourless choking acid gas – sulphur dioxide – is formed: $$S(s) + O_2(g) \longrightarrow SO_2(g)$$

Uses of oxygen

In medicine	To help breathing	In welding
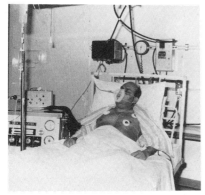		
A patient who is very ill or has a chest illness is helped by breathing oxygen.	This miner in rescue kit carries a cylinder of oxygen to breathe when there is very little oxygen in the air.	Hydrogen, or ethyne (acetylene), can be burned with oxygen to produce the very high temperatures used in welding.

4 Gases in the Air

Carbon dioxide

Where is carbon dioxide found?

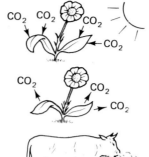

PLANTS
Plants take in carbon dioxide during photosynthesis.

Plants give out carbon dioxide during respiration.

ANIMALS
Animals breathe out carbon dioxide.

BURNING FUELS
Carbon dioxide is one of the products when coal, natural gas and other fuels are burned. The fuel burned in the last 200 years has made the amount of carbon dioxide in the air rise measurably. Some scientists think this may affect the world's weather.

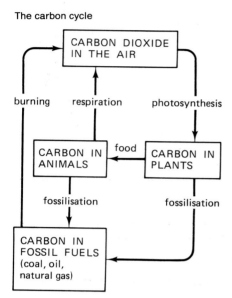

The carbon cycle

Making carbon dioxide in the laboratory

Carbon dioxide is made in the laboratory by reacting calcium carbonate with dilute hydrochloric acid:

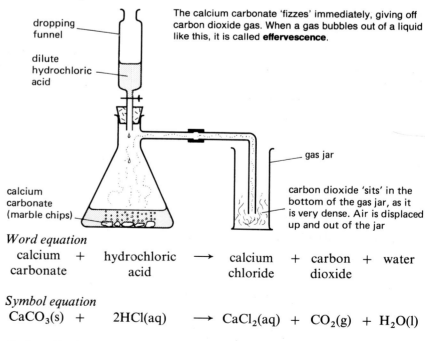

Word equation
calcium carbonate + hydrochloric acid → calcium chloride + carbon dioxide + water

Symbol equation
$$CaCO_3(s) + 2HCl(aq) \rightarrow CaCl_2(aq) + CO_2(g) + H_2O(l)$$

Carbon dioxide can be made by the action of other acids on carbonates. An exception to this is the reaction of dilute sulphuric acid with calcium carbonate. The reaction quickly stops, as insoluble calcium sulphate is formed. This stops the acid reacting with any more calcium carbonate.

4 Gases in the Air

Structure of carbon dioxide

Carbon dioxide gas contains small, separate triatomic molecules. Formula: CO_2

A precipitation reaction

When a solid is formed during a reaction in an aqueous solution, it is called a **precipitate**. Calcium hydroxide solution (limewater) going cloudy is an example of a **precipitation reaction**.

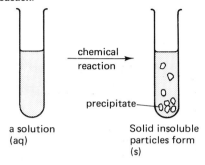

a solution (aq) → Solid insoluble particles form (s)

Properties of carbon dioxide

Physical properties   Colourless gas. More dense than air. Very slight 'sharp' smell.

Chemical properties   Calcium hydroxide (limewater)

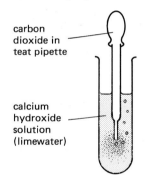

Calcium hydroxide solution (limewater) turns cloudy: small particles of calcium carbonate are formed.

Word equation calcium hydroxide + carbon dioxide → calcium carbonate + water

Symbol equation $Ca(OH)_2(aq) + CO_2(g) \rightarrow CaCO_3(s) + H_2O(l)$

Lighted splint

Carbon dioxide puts out a lighted splint. When a gas does not allow something to burn in it, the gas 'does not support combustion'.

Uses of carbon dioxide

Fizzy drinks

Fizzy drinks contain carbon dioxide dissolved in water under pressure.

Fire extinguishers

Dry ice

Dry ice is solid carbon dioxide. It is used to keep things cool. It is unusual as it turns straight from a solid to a gas – it sublimes.

Special effects

Clouds of carbon dioxide are specially made from dry ice to produce the 'fog' used in plays and discos.

4 Gases in the Air

Many old buildings were covered in soot produced from burning coal. Now the air is cleaner, it is worthwhile washing down the buildings to restore them.

Argon

Only 1% of the air is argon. This can be separated out during fractional distillation. Argon is very unreactive. It is used to fill light bulbs. Although the metal filament glows white hot, it does not react with argon.

Structure of argon

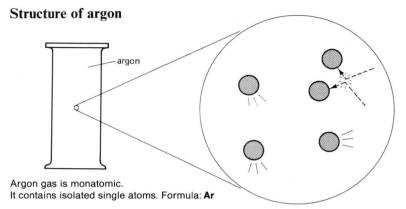

Argon gas is monatomic.
It contains isolated single atoms. Formula: **Ar**

Pollution of the air

Man has always polluted the air with fires. The first 'clean air' act was passed in England in 1273! The problem has become much more serious today as large factories burn millions of tonnes of fuel each year.

Fifty years ago nearly everyone burned coal to heat their houses. Coal was the main fuel in factories too. The fires were inefficient and produced a lot of smoke. Smoke contains a lot of small particles of carbon. This made the air very dirty, and buildings became blackened. Many countries have passed laws against producing too much smoke. As a result, the air in many cities has got much cleaner. It is possible to burn fuels in such a way that very little smoke is produced. When a good supply of oxygen from the air is provided, the fuel burns cleanly and efficiently, with no smoke.

Smoke is not the only substance that pollutes the air when fuels burn. Various unpleasant gases may be formed. When rain falls through the air, these gases dissolve into the rainwater, causing it to be polluted. Your rainwater may not be as pure as you think!

Dissolved gases in rainwater

Gas	Source	Effect
Carbon dioxide	Naturally present in air. Produced by burning fuel.	Forms dilute carbonic acid in rainwater.
Sulphur dioxide	Coal and oil contain sulphur. When burned, sulphur dioxide is formed.	Forms dilute sulphuric acid in rainwater.
Nitrogen dioxide	Formed when fuels burn.	Forms a mixture of dilute nitrous and nitric acids in rainwater.

Increased acidity of rainwater in the last 150 years has rapidly eroded stonework like this. As much erosion takes place in ten years today as used to take place in 200 years.

Rain falling near large industrial towns is sometimes called 'acid rain'. Acid rain can erode away the stonework on some buildings. It is also thought to affect the growth of crops and trees.

In cities where there is a lot of traffic, the exhausts from cars and lorries can pollute the air. Old cars and lorries with worn-out engines can produce unpleasant smoke. All vehicles produce **carbon monoxide** in their exhausts (formula CO). This is a very poisonous gas. Carbon monoxide combines with haemoglobin in the blood. This prevents enough oxygen from getting to the body and brain. The carbon monoxide forms a very bright red substance called carboxyhaemoglobin. Someone being poisoned by this gas will turn bright red!

Petrol often has **lead compounds** added to it. These make it cheaper and easier to burn. When the petrol burns in the engine, lead compounds are released in the exhaust. Where there is heavy traffic, there can be a lot of lead compounds in the air. Breathing in these lead compounds can be especially harmful to young children. The lead can cause brain damage.

Cars can run on lead-free petrol. The petrol is a little more expensive to make, and cars have to be adapted to run on the different petrol. Many countries have passed laws to reduce or ban the lead content of petrol.

Another gas in the air that has caused concern comes from **aerosol sprays**. In an aerosol, the hairspray, polish, deodorant or other liquid is forced out of the container under pressure. The gas most commonly used is called a 'freon'. It has the formula CF_2Cl_2. Large amounts of freons have been released into the air by the use of aerosol sprays. They eventually reach the **ozone layer** high up in the atmosphere. Molecules of ozone, O_3, contain three atoms of oxygen. The ozone layer protects the earth from the harmful ultra-violet rays of the sun. The freons are thought to be breaking down this layer. If too many ultra-violet rays reach the earth, they can lead to harmful effects such as skin cancer.

This Japanese policeman is measuring the amount of carbon monoxide in a vehicle's exhaust.

Aerosol sprays contain gases called freons. They are thought to break down the ozone layer of the earth's atmosphere.

Summary

1 Air is a mixture of gases. The main gases are:
nitrogen 78%
oxygen 20%

2 Air can be separated into a number of gases. It is liquefied and **fractionally distilled**.

3 Nitrogen is a very unreactive gas.

4 Oxygen is vital for the respiration of living things.
- *Laboratory preparation*
Decomposition of hydrogen peroxide solution with a manganese dioxide catalyst.
- *Chemical properties*
Relights a glowing splint.
Reacts with most metals and non-metals to make oxides.
- *Uses*
For breathing – in medicine, aircraft, mountaineering, etc.
In welding, e.g. oxyacetylene torch.

5 Carbon dioxide is a colourless gas, heavier than air.
- *Laboratory preparation*
Reaction of a dilute acid on a carbonate.
- *Chemical properties*
Puts out a lighted splint.
Turns calcium hydroxide solution (limewater) cloudy.
- *Uses*
Fizzy drinks.
Fire extinguishers.
Dry ice.

6 Pollution of the air comes from many sources:
smoke from inefficient burning of fuels;
carbon monoxide and lead compounds from car exhausts;
acid gases from fuels burning, e.g. sulphur dioxide;
freons from aerosol sprays.

4 Gases in the Air

Questions

1. (a) Make a list of the gases present in air, and their percentage by volume.
   (b) How are the gases in the air separated from each other?
   (c) Air contains small amounts of the gases neon (boiling point −246 °C) and krypton (boiling point −153 °C). Explain how samples of these two gases could be obtained from the air. **R**

2.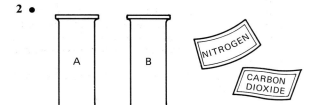

   The labels have fallen off gas jars A and B. You are given a sample of gas from each jar. What tests could you do to find out which is the correct label to put on each jar? **U**

3. Oxygen can be prepared in the laboratory by the following reaction:

   sodium peroxide + water → sodium hydroxide + oxygen

   $2Na_2O_2(s) + 2H_2O(l) \longrightarrow 4NaOH(aq) + O_2(g)$

   Water is added a drop at a time onto solid sodium peroxide. Draw a fully labelled diagram of the apparatus you would use to collect a few test-tubes of oxygen. What test could you do to prove that the gas was oxygen? **R**

4. Give an account of some of the ways in which the air is polluted by man. Discuss ways in which the air has been or could be made cleaner. **R**

5. (a) Which gas in the air is needed to keep plants and animals alive?
   (b) What test would you use in the laboratory to show the presence of this gas?
   (c) What volume of this gas would there be in 100 cm³ air? **R**

6. Statements about pollution are listed below:
   A The china clay industry produces large unsightly spoil heaps.
   B The waste products from nuclear reactors are radioactive and the disposal of these products presents long term difficulties.
   C 'Acid rain' produced by the large scale burning of fossil fuels is causing a reduction in the trout population of some Scottish lochs.
   D Phosphates, from domestic sewage, and nitrogenous fertilisers cause the uncontrolled growth of algae in lakes and streams.
   (a) (i) What is a spoil heap?
       (ii) Name one other industry that produces large spoil heaps.
       (iii) Why are spoil heaps unsightly?
   (b) What are the problems associated with the disposal of radioactive materials?
   (c) (i) Explain how the burning of fossil fuels causes acidity in rain.
       (ii) Give one other problem caused by this type of pollution.
   (d) (i) How do nitrogenous fertilisers get into lakes and streams?
       (ii) Which domestic product is the major source of the phosphates?
       (iii) Why, other than the appearance of the lake, are extensive surface growths of algae undesirable? (NEA) **H**

7. Read the following passage carefully. It will help you to answer the questions which follow.

   In the air there are many things which are harmful to animals, plants and buildings. These harmful substances include smoke, sulphur dioxide and exhaust fumes. These substances are said to pollute the atmosphere and cause pollution.

   Smoke and sulphur dioxide are made when fuels, such as coal and oil, are burned. Sulphur dioxide combines with water and oxygen to form sulphuric acid which produces 'acid rain'. As well as harming animals and plants, buildings can be damaged by this 'acid rain' because it destroys the stonework.

   Exhaust fumes, mainly from cars and lorries, contain a very poisonous gas called carbon monoxide. This gas is colourless and has no smell, but in large enough quantities and in a small space, it can kill a person. Exhaust fumes also contain lead compounds, which are poisonous and are thought to cause brain damage to young children.

   (a) Name **three** things which may be present in air which cause pollution.
   (b) What is meant by the word **pollution**?
   (c) Name **two** fuels which contain sulphur.
   (d) (i) Balance the equation for the reaction of water, sulphur dioxide and oxygen.
       $H_2O + SO_2 + O_2 \longrightarrow H_2SO_4$
       (ii) Explain how 'acid-rain' is produced.
   (e) Why are the lead compounds which are added to petrol considered to be a health hazard? (NREB) **H**

8. Air is a mixture of gases. The following experiment was done to find out about this mixture:

   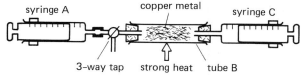

   100 cm³ of air was passed several times over the hot copper. The remaining gases were then passed into syringe A and cooled to room temperature.
   (a) Which gas in the air does copper react with?
   (b) What is the name of the compound formed in tube B?
   (c) What volume of gas would be left in syringe A at the end of the experiment?
   (d) What is the name of the main gas left in syringe A at the end of the experiment? **R**

9 ■ Use the names of the gases in the list below to answer questions (a) to (i).

ammonia
argon
carbon dioxide
carbon monoxide
hydrogen
methane
nitrogen
oxygen
sulphur dioxide

Which of these gases:
(a) is very unreactive and does not form any known compounds?
(b) dissolves in water to produce an acid solution, and is the major cause of 'acid rain'?
(c) is present in 'natural gas'?
(d) is very soluble in water, producing an alkaline solution?
(e) puts out a lighted splint, does not react with calcium hydroxide solution (limewater) and is the most abundant gas in the air?
(f) is a poisonous gas found in car exhausts, and causes blood to turn bright red?
(g) is formed as sugars ferment?
(h) re-lights a glowing splint?
(i) burns with a squeaky 'pop'? **R**

10 ■ Air is a mixture of gases. It consists mainly of oxygen and nitrogen, with small amounts of noble gases, carbon dioxide and water vapour. Certain areas of the world also have small amounts of pollutants in the air.
(a) What are the approximate percentages of oxygen and nitrogen in the air?
(b) State *two* ways in which carbon dioxide is released in the air.
(c) Why has the amount of carbon dioxide in the air increased over the past 100 years? Why might this be dangerous?
(d) Plants such as trees and algae in the sea take in carbon dioxide from the air.
  (i) What is the name of this process?
  (ii) Write a word equation for the chemical reaction that happens. **R**

11 ■ The percentage of carbon dioxide in the atmosphere remains fairly constant because much of it is absorbed by plants.
(a) Name a substance which is taken in by plants and which reacts with carbon dioxide.
(b) Name the two products formed when carbon dioxide reacts with the substance named in (a).
(c) Name a substance present in plants which is essential for this reaction of carbon dioxide.
(d) State one other essential condition required for this reaction to take place.
(e) Name the process taking place in the plants when they absorb and use carbon dioxide in this reaction.
(NEA) **R**

12 ■ (a) Oxygen can be prepared by the catalytic decomposition of hydrogen peroxide. This reaction is catalysed by manganese(IV) oxide.
  (i) Explain the term 'decomposition'.
  (ii) Given that manganese(IV) oxide increases the rate of reaction, what further experiment must be done to show that it is a catalyst for this reaction?
  (iii) Draw the apparatus that could be used to prepare and collect oxygen, produced by the decomposition of hydrogen peroxide.
(b) 100 cm^3 of a solution of hydrogen peroxide, whose concentration is 2.0 moles per litre, is decomposed by the addition of a catalyst. Calculate the volume of oxygen produced, measured at room temperature and pressure.
Molar volume of any gas at room temperature and pressure = 24 litres.
$$2H_2O_2 \longrightarrow 2H_2O + O_2$$
  (i) How many moles of hydrogen peroxide are there in 100 cm^3 of solution containing 2.0 moles per litre?
  (ii) How many moles of oxygen (O_2) are formed?
  (iii) Calculate the volume of oxygen produced.
(NEA) **U**

13 ■ The most abundant gas in the air is nitrogen.
(a) What percentage of the air is nitrogen?
(b) To obtain nitrogen, air must be cooled until it condenses to a liquid. Looking at page 18, find the boiling points of nitrogen and oxygen. Which of these gases is easiest to liquefy? Explain your answer.
(c) What is the name of the process that separates nitrogen from liquid air?
(d) Give one everyday use of nitrogen.
(e) How would nitrogen react with: (i) a lighted splint, (ii) calcium hydroxide solution (limewater), (iii) damp universal indicator paper? **R**

14 ▶ The following table shows some information about gases.

Name of gas	Formula	Relative molecular mass	Vol. of 1 g gas at rm. temp. and pressure/cm^3
ammonia	NH$_3$	17	1410
argon	Ar	40	600
carbon monoxide	CO	28	860
chlorine	Cl$_2$	71	340
methane	CH$_4$	16	1500
sulphur dioxide	SO$_2$	64	380

(a) Use this information to plot a graph of gas volume (vertical axis) against relative molecular mass (horizontal axis).
(b) Predict from the graph the volumes that would be occupied by 1 g of nitrogen (N$_2$) and 1 g of neon (Ne) at room temperature and pressure.
(Ne = 20 N$_2$ = 28)
(c) Find the formula of a gaseous hydrocarbon, 1 g of which occupies 545 cm^3 at room temperature and pressure. **H**

5 Metals and Non-metals

The position of metals and non-metals in the periodic table

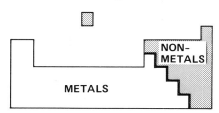

All elements are either metals or non-metals. There are 79 metallic elements and 26 non-metallic elements.

The properties of metals and non-metals are quite different as the following table shows.

Examples and physical properties of various metals and non-metals

Metals	*Non-metals*
Examples Nearly all metals are solids at room temperature:	Non-metals can be either solids, liquids or gases at room temperature:
Solids e.g. Copper Cu Iron Fe Magnesium Mg	**Solids** e.g. Iodine I_2 Sulphur S_8 Carbon C
Liquid Mercury Hg – the only liquid metal	**Liquid** Bromine Br_2 – the only liquid non-metal
	Gases Argon Ar Oxygen O_2 Nitrogen N_2
Physical properties All metals conduct electricity when solid or melted, e.g. copper is used in electrical wiring.	Non-metals do not conduct electricity, except for graphite.
All metals conduct heat well, e.g. aluminium saucepans.	Non-metals do not conduct heat very well.
Metals are strong and 'bendy'. Many metals are quite soft.	Non-metals are hard and brittle when solid.
All metals are shiny when polished. The shine is called a **lustre**.	Non-metals are mostly dull when solid.

The arrangement of atoms in metals

A tray of marbles close-packed together forms a regular pattern:

Metal atoms, although much smaller than marbles, are close-packed together in a similar way:

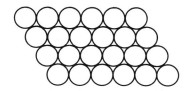

The arrangement of atoms in metals

The atoms inside a metal are packed together very tightly. The atoms are said to be 'close-packed'. The metal atoms are arranged in a very tidy and orderly way in layers. Each layer of metal atoms fits on top of another layer, like apples on a market stall. Atoms are so small that even a few grams of a metal will contain millions of layers of atoms all closely and regularly packed together. When a regular structure is repeated over and over again in a solid, it is called a **giant structure**.

The arrangement of atoms in non-metals

Atoms of non-metallic elements can be arranged in two ways. Most join together in small groups to form simple molecules.

Simple molecules formed by non-metallic elements

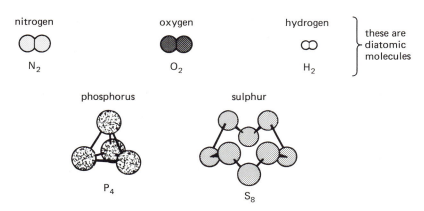

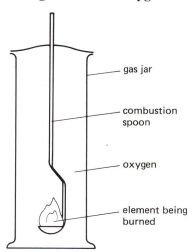

Burning elements in oxygen

A few non-metallic elements like carbon and silicon have giant structures. The atoms are arranged in a strong 3-dimensional pattern that is repeated throughout the structure. These are described in more detail in Chapter 20.

Oxides of elements

Nearly all metals and non-metals react with oxygen. A compound of an element and oxygen is called an **oxide**:

$$\text{ELEMENT} + \text{OXYGEN} \xrightarrow{\text{chemical reaction}} \text{OXIDE}$$

Many elements react so well with oxygen that they catch fire and burn. When an element or compound burns in oxygen, the reaction is called **combustion**.

Examples of some oxides

Metal oxides			Non-metal oxides		
		Is oxide water-soluble?			Is oxide water-soluble?
Calcium oxide	CaO	yes – pH 12	Carbon dioxide	CO_2	yes – pH 6
Iron oxide	Fe_2O_3	no	Sulphur dioxide	SO_2	yes – pH 1
Magnesium oxide	MgO	no	Phosphorus oxide	P_4O_{10}	yes – pH 1
Sodium oxide	Na_2O	yes – pH 14	Silicon dioxide	SiO_2	no
Some metal oxides are insoluble in water. Water-soluble metal oxides form alkaline solutions: (pH 8–14)			Non-metal oxides dissolve in water to form acidic solutions: (pH 1–6)		

5 Metals and Non-metals

Summary

1. All elements are either **metals** or **non-metals**.

2. **Metals:**
   - are all solids at room temperature, except mercury which is the only liquid metal.
   - conduct electricity.
   - are strong and bendy.
   - Metal atoms are arranged in a close-packed giant structure.
   - Some metal oxides are water-soluble. Others are insoluble. Soluble metal oxides form alkaline solutions in water.

3. **Non-metals:**
   - may be solids, liquids or gases at room temperature.
   - do not conduct electricity (except graphite).
   - are hard and brittle when solid.
   - Most non-metal atoms join together to form small molecules. Some form giant structures.
   - Most non-metal oxides are water soluble. Soluble non-metal oxides form acidic solutions in water.

Questions

1 ● Copy out the following table. Use the alphabetical list of elements at the back of this book to complete the missing information in the table. Assume that room temperature is 15°C. **H**

Element	Symbol	Metal or non-metal?	Melting point /°C	Boiling point /°C	Solid, liquid or gas at room temperature?
Example: Bromine	Br	non-metal	−7	59	liquid
Carbon			3700	4800	
Chlorine					
Copper					
	Pb				
Mercury					
		non-metal	−210	−196	
	Sn		232	2270	

2 ● (a) Draw a diagram to show how the atoms are arranged in
  (i) a typical metallic element.
  (ii) two non-metallic elements.
  (b) Underneath each diagram write a sentence to describe the arrangement of the atoms. **R**

3 ● Write out the following sentences, filling in the spaces with the correct word(s):
  (a) A compound of an element and oxygen is called _____.
  (b) When an element burns in oxygen, a _____ reaction occurs.
  (c) Carbon burns in excess oxygen to form _____. When this product dissolves in water, the solution is _____. (acidic or alkaline?)
  (d) When metal oxides are water soluble, the solution is _____. (acidic or alkaline?) **R**

4 ● Make out a table as follows:

Element	Symbol	Use

Enter on the table *four* metals and *two* non-metals. Write one or two sentences about each, describing an everyday use. **R**

6 Hydrogen and Water

Hydrogen

Hydrogen is the lightest of all gases. But it is not found in the air as an element. This is just as well, or every time you lit a match, the air around you would explode! Many hydrogen compounds occur in the world. Hydrogen forms more compounds than any other element – there are over two million of them!

Where is hydrogen found?

Water H_2O  Water covers four-fifths of the world's surface, and is essential for life.

Methane CH_4  Natural gas is mostly methane.

Making hydrogen in the laboratory

Hydrogen is made in the laboratory by reacting zinc metal with dilute sulphuric acid:

Structure of hydrogen

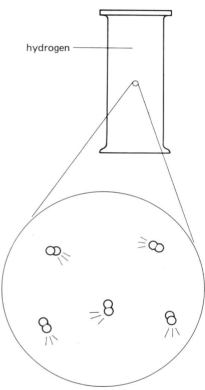

Hydrogen gas contains small, separate diatomic molecules. Formula: H_2

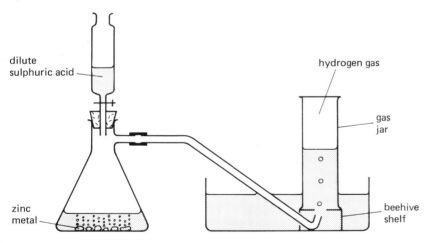

A little copper sulphate solution is often added to the acid, to make the reaction go faster. The copper from the copper sulphate acts as a catalyst.

Hydrogen gas does not dissolve in water. This is why it is usually collected over water like this.

Word equation   zinc + dilute sulphuric acid → zinc sulphate solution + hydrogen

Symbol equation $Zn(s) + H_2SO_4(aq) \rightarrow ZnSO_4(aq) + H_2(g)$

6 Hydrogen and Water

Properties of hydrogen

Physical properties Hydrogen is a colourless gas with no smell. It has a very low density – it is the lightest gas.

Chemical properties

Reaction with oxygen

Lighted splint

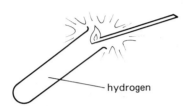

Burning hydrogen

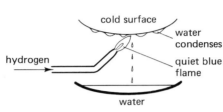

Hydrogen, mixed with oxygen in the air, burns with a squeaky 'pop'.

Hydrogen burns quietly in air to make water vapour. This can be condensed on a cold surface.

hydrogen + oxygen ⟶ water

$2H_2(g) + O_2(g) \longrightarrow 2H_2O(g)$

Reaction with chlorine

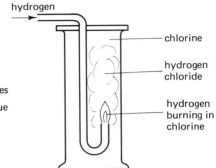

Hydrogen continues to burn in chlorine gas. Hydrogen chloride is formed.

hydrogen + chlorine ⟶ hydrogen chloride

$H_2(g) + Cl_2(g) \longrightarrow 2HCl(g)$

Launch of the Ariane rocket: a controlled explosion.

The author at work

6 Hydrogen and Water

Reaction with metal oxides: reduction

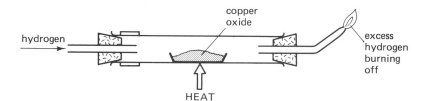

Some metal oxides react with hydrogen to form the metal and water:

Word equation   copper oxide + hydrogen ⟶ copper + water

Symbol equation $CuO(s) + H_2(g) \rightarrow Cu(s) + H_2O(g)$

Copper oxide is turned into copper metal. When a metal oxide reacts to form the metal in this way, it is said to be **reduced**. Reduction in this experiment is **the removal of oxygen** from the copper oxide. When any substance is reduced, another substance is always **oxidised**. Oxidation happens in this experiment when **oxygen is added** to a substance.

Oxidation	**Reduction**
is	is
adding oxygen	removing oxygen

Oxidation and reduction always happen together:

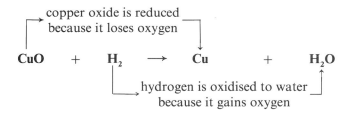

Oxidation and reduction can be explained in other ways. These are discussed in more detail in Chapter 24.

Uses of hydrogen

Making ammonia
Hydrogen is reacted with nitrogen in the Haber process to make ammonia:

hydrogen + nitrogen ⟶ ammonia

$3H_2(g) + N_2(g) \rightarrow 2NH_3(g)$

As a fuel
The reaction between hydrogen and oxygen is used to power some spacecraft and rockets. It is also used in welding.

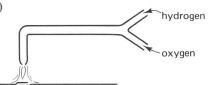

Using hydrogen safely

A mixture of hydrogen and oxygen in the air is dangerously explosive. In any experiment using hydrogen, it is very important that air is removed from the apparatus first. One way to do this is to pass a stream of unreactive nitrogen gas through the apparatus.

Hydrogen – the fuel of the future?

This car is fuelled by hydrogen. Hydrogen is difficult to store in the car, but the vehicle runs well on this fuel, and the main gas in the exhaust is steam!

Making margarine
Vegetable oils are 'hardened', or turned into solid margarine by reacting them with hydrogen.

6 Hydrogen and Water

Water

About 80% of the earth is covered by water. Only a very small amount of it is fit to drink. Sea water contains too many dissolved chemicals to be drinkable. In countries where there is plenty of rain, everyone takes water for granted. In hot, dry countries, it is valued much more. None of us can live more than a few days without fresh water to drink.

The formula for water is H_2O. This means that a water molecule contains two hydrogen atoms and one oxygen atom chemically joined together.

A water molecule

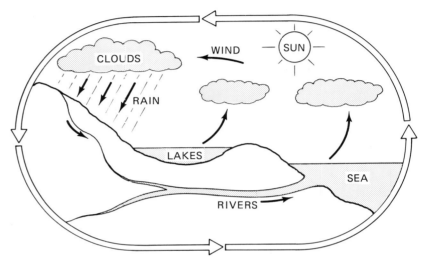

The 'water cycle' shows where fresh water supplies come from.

Water is a very unusual liquid. Many of its physical properties are unique, and make water so important for life.

Unusual physical properties of water – solid, liquid and gas

Water is the only common substance that exists as a solid, liquid and gas in everyday life on earth.

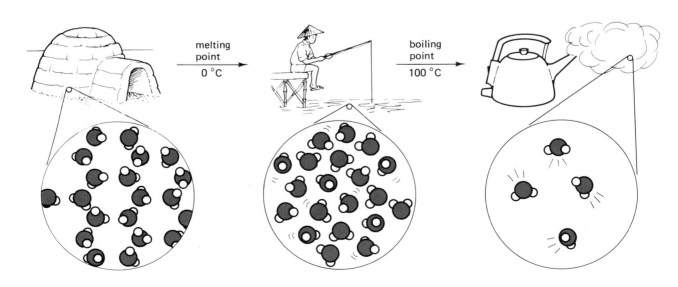

6 Hydrogen and Water

Water is a liquid at room temperature.

Other molecules of a similar size and mass are all gases at room temperature.

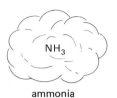

carbon monoxide   ammonia

Water expands as it freezes...

All other compounds contract as they freeze. In cold weather, water pipes can burst if the water inside them freezes. When the ice in the pipe melts, the pipe then leaks.

The **density** of a substance is the mass of 1 cm^3. Density is written

Density of water =

g stands for mass in grams   this means 'per cubic centimetre'

Here are the densities of some other substances:

Substance	Density
Aluminium	2.70 g cm^{-3}
Bromine	3.12 g cm^{-3}
Gold	19.32 g cm^{-3}
Mercury	13.55 g cm^{-3}
Sulphur	2.07 g cm^{-3}
Water	1.00 g cm^{-3}

...so ice floats on water.

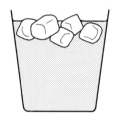

Density of ice = 0.92 g cm^{-3}

Density of water = 1.00 g cm^{-3}

In all other compounds, the solid form is more dense than the liquid, and sinks to the bottom:

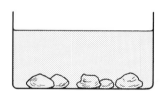

If ice were to sink, rivers and oceans would freeze from the bottom upwards, and become solid ice. Plant and animal life in the water would be impossible. When ice freezes on a river or pond, it forms an insulating layer that prevents the rest of the water from freezing, unless the weather is very cold.

Water is a good solvent. A solvent is a liquid that can dissolve other substances into itself.

Dissolving gases

Dissolved oxygen and carbon dioxide in water are essential for fish and water plants.

Dissolving solids

Water dissolves many solids.

Dissolving solids in water

Water is a good solvent for many solids. Imagine stirring spatulas full of copper sulphate crystals into water. At first it is easy to dissolve the solid in the water to make a solution. Eventually, as more crystals are stirred in to the solution, no more will dissolve. The solution is **saturated**. A saturated solution is one in which no more solute can dissolve at that temperature.

Making a solution

solvent + **solute** → **solution** → **saturated solution**

A solvent is the liquid that does the dissolving.

A solute is the substance that is dissolved.

A solution is formed when a solute is dissolved by a solvent.

A saturated solution is one that will dissolve no more solute at that temperature.

Chemists often need to know exactly how much solute is dissolved in a saturated solution. This is called the solubility. The **solubility** of a solid in water is the number of grams of that solid that will dissolve in 100 g of water. If the saturated copper sulphate solution were heated, much more solid could be dissolved in it. Most compounds dissolve more in hot water than in cold. Their solubility increases with increasing temperature. A graph can be plotted to show how the solubility of a compound changes with increasing temperature. This is called a **solubility curve**.

Solubility curves for various compounds

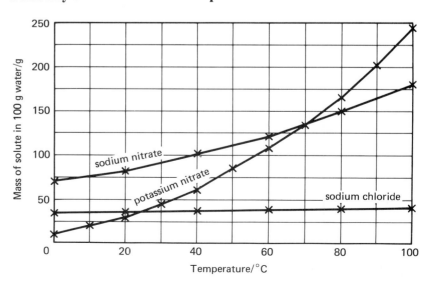

A solubility curve contains a number of useful bits of information:

- the solubility of most compounds increases quickly with temperature. For some, like sodium chloride, it hardly increases at all. A few substances actually get less soluble with increasing temperature.
- by looking at a solubility curve, the solubility of a substance at a particular temperature can be read off, e.g. for the sodium nitrate curve on the graph, at 40°C, its solubility is 102 g in 100 g of water.
- from a solubility curve, predictions can be made about what happens when a solution cools.

Solubility curve for copper sulphate

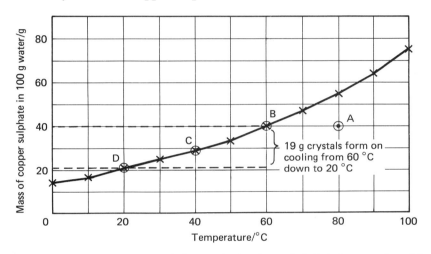

Solubility of copper sulphate at various temperatures

Temperature /°C	Mass of copper sulphate in 100 g water/g
0	14
10	17
20	21
30	25
40	29
50	33
60	40
70	47
80	55
90	64
100	75

Suppose some hot copper sulphate solution is cooled. It is known that this solution contains 40 g of crystals dissolved in 100 g of water.

	Point on graph	Temperature	What happens
solution cools	A	80 °C	Hot copper sulphate solution cools.
	B	60 °C	Solution is now saturated. Crystals start to form on cooling.
	C	40 °C	Solution stays saturated. 11 g of crystals have separated out.
	D	20 °C	Solution is still saturated. 19 g of crystals have formed.

Dissolving gases in water

Water is a solvent for gases as well as solids.
- Only a small amount of most gases dissolve in water.
- Some gases react chemically with water.

If some tap water is warmed, bubbles of air will be seen forming as the water is heated. This is because the solubility of the dissolved gases gets less as the water gets hotter. This is opposite to what happens to most solids.

Solubility of some gases in water

100 cm³ water at 20°C will dissolve:

   2 cm³ hydrogen
or 3 cm³ oxygen
or 1.6 cm³ nitrogen

100 cm³ water at 20 °C will dissolve:

   75 litres of ammonia
or 48 litres of hydrogen chloride
or 4.2 litres of sulphur dioxide
or 92 cm³ of carbon dioxide

Water of crystallisation

When some compounds are heated, they simply melt. Other compounds are seen to give off clouds of steam.

Heating various crystals

Tests for water

1 White anhydrous copper sulphate powder turns blue:

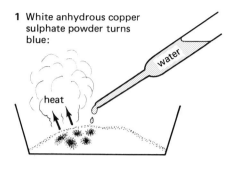

2 Blue cobalt chloride paper turns pink:

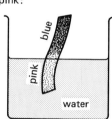

Sodium chloride crystals

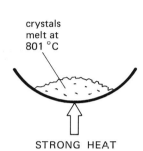

STRONG HEAT

Sodium chloride crystals are **anhydrous** – they contain no water of crystallisation.

Blue copper sulphate crystals

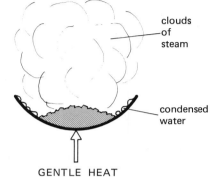

GENTLE HEAT

Copper sulphate crystals are **hydrated** – they contain water of crystallisation.

Hydrated copper sulphate crystals contain water of crystallisation. They do not feel wet to the touch because the water is joined chemically to the copper sulphate. The formula is written:

$$CuSO_4 \cdot 5H_2O$$

The raised dot shows that five water molecules are joined to each copper sulphate. Water is only loosely joined to copper sulphate. Mild heating drives off the water and leaves anhydrous crystals.

Water of crystallisation can be driven off by gentle heating

Blue hydrated copper sulphate crystals

White anhydrous copper sulphate powder

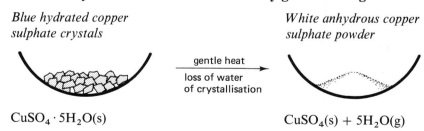

$CuSO_4 \cdot 5H_2O(s)$ $CuSO_4(s) + 5H_2O(g)$

This change can be easily reversed by adding water to the white powder. The blue crystals are formed again, and considerable heat is produced. Here are some other examples of compounds with water of crystallisation:

Name	Formula
Barium chloride	$BaCl_2 \cdot 2H_2O$
Calcium chloride	$CaCl_2 \cdot 6H_2O$
Zinc sulphate	$ZnSO_4 \cdot 7H_2O$
Sodium carbonate	$Na_2CO_3 \cdot 10H_2O$

6 Hydrogen and Water

Water in our daily lives

People living in countries where there is a lot of rain may use several hundred litres of water a day without even thinking about it. Water that comes out of the tap has been treated in several ways to make it safe and fit to drink.

Water treatment

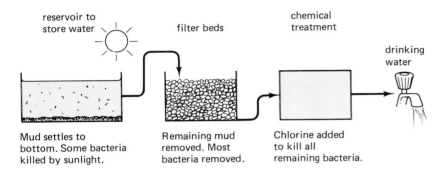

In the home, only a small amount of water is used for drinking. Most is used for washing, cleaning and flushing the toilet. Industry uses huge amounts of water, for example to wash and clean raw materials such as wood pulp, coal and iron ore. A lot of water is used in the food processing industry. Much water is also used for cooling. This is why many factories are built beside rivers.

Sewage treatment

Every time you pull the plug out of your bath, empty the washing-up water or flush the toilet, the water 'disappears' and you forget about it. In fact it enters a network of pipes which lead eventually to a sewage treatment plant. Here the sewage is treated to make it fit to pump into a river or the sea.

Sewage treatment

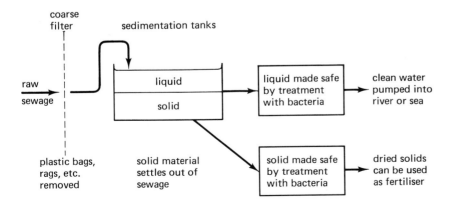

Pollution of water

Don't fall into the river in a large industrial town. Many rivers are badly polluted and poisoned by waste products from factories. Anyone falling into such a river would probably need to be taken to hospital to have their stomach pumped out.

A river in its natural state contains a balance of life between plants and animals. There are also useful bacteria which digest waste materials.

The natural balance in a river

[*Punch*, 1858]
Pollution of rivers is not a new problem. The River Thames in London was so badly polluted in 1858 that this was called the 'Year of the Great Stink'. Michael Faraday, a famous scientist, led a campaign to install a proper sewerage system in the city.

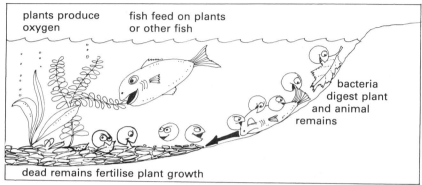

When a river becomes polluted, this natural balance is upset. Here are some of the man-made substances that cause pollution:

Industrial wastes From chemical companies, mining, paper mills, breweries, slaughterhouses, etc.

Fertilisers Washed off farming land by rainwater.

Detergents From washing clothes and dishes.

Oil From factories and ships.

Cleaning up the water that industry pumps into rivers costs a lot of money. This adds to the cost of products, which are then harder to sell. But money could be saved if waste products were collected from the water and recycled.

Pollution may upset the natural balance in a river

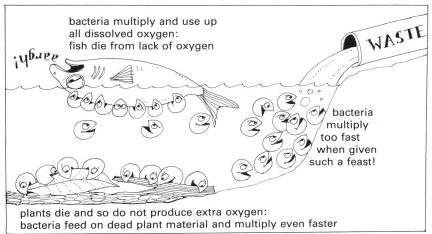

How can pollution be prevented?

Every water authority employs pollution control officers. These people collect samples of river water and test them. They also inspect factories and farms to check on what is pumped into rivers. Chemists in a water treatment plant analyse water samples. They continuously check the level of oxygen and other substances dissolved in the water. They also check for the presence of various poisons.

Many factories are very responsible and make their waste products safe before they dispose of them into rivers. Perhaps the only way to stop everyone from polluting rivers is by passing stricter laws to protect lakes and rivers.

It is easy to think that pollution can simply be got rid of once a river flows into the sea. The world's oceans are vast, and are the dumping ground not only for the waste from rivers, but for radioactive chemicals and poisonous substances that have been sunk in deep oceans. There is a limit though, to the amount of pollution an ocean can take, without its natural balance being upset. It is going to be much harder to 'clean up' a whole ocean than it is to clean up a river!

Thermal pollution

Power stations, like this one at High Marnham on the river Trent, use up to 200 000 000 litres of water an hour for cooling. The river is several degrees warmer downstream as a result. This means the water will contain less dissolved oxygen, and some fish may die as a result.

As on 'Thames Water', a floating laboratory, chemists in water treatment plants continuously check the purity of the water supplies.

Summary

1. **Hydrogen** is the lightest gas known.
   - *Laboratory preparation*:
     Reaction of zinc and sulphuric acid with copper sulphate catalyst. Collected over water.
     $$Zn(s) + H_2SO_4(aq) \longrightarrow ZnSO_4(aq) + H_2(g)$$
   - *Chemical properties*:
     - burns with squeaky 'pop' in air. A pure hydrogen flame burns quietly in air.
       $$2H_2(g) + O_2(g) \longrightarrow 2H_2O(g)$$
     - reacts with chlorine to make hydrogen chloride:
       $$H_2(g) + Cl_2(g) \longrightarrow 2HCl(g)$$
     - reduces some metal oxides:
       $$CuO(s) + H_2(g) \longrightarrow Cu(s) + H_2O(g)$$
   - *Uses*: to make ammonia (Haber process)
     to 'harden' oils into margarine
     as a fuel

2. **Water** has unusual properties:
   - It exists naturally as solid, liquid and gas.
   - It is a liquid at room temperature. Other similar molecules are all gases at room temperature.
   - Ice floats on water.
   - Water expands as it freezes.

3. **Water dissolves many solids.**
   - The **solubility** of a solid in water is the number of grams of solid that dissolve in 100 g water at a certain temperature.
   - A **saturated solution** is one in which no more solute can dissolve at that temperature.
   - A **solubility curve** shows how solubility changes with temperature. Most solids get more soluble as temperature is increased.

4. **Water dissolves many gases.**
   - Small amounts of most gases dissolve in water.
   - Some gases (e.g. ammonia) are very soluble in water because they react chemically with the water.

5. **Water of crystallisation** is chemically combined water. It is driven off by gentle heat, e.g. $CuSO_4 \cdot 5H_2O(s) \longrightarrow CuSO_4(s) + 5H_2O(g)$.

6. **Water for homes** is filtered and treated chemically to make it safe.

7. **Uses of water**   In the home: washing, cleaning, cooking, toilets.
   In industry: washing, cleaning, cooling.

8. **Sewage plants** make waste materials safe, and clean up water before it is discharged into rivers and the sea.

9. Water is **polluted** by waste products from industry. The natural balance in a river is upset.

6 Hydrogen and Water

Questions

1. ● (a) Magnesium metal will react with dilute sulphuric acid to make magnesium sulphate solution and hydrogen gas:

   $Mg(s) + H_2SO_4(aq) \rightarrow MgSO_4(aq) + H_2(g)$

   Draw and label a diagram to show the apparatus you would use to prepare and collect several test-tubes of hydrogen gas.
   (b) Underneath the diagram state **three** chemical reactions of hydrogen. Give an equation for each reaction.
   (c) State **three** uses of hydrogen. **R**

2. ● Copy out the sentences below, adding the correct missing word from the following list:

   ADDITION OXIDISED LOSES
   REMOVAL   REDUCED   GAINS

   Each word may be used once, more than once, or not at all.
   (a) When copper oxide reacts with hydrogen, it is _____ to copper metal.
   (b) Reduction is the _____ of oxygen.
   (c) Oxidation is the _____ of oxygen.
   (d) In the following reaction:

   iron oxide + hydrogen → iron + water
   FeO(s)   + H$_2$(g) → Fe(s) + H$_2$O(g)

   iron oxide is _____ to iron metal, because it _____ oxygen. Hydrogen is _____ to water, because it _____ oxygen. **U**

3. ● Discuss **four** of the unusual properties of water, giving examples of each property. **R**

4. ● Write one sentence about each of the following words to explain their meaning:
   (a) anhydrous   (e) solute
   (b) saturated solution (f) solution
   (c) solubility   (g) solvent
   (d) solubility curve (h) water or crystallisation **R**

5. ■ Plot a solubility curve for potassium chlorate from the following data.

   Temperature/°C   0   10 20 30 40 50 60 70
   Solubility/g per
   100g water   3.3 5.0 7.4 10.5 14.0 19.3 24.4 32.5

   Use the graph to find the following:
   (a) The solubility of potassium chlorate at (i) 45 °C, (ii) 65 °C.
   (b) A solution containing 14 g potassium chlorate per 100 g water is heated to 65 °C. Draw a cross marked 'A' at this point on the graph. As the solution is cooled, at what temperature do crystals first start to appear in the solution? Mark another cross at this point, and label it 'B'. The solution is cooled still further to 20 °C. Mark this point with a 'C'. What mass of crystals are formed in the solution on cooling from B to C? **H**

6. ● (a) Explain three ways in which rivers are polluted by man.
   (b) How is the natural balance in a river upset by this pollution?
   (c) How can this pollution be reduced or prevented? **R**

7. ● (a) Outline, with the help of a diagram, how water is treated before it reaches the home, to make it safe to use.
   (b) Give **two** uses of water in industry and **two** uses in the home.
   (c) Outline, with the help of a diagram, how water is treated after we have finished with it, to make it safe to discharge into rivers or the sea. **R**

8. ■ (a) Name a substance which when dissolved in water makes the water: (i) temporarily hard, (ii) permanently hard.
   (b) Name a type of substance which when added to hard water –
   (i) produces a lather but does not soften the water,
   (ii) produces a lather and forms a white precipitate.
   (c) State one method which –
   (i) can only be used for softening temporarily hard water,
   (ii) is used to soften water which is both temporarily and permanently hard.
   (d) State: (i) one advantage of hard water, (ii) one disadvantage of hard water. (NEA) **R**

9. ■ The following experiments were done to investigate the effect of adding salt to ice:

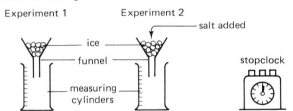

Readings of the volume of water collected were taken every two minutes, as follows:

Time/min	Volume of water/cm³	
	Experiment 1	Experiment 2
0	0	0
2	0	6.5
4	0	10.8
6	0.2	14.7
8	0.3	18.0
10	0.6	20.8
12	1.8	23.5
14	3.5	25.6
16	5.2	27.6
18	7.3	29.7
20	10.0	31.2

(a) Plot a graph of the volume of water collected (vertical axis) against time (horizontal axis), putting the results of both experiments on the same graph. Label the lines 'Experiment 1' and 'Experiment 2'.
(b) Use your graph to estimate the volume of water produced after 15 minutes in both Experiment 1 and Experiment 2.
(c) In which experiment did the ice melt more quickly?
(d) Give two reasons why rock salt is spread on icy roads.
(e) State one disadvantage of using salt on icy roads. **R**

7 Competition among Metals

Tarnishing happens when metals react with oxygen in the air. A coat of metal oxide forms on the metal, and it loses its shine and becomes dull.

Imagine you are rich enough to buy a new car and it arrives gleaming and polished! Great care has been taken to cover the steel bodywork with many coats of paint. Underneath, it has been protected with a thick black coating. If the car had been delivered without these protective coats it would quickly become a rusting wreck! The car is made from steel which contains iron plus small amounts of a few other elements. Rainwater and oxygen in the air react with the iron to make rust.

Iron is a fairly **reactive** metal. If you were rich enough to have your car gold plated, no coats of protective paint would be needed at all. Gold is a very **unreactive** metal, and stays shiny for years. Each metal has its own **reactivity**, and this is shown in some of the experiments in this chapter.

Reaction of metals with oxygen

Nearly all metals react with oxygen to form **oxides**. Pure oxygen reacts very strongly with most metals, but the 20% of oxygen in the air is enough for most metals to react to form oxides:

$$\text{METAL} + \text{OXYGEN} \rightarrow \text{METAL OXIDE}$$

e.g. magnesium + oxygen → magnesium oxide

$$2Mg(s) + O_2(g) \rightarrow 2MgO(s)$$

When a metal is pure, it is bright and shiny. If it reacts with oxygen in the air, it forms a coat of metal oxide on the surface. It then looks dull. This is called **tarnishing**. When a metal reacts with oxygen in this way, it has been oxidised – it has added on oxygen.

Reaction of some metals with oxygen

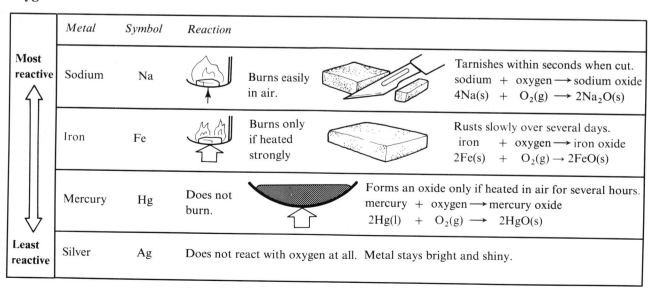

The metals in the table have been put in order of their reactivity with oxygen.

Reaction of metals with water

Some metals react chemically with water. When this happens a metal hydroxide or oxide is formed and hydrogen gas is given off:

METAL + WATER ⟶ METAL HYDROXIDE + HYDROGEN
(or OXIDE)

Reaction of some metals with water

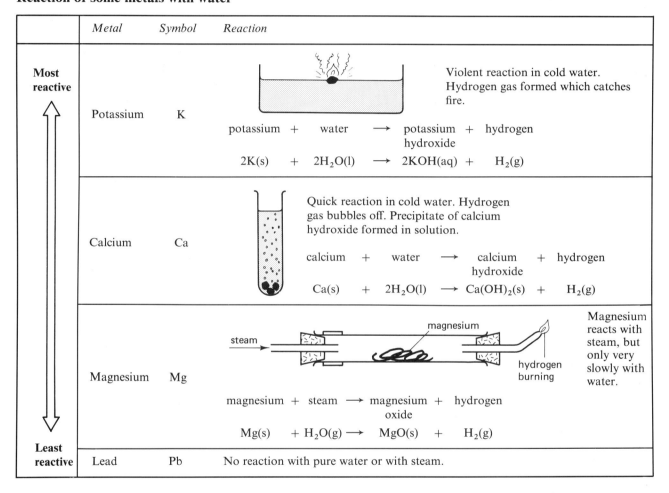

	Metal	Symbol	Reaction	
Most reactive ↑ ↓ **Least reactive**	Potassium	K	Violent reaction in cold water. Hydrogen gas formed which catches fire. potassium + water ⟶ potassium hydroxide + hydrogen $2K(s) + 2H_2O(l) \rightarrow 2KOH(aq) + H_2(g)$	
	Calcium	Ca	Quick reaction in cold water. Hydrogen gas bubbles off. Precipitate of calcium hydroxide formed in solution. calcium + water ⟶ calcium hydroxide + hydrogen $Ca(s) + 2H_2O(l) \rightarrow Ca(OH)_2(s) + H_2(g)$	
	Magnesium	Mg	magnesium + steam ⟶ magnesium oxide + hydrogen $Mg(s) + H_2O(g) \rightarrow MgO(s) + H_2(g)$	Magnesium reacts with steam, but only very slowly with water.
	Lead	Pb	No reaction with pure water or with steam.	

In all of these reactions, a competition is going on. The metal and the hydrogen in water are competing for the oxygen. In the first three examples in the table, the metal wins the competition when it takes the oxygen from water (H_2O), and hydrogen gas is formed (H_2).

Some metals such as lead and copper do not react with water at all. In these cases, the metal loses the competition, and the hydrogen in water keeps its oxygen atom.

When metals react with water, a competition goes on to see which element can 'win' the oxygen. Very reactive metals like potassium and calcium easily win the oxygen in water: the oxide produced goes on to form a hydroxide.

Less reactive metals like lead lose the competition for oxygen and the hydrogen and oxygen in water stay joined together.

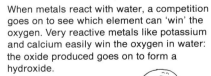

7 Competition among Metals

When the word 'salt' is used in everyday language, it means the white crystals you sprinkle on your chips.

For the chemist, this particular salt is called sodium chloride. There are many thousands of different 'salts', each with its own chemical name.

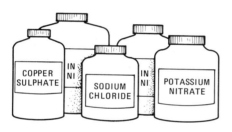

Reaction of metals with acids

Many metals react with acids. When this reaction happens, a new substance called a **salt** is formed:

METAL + ACID ⟶ SALT + HYDROGEN

Which salt is formed depends on which metal and which acid are used.

Common acids and the salts formed from them

Acid	Name of salt	Example	
Hydrochloric acid	Chlorides	Sodium chloride	NaCl
		Calcium chloride	$CaCl_2$
Nitric acid	Nitrates	Potassium nitrate	KNO_3
		Zinc nitrate	$Zn(NO_3)_2$
Sulphuric acid	Sulphates	Copper sulphate	$CuSO_4$
		Magnesium sulphate	$MgSO_4$

Acids are often diluted with water before they are reacted with metals.

Nitric acid reacts in an unusual way with many metals. Nitrogen oxides are formed instead of hydrogen. The equations are usually quite complicated, e.g.

copper + concentrated nitric acid ⟶ copper nitrate + nitrogen dioxide + water

$Cu(s) + 4HNO_3(l) \longrightarrow Cu(NO_3)_2(aq) + 2NO_2(g) + 2H_2O(l)$

Reaction of some metals with acids

	Metal	Symbol	Reaction
Most reactive ↑ ↓ **Least reactive**	Sodium	Na	Dangerously explosive reaction. This should never be attempted in the laboratory. sodium + hydrochloric acid ⟶ sodium chloride + hydrogen $2Na(s) + 2HCl(aq) \longrightarrow 2NaCl(aq) + H_2(g)$
	Zinc	Zn	Moderately fast reaction – hydrogen bubbles off. zinc + sulphuric acid ⟶ zinc sulphate + hydrogen $Zn(s) + H_2SO_4(aq) \longrightarrow ZnSO_4(aq) + H_2(g)$
	Lead	Pb	Slow reaction with concentrated acids. lead + hot concentrated hydrochloric acid ⟶ lead chloride + hydrogen $Pb(s) + 2HCl(aq) \longrightarrow PbCl_2(s) + H_2(g)$
	Platinum	Pt	No reaction with most acids, even when hot and concentrated.

7 Competition among Metals

When metals react with acids, another competition reaction is going on. These acids are all compounds containing hydrogen. The hydrogen in the acid competes with the metal.

Competition between magnesium and sulphuric acid

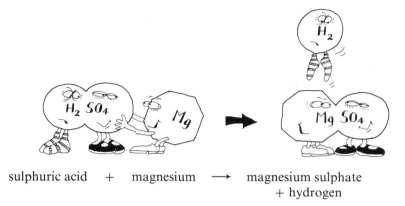

sulphuric acid + magnesium ⟶ magnesium sulphate + hydrogen

When magnesium reacts with sulphuric acid, the magnesium 'wins' the competition. Hydrogen gas bubbles off and magnesium sulphate solution is formed.

Competition between platinum and sulphuric acid

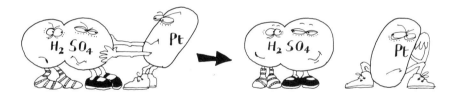

sulphuric acid + platinum ⟶ no reaction

When platinum and sulphuric acid meet, there is no reaction. The platinum 'loses' this competition, and the hydrogen holds on to the sulphate in sulphuric acid.

The reactivity series

Some metals react very well with air, water and acids. Others are less reactive. Metals can be put into a reactivity series. This series arranges metals in order of their **reactivity**.

Reactivity series of metals

Metal	Symbol	
Potassium	K	**Most reactive**
Sodium	Na	⇧
Calcium	Ca	
Magnesium	Mg	
Aluminium	Al	
Zinc	Zn	
Iron	Fe	
Tin	Sn	
Lead	Pb	
Copper	Cu	
Mercury	Hg	
Silver	Ag	
Gold	Au	⇩
Platinum	Pt	**Least reactive**

Unreactive metals
like silver, gold and platinum are found naturally in rocks (in very small quantities!)

Moderately reactive metals
like iron, zinc and copper are found as ores.
The metal is obtained by reducing the ore with carbon or carbon monoxide (see Chapter 19).

Very reactive metals
like aluminium and sodium can only be extracted from their ores by melting and electrolysis.

Reacting metal oxides with hydrogen

Some metal oxides react with hydrogen. The hydrogen **reduces** the metal oxide to the metal:

METAL OXIDE + HYDROGEN → METAL + WATER

oxidation (hydrogen gains oxygen)

e.g. copper oxide + hydrogen → copper + water
$CuO(s) + H_2(g) \rightarrow Cu(s) + H_2O(g)$

reduction (loss of oxygen)

The hydrogen brings about reduction. Hydrogen is called a **reducing agent**.

Reaction of some metal oxides with hydrogen

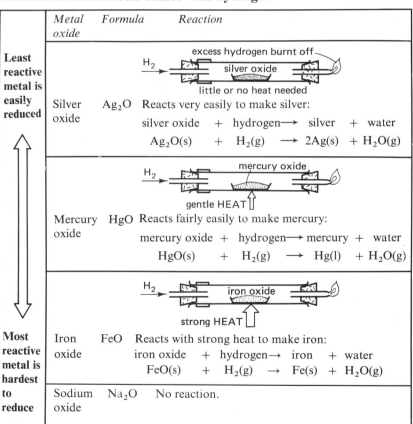

Compare this table to the table at the start of this chapter (page 44) showing the reaction of some metals with oxygen.

Have you noticed that the order is reversed? Sodium is a very reactive metal. It 'likes' to react with other elements like oxygen. Once it has combined with oxygen, it does not easily 'let go'. Silver however is a very unreactive metal. It is hard to get it to react with elements such as oxygen. If it *has* combined with oxygen, it easily 'lets go' and goes back to pure silver. Silver oxide is so easily reduced to silver, it doesn't even need hydrogen to react with. When silver oxide is gently warmed, it breaks down into silver and oxygen.

7 Competition among Metals

Growing metal crystals: displacement reactions

Suppose a strip of zinc metal is suspended in blue copper sulphate solution. After a few minutes, crystals of copper metal start to grow on the zinc strip.

Reaction of zinc metal and copper sulphate solution

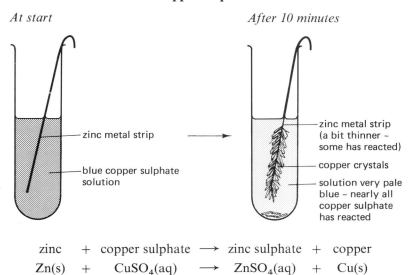

Zinc and copper sulphate solution – a displacement reaction

Before reaction:
copper and sulphate are quite 'happy' together – nothing else is there to compete.

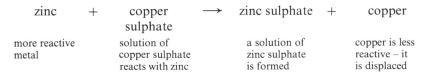

Zinc is a more reactive metal than copper. It is higher in the reactivity series than copper. The zinc **displaces** the copper. A **displacement reaction** happens when a more reactive metal displaces a less reactive metal from a solution of its salt.

zinc	+	copper sulphate	→	zinc sulphate	+	copper
more reactive metal		solution of copper sulphate reacts with zinc		a solution of zinc sulphate is formed		copper is less reactive – it is displaced

When zinc is added:
zinc is more reactive than copper. Zinc wins the competition and copper is displaced or 'thrown out' on its own.

Similar displacement reactions can happen with other metals. Study this small part of the reactivity series:

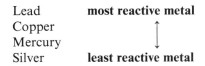

This list shows that lead is more reactive than either copper, mercury or silver. Lead will therefore displace any of these metals, e.g.:

    lead + copper chloride ⟶ lead chloride + copper
    lead + mercury nitrate ⟶ lead nitrate + mercury
    lead + silver nitrate ⟶ lead nitrate + silver

Silver on the other hand is less reactive than either lead, copper or mercury. It cannot displace the metals from solutions of any of their salts, e.g.:

    silver + copper sulphate ⇸ no reaction
    silver + lead nitrate ⇸ no reaction

Summary

1. Every metal has its own **reactivity**. Metals can be arranged in order in the **reactivity series**.

2. Nearly all metals react with oxygen to form **oxides**:

    METAL + OXYGEN ⟶ METAL OXIDE

    e.g. copper + oxygen ⟶ copper oxide
    $2Cu(s) + O_2(g) \longrightarrow 2CuO(s)$

3. Some metals are so reactive that they can take the oxygen out of **water**. Hydrogen gas comes off:

    METAL + WATER ⟶ METAL HYDROXIDE + HYDROGEN

    e.g. sodium + water ⟶ sodium hydroxide + hydrogen
    $2Na(s) + 2H_2O(l) \longrightarrow 2NaOH(aq) + H_2(g)$

4. Many metals react with **acids** to make a **salt** and hydrogen:

    METAL + ACID ⟶ SALT + HYDROGEN

    e.g. magnesium + sulphuric acid ⟶ magnesium sulphate + hydrogen
    $Mg(s) + H_2SO_4(aq) \longrightarrow MgSO_4(aq) + H_2(g)$

5. Some **metal oxides** can be **reduced** with hydrogen:

    METAL OXIDE + HYDROGEN ⟶ METAL + WATER

    e.g. lead oxide + hydrogen ⟶ lead + water
    $PbO(s) + H_2(g) \longrightarrow Pb(s) + H_2O(g)$

6. **Displacement reactions** happen when a more reactive metal displaces a less reactive metal from a solution of its salt, e.g.:

    mercury + silver nitrate ⟶ mercury nitrate + silver
    $Hg(l) + AgNO_3(aq) \longrightarrow HgNO_3(aq) + Ag(s)$

Questions

1. • What is tarnishing? Write out and complete the following equations, by filling in the missing words or formulae:

    (a) potassium + oxygen ⟶ _____
    $K(s) + \underline{} \longrightarrow KO_2(s)$

    (b) _____ + _____ ⟶ magnesium oxide
    _____ + _____ ⟶ $2MgO(s)$

    (c) copper + oxygen ⟶ _____
    $2Cu(s) + \underline{} \longrightarrow \underline{}$ **R**

2. • Zinc metal reacts with steam when heated. Draw a labelled diagram of the apparatus you would use to show this reaction. Underneath the diagram write an equation for the reaction in words and symbols.   **R**

3. • Six different strips of metal were hung in solutions of some metal nitrates to see if there was any reaction. The results are shown in the next column.
    Put the metals **P** to **U** in order of their reactivity with the most reactive metal first.   **H**

Metal	P nitrate	Q nitrate	R nitrate	S nitrate	T nitrate	U nitrate
P	—	✓	✓	✓	✗	✓
Q	✗	—	✗	✗	✗	✗
R	✗	✓	—	✓	✗	✗
S	✗	✓	✗	—	✗	✗
T	✓	✓	✓	✓	—	✓
U	✗	✓	✓	✓	✗	—

✓ = metal displaced   ✗ = no reaction

4. • A pupil was finding out about the reactivity of some metals. The following table shows some of the results. Study the table and put the five metals **A** to **E** in order of their reactivity with the most reactive first.

The reactivity series

	Element	Symbol	Reaction of metal with oxygen in the air	Reaction of metal with water	Reaction of metal with dilute hydrochloric acid	Reaction of oxide with hydrogen
Most reactive ↑	Potassium	K	burn easily with bright flame	burns violently in the cold	dangerous violent reaction	no reaction
	Sodium	Na		fast reaction in the cold		
	Calcium	Ca		slow reaction in the cold		
	Magnesium	Mg		reacts with steam	react quite well	
	Aluminium	Al		reaction stopped by oxide layer		
	Zinc	Zn		reacts with steam		
	Iron	Fe	react slowly with heating	reacts reversibly with steam		reduced reversibly
	Lead	Pb			slow reaction with concentrated acid	slow reduction
	Copper	Cu		no reaction with water or steam		rapid reduction
	Mercury	Hg			no reaction	oxides reduced to metal very easily
	Silver	Ag				
↓ Least reactive	Gold	Au	no reaction			
	Platinum	Pt				

Metal	Reaction with water	Reaction with dilute acid
A	no reaction	no reaction
B	reacts only with steam	reacts quite well
C	no reaction	slow reaction with conc. acid
D	reacts violently in cold water	violent reaction
E	reacts only with steam	slow reaction with conc. acid U

5 ■ (a) Zinc is reacted with steam using an apparatus illustrated in the diagram.

Gas A, when mixed with air and ignited, gave a small explosion. A solid B, which is yellow when hot and white when cold, remained in the reaction tube.
 (i) Name gas A.
 (ii) Name the product formed when gas A burns in air.
 (iii) Name solid B.
 (iv) Write a symbol equation for the reaction between zinc and steam.
 (v) Name another metal which could be used safely in place of the zinc, to produce another sample of gas A.
(b) Gas A is also produced when zinc reacts with dilute hydrochloric acid. Write the **name** and **formula** of the other product of this reaction.
(c) (i) Name one metal which reacts vigorously with cold water to produce gas A.
 (ii) Name the other product of this reaction. (NEA) **R**

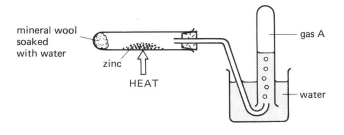

8 Solids, Liquids and Gases

The three states of matter

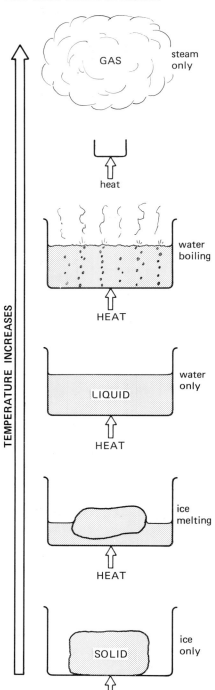

There are only three states in which a pure chemical can exist. It may be a solid, a liquid or a gas. These three **states of matter** cause chemicals to have different appearances. Solids, for example, have a definite shape. A block of ice taken out of the fridge has the shape of the mould in which it was made. If the ice melts, the shape changes. The water spreads out to fill the bottom of the container. Water is a liquid, and all liquids spread out like this.

When water is boiled, a gas is produced. This is steam or water vapour. Gases are much more difficult to store than liquids because they spread out to fill the whole container. If the container is a kettle, the gas escapes from the open spout to fill the room. If the room has open doors and windows, the gas escapes outside to try and fill the atmosphere. Water does not always need to be boiled for it to turn into a gas. A puddle of water in the open air will soon evaporate into water vapour.

Chemists need to be able to understand the reasons why solids, liquids and gases behave in these different ways. There is a lot of evidence to suggest that everything is made of particles – you, your clothes, the air you breathe and the ground you stand on! This chapter looks at some of that evidence.

Water can exist in three states of matter – solid, liquid and gas. The three states can exist together. Here the iceberg is solid water, the sea is liquid water, and the surrounding air contains water vapour.

Gases

If a balloon is filled with hydrogen gas, it floats up into the sky. Another balloon filled with carbon dioxide gas sinks to the ground. This happens because hydrogen is lighter than air and carbon dioxide is heavier. What happens if two gas jars are joined together, one containing hydrogen, the other air?

Since hydrogen is lighter than air, it ought to stay in the top jar and air stay in the bottom jar. After several minutes though, both jars burn with a squeaky pop. A mixture of hydrogen and air must be in both jars. Some of the hydrogen must have moved downwards, even though it is lighter than air. Some of the air must have moved upwards, even though it is heavier than hydrogen. This can be explained by suggesting that each gas is made up of molecules. These molecules are constantly moving, bumping into each other and into the walls of the jar. When the two jars are joined, this movement causes the two gases to mix up completely. This rapid, random movement of particles in a gas is called **diffusion**.

Joining gas jars of hydrogen and air

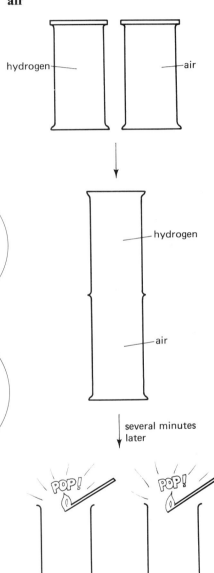

A mixture of hydrogen and air is found in both gas jars.

Diffusion of the molecules in hydrogen and air

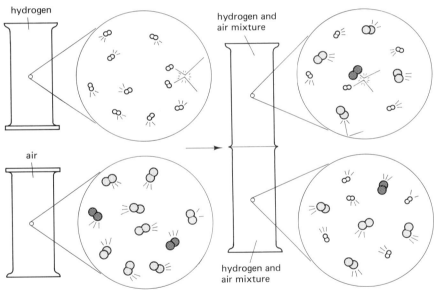

Key
- ∞ H_2 a hydrogen molecule
- ●● O_2 an oxygen molecule } air is mainly a mixture of nitrogen and oxygen molecules
- ○○ N_2 a nitrogen molecule

8 Solids, Liquids and Gases

Most gases are made of molecules

A molecule contains two or more atoms chemically joined together. Here are some examples:

H_2 Hydrogen molecule

HCl Hydrogen chloride molecule

N_2 Nitrogen molecule

NH_3 Ammonia molecule

O_2 Oxygen molecule

CO_2 Carbon dioxide molecule

The smoke cell

Gas molecules are very, very small. They are so small that they cannot be seen, even under a microscope. But it is possible to do an experiment to see collisions happening. Looking down a microscope into a **smoke cell** reveals tiny, bright white spots. The smoke itself is not a gas, but a collection of very small particles of carbon. The bright spots are caused by light being reflected from these particles of smoke. The spots are always moving in small 'zig-zag' steps. The reason is that air molecules keep bumping into the smoke particles, knocking them about. The air molecules are also bumping into each other, but they are too small to be seen, even under the microscope. What is seen is the effect of the air molecules when they collide with the smoke particles. You are being bombarded by air molecules at this moment travelling at over 1000 miles an hour! You don't get knocked around like the smoke particles because you are much bigger and heavier than they are.

A smoke cell

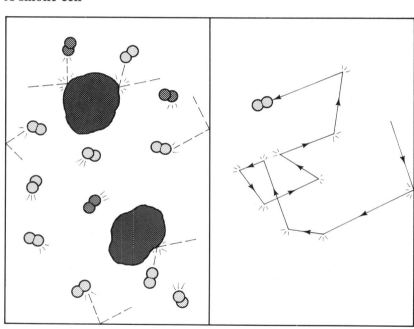

Smoke particles being bombarded by air molecules.

The path taken by a single gas molecule is 'zig-zag' and random. As it travels, it bumps off other molecules, and the sides of the vessel.

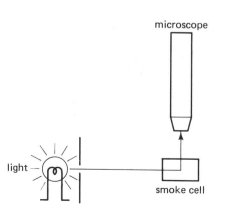

In the smoke cell, light is reflected off smoke particles. These are seen as tiny bright moving dots.

The molecules of different gases move at different speeds. This can be shown with a simple experiment using two gases – ammonia and hydrogen chloride. These two gases react with each other to form a white powder called ammonium chloride:

ammonia + hydrogen chloride ⟶ ammonium chloride
$NH_3(g)$ + $HCl(g)$ ⟶ $NH_4Cl(s)$

Diffusion of ammonia and hydrogen chloride

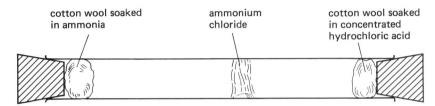

This reaction happens in the glass tube when the two gases diffuse from each end. However, the ring of white powder does not form in the middle of the tube. It is found about two-thirds of the way along the tube, nearer the cotton wool soaked in concentrated hydrochloric acid. This shows that in the same time the ammonia molecules have travelled further than the hydrogen chloride molecules. Ammonia molecules must travel faster than hydrogen chloride molecules. Ammonia molecules are lighter than hydrogen chloride molecules. Lighter molecules always travel faster than heavier ones at the same temperature.

Bromine diffusion

Bromine is a liquid which easily evaporates to give a dark red gas. When bromine is placed in a gas jar containing air, molecules of bromine bump into air molecules as they spread through the jar. This slows down their movement. When the bromine is in a vacuum, there are no air molecules to bump into, so the bromine spreads quickly. It is like the difference between being in a crowded shopping street on a Saturday afternoon and the same street on a Sunday morning. It is much easier to travel from one end to the other on a Sunday – there are fewer people to bump into!

Gases can move rapidly through a vacuum, but diffuse more slowly in air. It is like walking up an empty street on a Sunday morning compared to the same street on a Saturday afternoon.

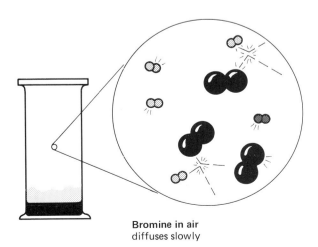

Bromine in air diffuses slowly

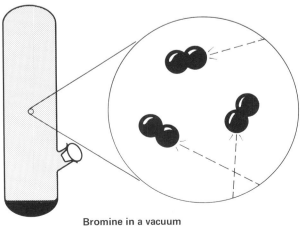

Bromine in a vacuum colour spreads instantly

8 Solids, Liquids and Gases

Liquids

When a liquid boils, a gas is produced. The volume of gas is always much larger than the liquid from which it was produced. Since the gas and the liquid must contain the same number of particles, the particles in a liquid must be much closer together than those in a gas.

A crystal of purple potassium permanganate placed in water leads to the purple colour spreading slowly through the water. After several days the solution is completely purple. If hot water is used instead, the colour spreads much faster. The solution becomes purple in only a few hours.

The purple colour has **diffused** through the liquid. This is caused by the water molecules bumping into the potassium permanganate crystals, and knocking off some of the purple particles. As these get carried into the water, they are bumped into by other water molecules, so that the colour eventually spreads throughout the whole solution.

Movement of molecules in a beaker of water

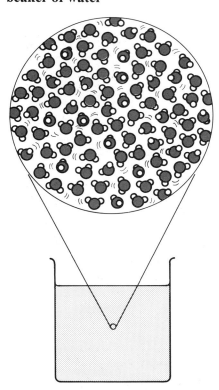

Diffusion of potassium permanganate in water

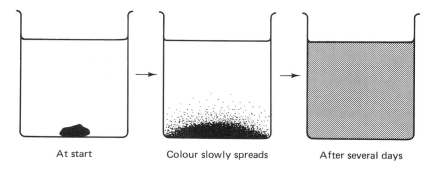

At start   Colour slowly spreads   After several days

The idea of how the particles in a liquid move can be seen in an experiment similar to the smoke cell. If pollen grains are mixed with water, and looked at under a microscope, they too can be seen to move about randomly. The movement is much slower than in a smoke cell. It is caused by water molecules bumping into the much larger pollen grains. The water molecules are too small to be seen, but their movement can be detected when they bump into the pollen grains. This effect was first noticed in 1827 by a botanist called Robert Brown. It is called **Brownian movement**.

This evidence gives an idea of how the molecules in a liquid behave. They move in a random way like gas molecules, but they are much closer together. They also move much more slowly. If the liquid is heated, the molecules have more energy, and so they move faster. However, the particles in liquids always move much slower than those in a gas. This also explains why the colour of the potassium permanganate spreads faster in hot water than in cold. The particles of the crystal are being bombarded more often by the water molecules. Movement of particles in liquids is rather like the movement of dancers in a crowded disco!

Movement of molecules in liquids can be compared to the movement of dancers in a crowded disco.

8 Solids, Liquids and Gases

Solids

There is no evidence to suggest that the particles in a solid are moving in the same way as in liquids or gases. If a crystal of potassium permanganate is placed on a solid sheet of glass, the purple colour does not spread into the glass. Solids hardly diffuse at all. The shape of crystals does give some evidence about the arrangement of the particles in a solid. Different crystals have different shapes, but the shapes are always regular. These shapes can be explained by the fact that the particles in the solid are packed together in a regular way. Crystals of one substance are always the same shape, but they can be different sizes. Sodium chloride crystals are always cube-shaped, but some crystals are bigger than others. As a crystal gets larger, the particles are arranged in the same pattern, but there are many more of them.

Shapes of crystals

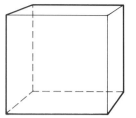

A cube-shaped crystal...

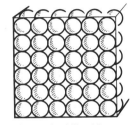

...may contain particles packed like this.

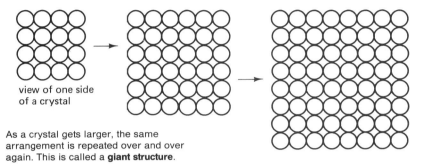

view of one side of a crystal

As a crystal gets larger, the same arrangement is repeated over and over again. This is called a **giant structure**.

The precise arrangement of particles in a solid is found by a process called **X-ray diffraction**. X-rays are shone onto a crystal, and they come through the crystal onto some photographic film. When the film is developed, there is a pattern of dots. From these dots, scientists can work out the exact arrangement of the particles in the crystal.

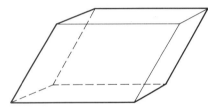

A diamond-shaped crystal...

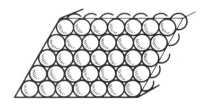

...may contain particles packed like this.

X-ray diffraction

An X-ray photograph of some sodium chloride forms a pattern of dots that looks like this:

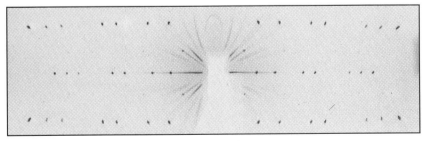

From the pattern of dots, the exact structure of sodium chloride has been worked out.

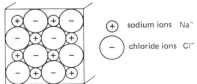

sodium ions Na⁻
chloride ions Cl⁻

Professor Dorothy Hodgkin. She won the Nobel Prize in 1964 for her work on X-ray crystallography.

All this evidence about solids shows that particles in a solid do not move around in the same way as those in liquids and gases. In solids the particles are locked into position. They wobble around a little – they are said to **vibrate**. They do not move from their main position.

8 Solids, Liquids and Gases

Changes of state

When a solid changes to a liquid, there is a change of state. It has been changed from the solid state to the liquid state. When a liquid changes to a gas, there is also a change of state. The following are examples of what happens when there is a change of state.

Melting and boiling

When a solid is heated, it gets hotter and hotter. The particles in the solid vibrate more and more, until the particles begin to break away from one another. This happens at the **melting point**. At this point, the temperature of the solid does not rise any more, even though heating continues. Instead, energy is used to break the bonds between the solid particles. As this happens, the solid melts to a liquid, and more and more particles become free to move. When all the solid has melted, the temperature of the liquid starts to rise.

When a liquid is heated, the particles in the liquid move faster and faster as the temperature rises. A few particles at the surface have enough energy to escape as a gas. This is called **evaporation**.

As more heat energy is given to the liquid, it reaches its **boiling point**. At this point, particles throughout the liquid have enough energy to break away from their neighbours and escape as gas particles. When a liquid is boiling, bubbles of gas form in the liquid and rise to the surface. The temperature of the liquid does not rise above the boiling point, but stays at that temperature until all the liquid has turned to a gas. If the gas is heated further, the temperature of the gas will continue to rise.

Temperature changes when a solid is heated

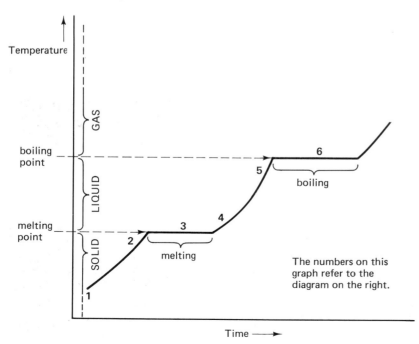

The numbers on this graph refer to the diagram on the right.

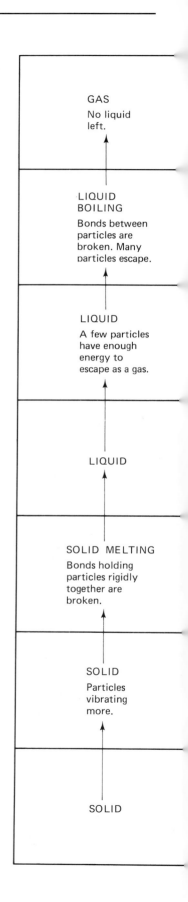

8 Solids, Liquids and Gases

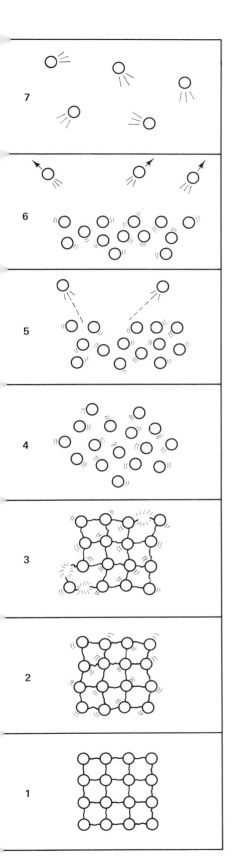

Sublimation

Sometimes, when a solid is warmed, it turns directly into a gas. It does not go through the liquid state in between. Similarly, when the gas is cooled, it turns directly into a solid. This process is called **sublimation**. Iodine is an example of a solid that sublimes.

Sublimation of iodine

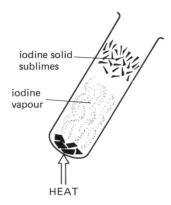

Solutions

When a solid dissolves in a liquid, a solution is formed. It is important to understand the difference between dissolving and melting. The following examples are useful:

Ice **melts** to form water. Water is a pure **liquid**.
Sodium chloride (common salt) **dissolves** in water to make brine. Brine is a solution.
When sodium chloride is heated strongly, it **melts**. Hot melted sodium chloride is a **liquid**.

Melting and dissolving

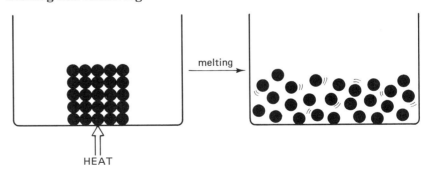

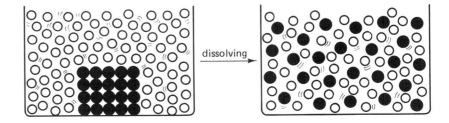

Summary

1. **Diffusion in gases** is caused by rapid, random movement of gas molecules. The gas spreads out to fill whatever container it is in. Heavy gas molecules move more slowly than lighter ones. Lighter gas molecules diffuse faster than heavier ones.

2. Movement of gas molecules can be seen in a **smoke cell**. Smoke particles move as they collide with air molecules.

3. **Diffusion in liquids** occurs more slowly than in gases.

4. Movement of particles in a liquid can be seen by watching pollen grains vibrating in water. This is called **Brownian movement**.

5. **Solid** particles are held close together in a rigid, regular arrangement. The particles are not free to move – they can only vibrate.

6. The **regular arrangement** of particles in a solid leads to the regular shapes of crystals.

7. **Changes of state** can occur between solids, liquids and gases.

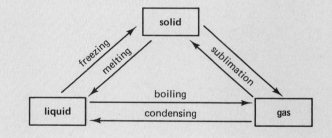

8 The properties of the three **states of matter** are summed up in the table below.

Solid	Liquid	Gas
regular arrangement	random arrangement	random arrangement
particles very close together	particles still very close together	particles far apart
definite shape	no shape – liquids fill container from the bottom	no shape – gases fill whole container
definite volume	definite volume	no fixed volume – gas occupies whole container
particles vibrate	particles move randomly and quite slowly	particles move randomly and quickly
little diffusion	slow diffusion	rapid diffusion
cannot be compressed	cannot be compressed	easily compressed

Questions

1. If two pairs of test-tubes were set up as shown in the diagram below, what gas or mixture of gases would you expect to find after a few minutes in each of test-tubes A, B, C and D?

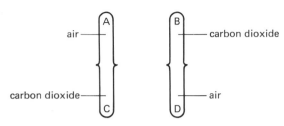

Explain your answer in terms of the movement of particles. How would you test for the presence of carbon dioxide? **U**

2. Rewrite the following statements, filling in the blanks with one of these words:

VIBRATE GAS DISSOLVE FASTER SUBLIMATION
RANDOM DIFFUSION SOLID SLOWER

   (a) Some glues cause plastics to _____.
   (b) Sugar dissolves in hot water _____ than it does in cold water.
   (c) The zig-zag movement of gas particles is called _____ motion.
   (d) The spacing of particles in a _____ is greater than in a _____.
   (e) It is easy to compress a _____.
   (f) Heavy gases move _____ than light ones.
   (g) When gases mix, the process is called _____.
   (h) In solids, the particles _____.
   (i) Iodine changes directly into a gas when heated gently. This is called _____. **U**

3. If $0.05\,cm^3$ water is put into a syringe and heated to about $110°C$, the plunger of the syringe moves out to about $100\,cm^3$.
   (a) What has happened to the water?
   (b) What has happened to the spacing between the particles?
   (c) What would happen if the syringe was cooled to about $50°C$? **U**

4. The diagram shows how particles are arranged in a liquid.

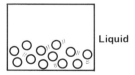

Copy out this diagram and, using the same sized particles, draw similar diagrams for the arrangement of particles in a solid and in a gas. Explain why it is easy to push in the plunger of a sealed syringe containing a gas, but difficult to push in the plunger of a sealed syringe containing a liquid. **R**

5. The diagrams labelled **A** and **C** represent particles in two states of matter.

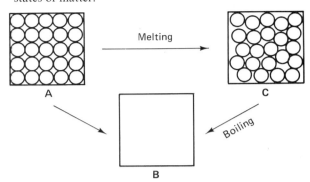

   (a) Copy out and complete the diagram labelled **B** to show the arrangement of particles in this state.
   (b) The particles in **C** are in the liquid state. In what state are the particles in **A**?
   (c) What is the difference in the behaviour of the particles in state **A** and those in state **C** which cannot be shown in the diagram?
   (d) Name the process by which state **A** changes straight to state **B**.
   (e) How could state **C** be converted to state **A**?
   (NREB) **U**

6. (a) Copy out and complete the labelling of the following diagram.
   (b) What do you *see* when the ice cube is gently warmed?
   (NREB) **U**

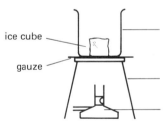

7. The following diagram shows the changes between the three states of matter with water as an example. The letters **A**, **B** and **C** represent changes of state.

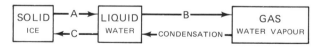

   (a) Name the changes of state **A**, **B** and **C**.
   (b) In which state of matter are the particles of water furthest apart?
   (c) (i) What is the boiling point of pure water?
       (ii) What is the freezing point of pure water?
   (d) Name the process for a solid changing to a gas without going through the liquid state.
   (NREB) **U**

8 ● The following is a list of terms used in chemistry. Use this list in answering questions (a) to (f).

  A Evaporating
  B Condensing
  C Melting
  D Subliming
  E Dissolving

Which word describes the process taking place in each of the following?
(a) The forming of a liquid from a vapour.
(b) The producing of water vapour from a solution of salt water.
(c) The change from solid sodium chloride to liquid sodium chloride by strong heat.
(d) The converting of molecules of water at room temperature from being closely packed to being very widely spaced.
(e) The changing of a solid to a gas on heating and back to a solid on cooling with no liquid state.
(f) The use of water to break down the ionic crystal structure of sodium chloride.   (NWREB)   **R**

9 ■ When the following experiment is set up, a ring of yellow powder is seen in the tube:

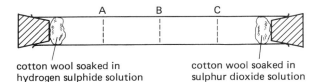

cotton wool soaked in hydrogen sulphide solution

cotton wool soaked in sulphur dioxide solution

It is known that hydrogen sulphide gas and sulphur dioxide gas react together as follows:

hydrogen   +   sulphur   →   sulphur   +   water
sulphide   dioxide

$2H_2S(g) + SO_2(g) \rightarrow 3S(s) + 2H_2O(g)$

Sulphur dioxide molecules are approximately twice as heavy as hydrogen sulphide molecules.
(a) What is the yellow powder formed in the tube?
(b) Where does the ring of powder form – at A, B or C?
(c) Which travels faster, hydrogen sulphide or sulphur dioxide?
(d) Draw the path you would expect a hydrogen sulphide molecule to take on its way down the tube.   **U**

10 ■ A strong sealed container full of ice was gently heated until only steam was present. The following graph shows the temperature changes that occurred.

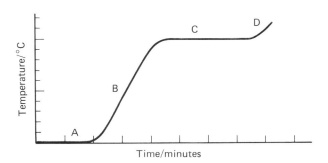

(a) What will be the temperature at (i) point A, (ii) point C?
(b) At which of the points A–D will the container have (i) only water, (ii) only steam, (iii) a mixture of water and steam?
(c) Describe what is happening to the water molecules at C.   **H**

11 ■ (a) The Kinetic Theory of Matter states that all substances contain particles which are moving. Use this theory to explain the following.
 (i) A solid has its own shape, but a liquid takes up the shape of its container.
 (ii) The pressure exerted by a gas in a sealed container increases with the temperature of the gas.
 (iii) A gas will move to fill any container.
(b) Pollen grains suspended in water are observed using a microscope. Smoke particles in air are also observed.
 (i) What would you see in both cases?
 (ii) How would the behaviour of the smoke particles differ from that of the pollen grains?
 (iii) What causes the particles to behave in the way you have described in b(i)?   (NEA)   **U**

9 Rates of Reaction

Rates of various reactions

Balloon full of hydrogen burning

very fast rate

Cake baking

quite slow rate

Apple ripening

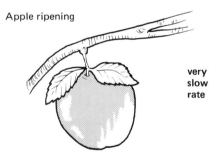

very slow rate

If a burning splint is put near a balloon full of hydrogen, there is a very loud bang! A chemical reaction has happened. Hydrogen has burned in air to make water vapour. The reaction happens very fast indeed. When a cake is being cooked in the oven, a series of chemical reactions are happening. They happen only slowly – it may take 30 minutes or more to cook the cake. All the time an apple is ripening on a tree, chemical reactions are happening. The acids that make the unripe apple sour, are being replaced by sugars. Apples ripen very slowly and this may take several months.

In each of these three examples, chemical reactions are happening at different **rates**. The rate of a chemical reaction is a measure of **how fast** it happens.

Measuring reaction rates

To find out how fast a reaction is happening, some measurements have to be made. Measurements are easy to make in the following reaction:

calcium + dilute hydrochloric → calcium + water + carbon
carbonate   acid   chloride   dioxide

$CaCO_3(s)$ + $2HCl(aq)$ → $CaCl_2(aq)$ + $H_2O(l)$ + $CO_2(g)$

The calcium carbonate in this reaction is usually in the form of marble chips. As the reaction happens, carbon dioxide gas is produced. There are two possible ways to measure how fast this reaction is happening. The carbon dioxide produced could be collected in a gas syringe, and readings of the volume of gas in the syringe be taken at regular time intervals. Here two readings are taken – **gas volume** and **time**. The other way to follow the rate of reaction is to measure the mass of the flask at regular intervals. As the carbon dioxide gas is given off, the flask gets lighter. Two readings are taken in this experiment – **mass of flask** and **time**.

In order to study the rate of any reaction, similar sets of readings must be taken. In other reactions, there may be different things to measure. For example, if a reaction involves an acid, changes in the pH could be measured at regular time intervals. The results from any such experiment are often plotted on a graph.

The reaction of a high explosive happens at a very fast rate.

9 Rates of Reaction

Following rate of reaction by measuring gas volume

The marble chips and dilute hydrochloric acid are put into a conical flask. This is connected to a gas syringe, which collects and measures the volume of gas formed. At regular time intervals, say every 10 seconds, a reading is taken of the volume of gas collected.

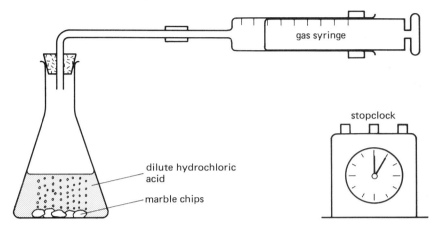

Results of measuring the reaction rate of marble chips and dilute hydrochloric acid.

Time/seconds	Gas volume/cm^3
0	0
10	10
20	26
30	44
40	63
50	78
60	86
70	90
80	90
90	90

Measurements made are: **gas volume** and **time**.

Here are the results of this experiment plotted on a graph.

Graph of volume of carbon dioxide collected against time

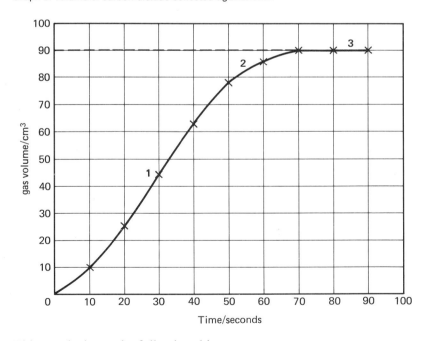

This graph shows the following things:

1. The graph is a straight line – gas is coming off at a steady rate.
2. The graph starts to level off as the reaction slows down.
3. The graph is a horizontal straight line. No more gas comes off. The reaction has stopped. Tracing the line back to the vertical axis shows that 90 cm^3 of gas has been collected.

Following rate of reaction by measuring mass

The rate of this same reaction may be followed by taking a series of readings of the mass of the flask. During the reaction carbon dioxide gas is given off. This makes the flask get steadily lighter. The flask is stood on a balance, and readings are taken of the mass every 10 seconds.

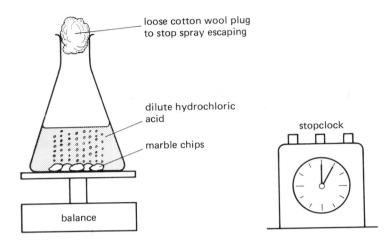

Results of measuring the reaction rate of marble chips and dilute hydrochloric acid

Time/seconds	Loss in mass/g
0	0.000
10	0.018
20	0.048
30	0.081
40	0.116
50	0.143
60	0.158
70	0.165
80	0.165
90	0.165

The **loss in mass** is plotted on the graph. This is found by measuring the mass of the flask and contents every 10 seconds, eg:

At start,
mass of flask + contents = 152.300 g
After 10 seconds,
mass of flask + contents = 152.282 g
In first 10 seconds,
  loss in mass = 0.018 g

Measurements made are: **mass** and **time**.

Here are the results of this experiment plotted on a graph.

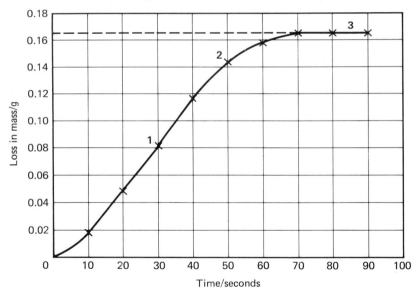

Graph of loss in mass of flask against time

This graph shows the following things:

1. The graph is a straight line – there is a steady loss in mass.
2. The graph starts to level off as the reaction slows down.
3. The graph is a horizontal straight line. There is no further loss in mass. The reaction has stopped. Tracing the line back to the vertical axis shows that 0.165 g of gas has been given off.

9 Rates of Reaction

Changing the rate of a reaction

There are several ways in which the rate of a chemical reaction can be changed. These are discussed below.

Changing temperature

Changing the temperature is often the best way to change the rate of a chemical reaction. A good experiment to show this is the reaction between dilute hydrochloric acid and sodium thiosulphate solution. These two clear, colourless solutions react to form pale yellow particles of sulphur. This causes the solution to go cloudy. If a flask containing these two solutions is stood on a cross marked on some paper, the cross eventually cannot be seen. The time taken for the cross to disappear at different temperatures is noted.

The effect of temperature on reaction rate

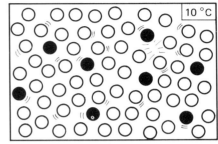

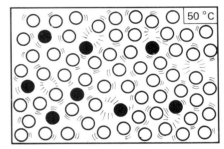

Particles at higher temperatures have more energy. They move faster and collide more often. Particles with more energy are more likely to react when they do collide.

Experiment to show the effect of temperature on reaction rate

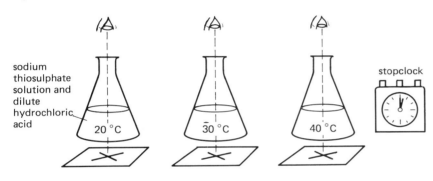

Time taken for cross on paper to disappear:

200 seconds   100 seconds   50 seconds

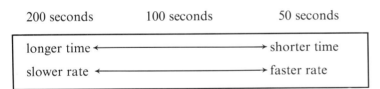

The hottest solution, at 40 °C, goes cloudy first. Increased **temperature** causes an increased reaction rate. The hotter the particles in a chemical reaction are, the more **energy** they have. Particles with more energy move around faster and so are more likely to bump into each other. When particles have more energy, they are also more likely to react when they do bump into each other. In a similar way, cooling down a chemical reaction will slow down the reaction rate. The particles have less energy and react more slowly.

Food is kept in a refrigerator so that it will stay fresh longer. The cold temperature slows down the chemical reactions that make the food go bad.

Changing concentration

Changing the concentration of a substance in a chemical reaction will affect the rate of reaction. The following is an example:

$$\text{magnesium} + \text{hydrochloric acid} \longrightarrow \text{magnesium chloride} + \text{hydrogen}$$

$$Mg(s) + 2HCl(aq) \longrightarrow MgCl_2(aq) + H_2(g)$$

A series of experiments is carried out, using acid of different concentrations. In each experiment, an **excess** of acid is used. This means that there is more than enough acid to react with all the magnesium. There is unused acid left over at the end, as well as magnesium chloride solution.

Experiment to show the effect of concentration on reaction rate

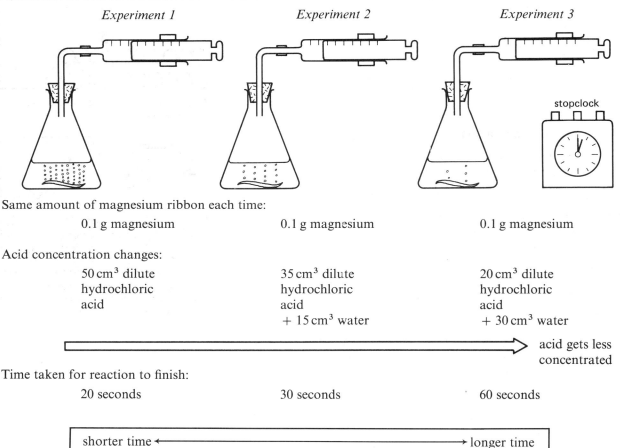

Same amount of magnesium ribbon each time:
  0.1 g magnesium   0.1 g magnesium   0.1 g magnesium

Acid concentration changes:
  50 cm³ dilute   35 cm³ dilute   20 cm³ dilute
  hydrochloric   hydrochloric   hydrochloric
  acid   acid   acid
       + 15 cm³ water + 30 cm³ water

⟶ acid gets less concentrated

Time taken for reaction to finish:
  20 seconds   30 seconds   60 seconds

| shorter time ← | → longer time |
| faster rate ← | → slower rate |

The most concentrated acid reacts the quickest. The greater the **concentration**, the faster the reaction rate. When the acid is more concentrated, there are more particles of the acid present in the same volume. This means that particles will be closer together and more likely to collide with the magnesium and react. When more water is added, the acid becomes more dilute. Acid particles become more spaced out, and are less likely to collide and react.

A graph may be plotted of the results of each of these three experiments. For each reaction, a series of readings of volume of gas collected against time are taken.

Graphs to show the effect of concentration on reaction rate

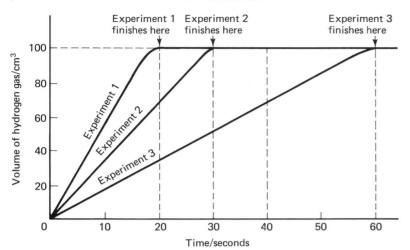

The effect of concentration on reaction rate

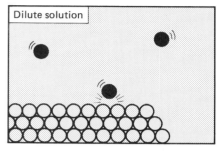

Particles are far apart and are less likely to meet and react.

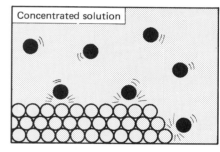

More particles are present in the same volume, so they are closer together. They are more likely to meet and react.

These three graphs show a number of things:

In each experiment, 100 cm^3 of hydrogen gas was produced. This was because the same mass of magnesium was used in each experiment.

The time taken for each reaction to finish was different:

Experiment 1 (most concentrated)	finished in 20 seconds
Experiment 2	finished in 30 seconds
Experiment 3 (least concentrated)	finished in 60 seconds

These results can be read off the graph.

The rate of each reaction is shown by how steep the slope of the graph is. In Experiment 1, the line shows a very steep 'climb' upwards. A large amount of gas is coming off in a short time. This means that the reaction is happening quite quickly. In Experiment 3, the line shows only a slow 'climb' upwards. The same amount of gas comes off, but in a longer time. This reaction is happening more slowly.

There is a similar effect for reactions involving **gases**. Changing the pressure on a gas is similar to changing the concentration of a solution. Increasing the **pressure** on a gas, increases the rate of reaction.

Effect of pressure on reaction rate for gases

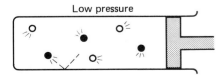

Particles are far apart and less likely to meet and react.

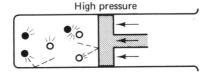

Same number of particles are closer together in a smaller volume. They are more likely to meet and react.

Changing surface area

When a solid reacts chemically with a liquid or a gas, its surface area can affect the reaction rate. The following reaction is an example:

calcium + dilute hydrochloric → calcium + carbon + water
carbonate   acid   chloride   dioxide
(chalk or
marble chips)

$$CaCO_3(s) + 2HCl(aq) \rightarrow CaCl_2(aq) + CO_2(g) + H_2O(l)$$

Experiment to show the effect of surface area on reaction rate

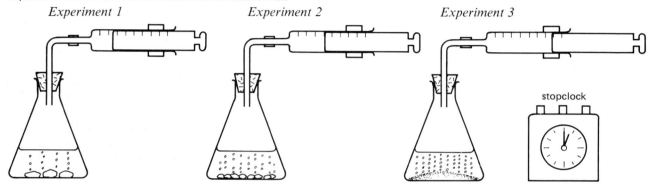

Experiment 1 *Experiment 2* *Experiment 3*

Same amount of acid each time:
  50 cm³ dilute hydrochloric acid   50 cm³ dilute hydrochloric acid   50 cm³ dilute hydrochloric acid

Same mass calcium carbonate each time:
  10 g   10 g   10 g

Size of particles:
  large marble chips   small marble chips   powdered chalk

Time for reaction to finish:
  6 minutes   3 minutes   20 seconds

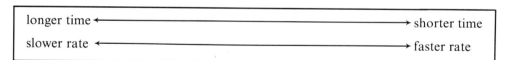

longer time ← → shorter time
slower rate ← → faster rate

Graph to show the effect of surface area on reaction rate

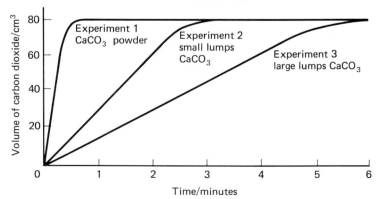

In each experiment, the same amount of acid and calcium carbonate was used. Only the size of the particles differed. The smaller particles have a larger **surface area** than the same mass of large particles. The greater the surface area, the faster the reaction rate. A powder is made from a large number of very small particles. This means that their surface area is very large. Powders can react very quickly indeed.

Catalysts

The rate of some chemical reactions can be changed by adding a substance called a catalyst.

Hydrogen peroxide solution decomposes or breaks down to give water and oxygen. The reaction happens only slowly at room temperature. Adding a small amount of black manganese dioxide powder suddenly makes the reaction happen much faster.

The effect of surface area on reaction rate

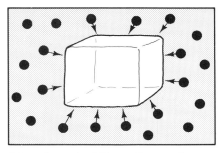

A large lump of solid has quite a small surface area. The reaction can only happen at the outside surface.

The effect of a catalyst on the decomposition of hydrogen peroxide

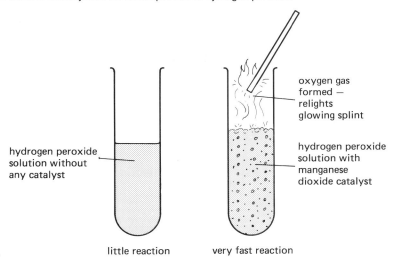

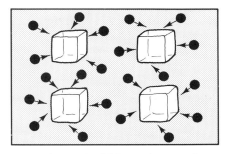

Smaller lumps of solid have a larger surface area at which the reaction can happen. The reaction rate is much faster.

hydrogen peroxide ⟶ water + oxygen
$$2H_2O_2(aq) \longrightarrow 2H_2O(l) + O_2(g)$$

Only a very small amount of manganese dioxide catalyst is needed. The catalyst is not 'used up' during the reaction. There is the same amount of catalyst at the end of the reaction as at the beginning. A **catalyst** is a substance that speeds up the rate of a chemical reaction. Its mass is unchanged at the end of the reaction.

The decomposition of hydrogen peroxide is also catalysed by other substances. A small potato peeling or a few drops of blood from your finger will do the job as well! The potato is a plant that contains a catalyst. Blood in animals also contains a catalyst. All living things – both plant and animal – contain many biological catalysts. A biological catalyst is called an **enzyme**.

Catalysts are very important in making chemicals on a large scale. Using a catalyst means that a chemical can be produced faster and more cheaply.

9 Rates of Reaction

Examples of large-scale use of catalysts

Making ammonia: Haber process

nitrogen + hydrogen ⟶ ammonia

$N_2(g) + 3H_2(g) \longrightarrow 2NH_3(g)$

Catalyst used

Iron Fe

Making sulphur trioxide: part of Contact process to make sulphuric acid

sulphur dioxide + oxygen ⟶ sulphur trioxide

$2SO_2(g) + O_2(g) \longrightarrow 2SO_3(g)$

Vanadium oxide V_2O_5

Making nitrogen oxide: part of manufacture of nitric acid and nitrate fertilisers

ammonia + oxygen ⟶ nitrogen monoxide + water

$4NH_3(g) + 5O_2(g) \longrightarrow 4NO(g) + 6H_2O(g)$

Platinum and Rhodium Pt + Rh

In each of these examples, the **surface area** of the catalyst is made as large as possible. This makes the catalyst more effective.

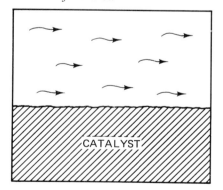

This is the catalyst alumina (aluminium oxide) used in several industrial processes. The particles are small to increase the surface area available to the reactants.

Effect of surface area of a catalyst

Small surface area

Mixture of gases passing over surface of catalyst. Only a small surface area is exposed to the gases.

Large surface area

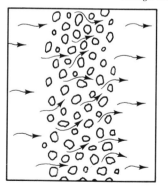

Mixture of gases passing through small pellets of catalyst.

Mixture of gases passing through catalyst gauzes.

Large surface area of catalyst is exposed to the gases.

Not all catalysts speed up chemical reactions. Some can be used to slow them down. These are called negative catalysts.

Using catalysts to control pollution

In Los Angeles, California, there are more cars per person than anywhere else in the world. Los Angeles is in a valley and the weather conditions combined with car exhaust fumes cause an unpleasant 'smog' to hang over the city. To help combat this pollution, all cars registered in California must be fitted with a special catalyst chamber in the exhaust pipe. The catalyst is usually in the form of platinum coated onto a network of tiny honeycomb-like tubes. Exhaust gases normally pollute the air with a mixture of unburned oil and petrol, carbon monoxide and oxides of nitrogen. The catalyst chamber converts these into harmless gases – nitrogen, oxygen, water vapour and carbon dioxide. The use of catalyst chambers on cars has steadily reduced the air pollution in Los Angeles. This process is only possible in countries where petrol does not contain lead compounds. Lead acts as a 'poison' to catalysts and makes them useless.

Summary

1 The **rate** of a chemical reaction measures how fast it is happening.

2 To find the rate of a reaction, some **change** is measured, e.g. mass or gas volume, at regular time intervals.

3 A reaction rate can be altered by:
   – temperature
   – concentration
   – pressure (for gases)
   – surface area of a solid
   – use of a catalyst

4 Measurements of reaction rate can be plotted on a **graph**:

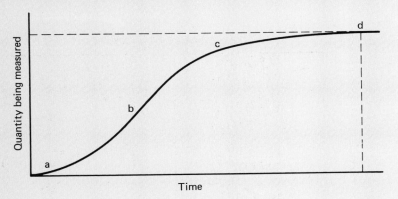

5 The **shape** of the graph shows useful information about the reaction:
   a Shallow slope – reaction is slow at the start.
   b Steep slope – fast reaction rate.
   c Slope starts to level off. Reaction slows down as chemicals are nearly all used up and their concentration falls.
   d Reaction has stopped. The time at which this happens and the final quantity measured can be read off the graph.

9 Rates of Reaction

Questions

1 ● The following graph shows the results of three experiments involving the reaction of magnesium and dilute hydrochloric acid:

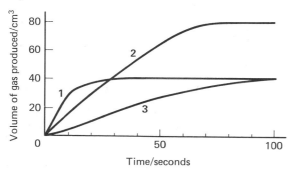

Answer the following questions, giving a reason for each of your responses.
(a) Which experiment had the fastest initial rate?
(b) Which experiment produced the greatest final volume of gas?
(c) Which experiment used the most concentrated acid? **H**

2 ■ A pupil carried out three experiments, all at 20 °C, to examine the rate of reaction between marble chips and hydrochloric acid. In each case he used the same mass of marble chips but the size of the chips differed. He used the same volume of acid in each experiment. The graphs of his results are shown below.

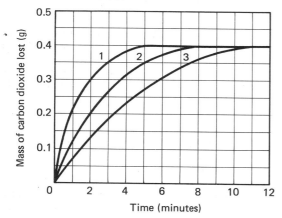

(a) (i) Which experiment gave the fastest reaction?
(ii) Give a reason for your answer.
(b) (i) In which experiment did he use the largest marble chips?
(ii) Give a reason for your answer.
(c) How much carbon dioxide was lost in **Experiment 2** after: (i) 2 minutes, (ii) $4\frac{1}{2}$ minutes?
(d) After how many minutes did the reaction in **Experiment 1** stop?
(e) What was the total mass of carbon dioxide lost in **Experiment 3**?
(f) Sketch the curve of the results you would expect if he had carried out **Experiment 2** at 50 °C instead of at 20 °C. Sketch this curve on the same graph as the other curves. (NREB) **U**

3 ■ A student studied the rate of the following reaction:

sodium carbonate + nitric acid $\longrightarrow$ sodium nitrate + water + carbon dioxide

$Na_2CO_3(s) + 2HNO_3(aq) \longrightarrow$
$\qquad 2NaNO_3(aq) + H_2O(l) + CO_2(g)$

The following results were obtained:

Time/seconds	0	10	20	30	40	50	60	70
Volume CO_2/cm^3	0	8	28	57	78	87	90	90

(a) Plot a graph of gas volume (vertical axis) against time (horizontal axis).
(b) At which of the following times was the reaction rate the fastest? (i) 10 secs (ii) 25 secs (iii) 45 secs (iv) 65 secs.
(c) Use your graph to find the volume of gas produced after: (i) 25 seconds (ii) 45 seconds.
(d) After how long did the reaction stop? What was the final volume of gas produced?
(e) Suggest two ways in which the rate of this reaction could have been increased. **H**

4 ■ Hydrogen peroxide (H_2O_2) can be decomposed using a catalyst of manganese(IV) oxide. The apparatus shown is used to measure the volume of oxygen produced at regular intervals during the course of the reaction.

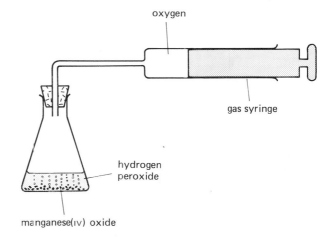

(a) What does a catalyst do to the speed of a chemical reaction?
(b) How would it be seen that the reaction was complete?
(c) 1 g of catalyst was used in the experiment. What mass of catalyst would remain after the hydrogen peroxide had completely decomposed? Explain your answer.
(d) Complete the equation for the decomposition of hydrogen peroxide.

$$2H_2O_2 \longrightarrow \underline{\qquad} + O_2$$

(NREB) **U**

5 ■ A pupil took a lump of limestone (calcium carbonate) weighing exactly 1 g and dissolved it in an excess of hydrochloric acid. The gas given off during this reaction was collected and its volume was measured at regular intervals. The experiment was repeated using small fragments of limestone. The table below gives the results:

Time/mins	Experiment A Vol. of gas/cm³	Experiment B Vol. of gas/cm³
0	0	0
1	11	18.5
2	22	37.5
3	33	54.5
4	43.5	67.5
5	53.5	74.5
6	63	78.5
7	71	80
8	77.5	80
9	79.5	80
10	80	80
11	80	80
12	80	80

(a) The experiment was designed to show the effect of using different sized particles. How should it be arranged to make sure that other factors (e.g. amount of substance, concentration, temperature etc.) did not affect the results?

(b) Draw and label a graph of the results. On the graph, sketch the line for results you would expect if 1 g of finely powdered limestone was used in the same experiment.

(c) With reference to the results of these experiments, write brief notes to explain **three** of the following.
  (i) Aluminium foil can be stored safely but containers of aluminium dust carry the hazard warning 'DUST EXPLOSION POSSIBLE'.
  (ii) Twigs are better for lighting fires than logs.
  (iii) Wheat grains do not easily catch fire, but flour dust in the air in flour mills sometimes causes explosions.
  (iv) An iron poker can be safely used to poke a fire, but when iron filings are sprinkled through a bunsen flame they burn brightly. (MEG) U

6 ▶ (a) In an experiment to investigate the rate of a reaction a sample of calcium was reacted with an excess of water at room temperature (20 °C) and atmospheric pressure. Hydrogen was given off and the volumes obtained at different time intervals are shown in the following table.

Times (minutes)	0	1	2	3	4	5	6
Volume of hydrogen (cm³)	0	29	44	53	59	60	60

(i) Draw a diagram of an apparatus suitable for carrying out this experiment.
(ii) Plot the results on graph paper. Label this graph **X**.
(iii) Explain why the first part of the graph has the steepest gradient.
(iv) Explain why the last part of the graph is a horizontal line.
(v) After what time was the reaction half completed?
(vi) Sketch on the same axes the graphs you would obtain if **only** the following changes were made in the original conditions.
  A The reaction temperature was 40 °C. Label this graph **Y**.
  B Half the original mass of calcium was used. Label this graph **Z**.

(b) The equation for the reaction between calcium and water is
$$Ca + 2H_2O \longrightarrow Ca(OH)_2 + H_2$$
(Relative atomic mass of Ca=40. The volume of one mole of a gas at room temperature and pressure is 24 litres).
Using the information given on graph **X**, calculate the mass of calcium used in the original experiment.

(c) Calcium reacts with hydrochloric acid to form hydrogen. The equation for the reaction is
$$Ca + 2HCl \longrightarrow CaCl_2 + H_2$$
(i) If the same mass of calcium as in part (b) was used to react with excess hydrochloric acid, what volume of hydrogen would be formed?
(ii) Explain why the rate of reaction of calcium with hydrochloric acid is faster than the rate of reaction of calcium with water.

(d) A solid **M** decomposes on heating into a gas and another solid **N** which is soluble in water.
When a mixture of solid **M** and an insoluble solid **Q** is heated, the same gas is given off at a faster rate than when **M** is heated alone.
(i) State **one** additional piece of evidence which would be required before **Q** could correctly be called a catalyst.
(ii) Describe how you would carry out an experiment to obtain the evidence stated in your answer to (d)(i).
(NEA) H

10 Atomic Structure

Particles in an atom

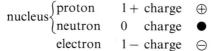

Atoms are so very small that no matter how hard you try to imagine their size, you never can! Even though atoms are so small, there is yet more to stretch the imagination. Scientists have discovered that each atom is itself made of a number of even smaller **sub-atomic particles**.

Particles in an atom

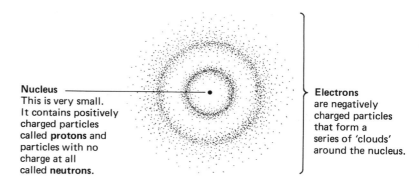

Nucleus — This is very small. It contains positively charged particles called **protons** and particles with no charge at all called **neutrons**.

Electrons are negatively charged particles that form a series of 'clouds' around the nucleus.

Most of the 'space' in an atom is filled by the negatively charged electrons. Imagine an atom to be the size of a large sports stadium. The nucleus would be the size of a pea in the centre of the field. The nucleus itself is very heavy for its size. Nearly all the mass of an atom comes from the nucleus. Some stars are thought to be made from neutrons – one of the particles in the nucleus. Scientists have estimated that a teaspoonful of neutrons would weigh 50 million tons!

Each atom has its own special arrangement of particles. Here is a helium atom.

A helium atom

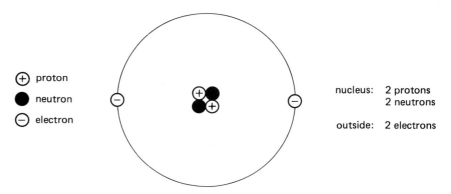

In an ordinary atom, there are always exactly the same number of protons and electrons. The positive and negative charges are balanced. The atom has no overall charge. The number of neutrons in the nucleus can vary. There is no easy way to predict how many neutrons there will be in an atom.

Measuring the size of atoms

Chemists have devised equipment that will measure the size of atoms. This page tries to give an idea of how small atoms are. The size of atoms is measured in **nanometres** (nm). One nanometre is a metre divided by ten, nine times over:

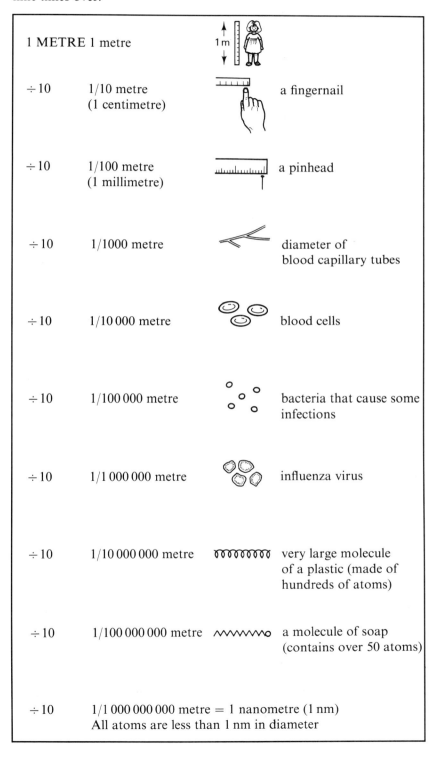

The size of some atoms in nanometres

hydrogen atom — 0.074 nm

carbon atom — 0.15 nm

magnesium atom — 0.32 nm

copper atom — 0.26 nm

Hydrogen atoms are so small that about 14 000 000 000 hydrogen atoms in a line would measure a metre!

Each of the 105 elements in the periodic table has its own number and arrangement of protons, neutrons and electrons. Elements in the periodic table are arranged in order of their atomic number. The **atomic number** is the number of protons in the nucleus of an atom. Each element has its own special atomic number. Carbon for example has an atomic number of 6. This is because carbon has six protons in its nucleus. If an atom had seven protons in the nucleus, it would be an atom of nitrogen – element number 7.

Sub-atomic particles of the first ten elements

Name	Symbol	Atomic number	In the nucleus: no. protons	no. neutrons	Number of electrons
Hydrogen	H	1	1	0	1
Helium	He	2	2	2	2
Lithium	Li	3	3	4	3
Beryllium	Be	4	4	5	4
Boron	B	5	5	6	5
Carbon	C	6	6	6	6
Nitrogen	N	7	7	7	7
Oxygen	O	8	8	8	8
Fluorine	F	9	9	10	9
Neon	Ne	10	10	10	10

Some atoms can have varying numbers of neutrons. This gives rise to **isotopes**. These are described in Chapter 29.

The electrons around the nucleus also have a special arrangement. Electrons exist in a number of cloud-like 'shells', one inside the other. The first, innermost shell is only small and can hold either one or two electrons, but no more. The second shell surrounding it is larger and can hold up to eight electrons. The following pages show the arrangement of electrons in the first 20 elements of the periodic table.

Summary

1 Atoms are very small. They are measured in **nanometres**.

2 Each atom is made from even smaller **sub-atomic particles**.

3 The central **nucleus** of an atom is very small. It contains positively charged protons, and neutrons which have no charge.

4 The nucleus is surrounded by cloud-like shells of **electrons**. Electrons are negatively charged.

5 In a neutral atom, number of protons (+ charge) equals number of electrons (− charge). The atom therefore has **no overall charge**.

6 Each element has an **atomic number**. The atomic number is the number of protons in the nucleus. Elements in the periodic table are arranged in order of their atomic numbers.

7 Electrons are arranged in a special way in a series of **shells**. These are one inside another. Each element has its own special arrangement of electrons.

10 Atomic Structure

The arrangement of electrons in the first twenty elements

Element	Symbol	Atomic no.	Configuration
Hydrogen	H	1	1
Helium	He	2	2
Lithium	Li	3	2,1
Beryllium	Be	4	2,2
Boron	B	5	2,3
Carbon	C	6	2,4
Nitrogen	N	7	2,5
Oxygen	O	8	2,6
Fluorine	F	9	2,7
Neon	Ne	10	2,8
Sodium	Na	11	2,8,1
Magnesium	Mg	12	2,8,2
Aluminium	Al	13	2,8,3
Silicon	Si	14	2,8,4
Phosphorus	P	15	2,8,5
Sulphur	S	16	2,8,6
Chlorine	Cl	17	2,8,7
Argon	Ar	18	2,8,8
Potassium	K	19	2,8,8,1
Calcium	Ca	20	2,8,8,2

The numbers under each atom show the way the electrons are arranged for that element. This is called its **electronic configuration**.

The electronic configuration of aluminium is 2, 8, 3. This means it has two electrons in the first shell, eight electrons in the second shell and three electrons in the third shell.

11 Ionic and Covalent Bonding

Salt and sugar are two white solids that we eat every day. Salt helps the nerves of the body to function and improves the taste of food. Sugar is an energy-giving substance that is added to food as a sweetener. These two white solids have very different properties.

Properties of salt and sugar

Property	Salt	Sugar
Chemical formula	NaCl a compound of sodium and chlorine	$C_{12}H_{22}O_{11}$ a compound of carbon, hydrogen and oxygen
Melting point	801 °C	180 °C
Does compound conduct electricity when melted?	yes	no
Is it soluble in water?	yes	yes
Does aqueous solution conduct electricity?	yes	no

How can these different properties be explained? Salt and sugar are both compounds. The atoms in these two compounds, however, are joined together in very different ways. Understanding how atoms join together can explain the properties of a substance. This chapter explains the different ways in which atoms can join together.

Noble gases – The 'unsociable' atoms

Nearly all atoms tend to join together with other atoms. The noble gases are the exception to this. These gases contain only isolated single atoms. A very reactive element like fluorine can 'force' a few noble gases to form compounds.

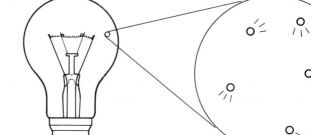

Argon is a **noble** gas used to fill light bulbs. Argon atoms do not combine with other atoms. They exist as isolated single atoms. Argon is said to be a **monatomic** gas, meaning it is made of isolated single atoms.

The behaviour of noble gases can be explained by looking at the way electrons are arranged in these gases.

Electronic configurations of some noble gases

Name	Helium He	Neon Ne	Argon Ar
Electronic configuration	2	2, 8	2, 8, 8
	The first shell can hold a maximum of 2 electrons.	The second shell can hold a maximum of 8 electrons.	The third shell can hold up to 8 electrons.
	In helium, the first shell is full.	In neon, the second shell is full.	In argon, the third shell is full.

A full shell of electrons has a special stability. Noble gas atoms are very stable as they are. Combining with other atoms would mean losing this stable arrangement of electrons. Atoms of other elements do not have full shells of electrons. When atoms of other elements join together, they do so in such a way as to form stable full shells of electrons. This usually happens in one of two ways. Electrons may be **transferred** from one atom to another, or they may be **shared** between atoms.

Ionic compounds: electron transfer

When atoms join together with the **transfer** of electrons, an ionic compound is formed. An example of this is the formation of sodium chloride from its elements:

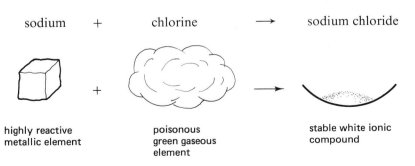

To understand how ions are formed, the arrangement of electrons in sodium and chlorine atoms needs to be looked at.

Making sodium chloride

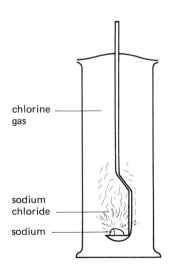

Sodium burns brightly in chlorine gas to make the ionic compound sodium chloride.

	A sodium atom (part of a giant structure of sodium atoms) Atomic number 11	*A chlorine atom* (in chlorine gas this is part of a chlorine molecule Cl$_2$) Atomic number 17
Electronic configuration	2, 8, 1	2, 8, 7
Number of protons in nucleus (1+ charge each)	11+	17+
Number of electrons (1− charge each)	11−	17−
Overall charge	0	0
	A sodium **atom** has 11 electrons. The outermost electron is in the third shell on its own.	A chlorine **atom** has 17 electrons. It is one electron short of a full outer shell.

When sodium and chlorine react together, the single outer electron in the sodium atom is **transferred** to the chlorine atom.

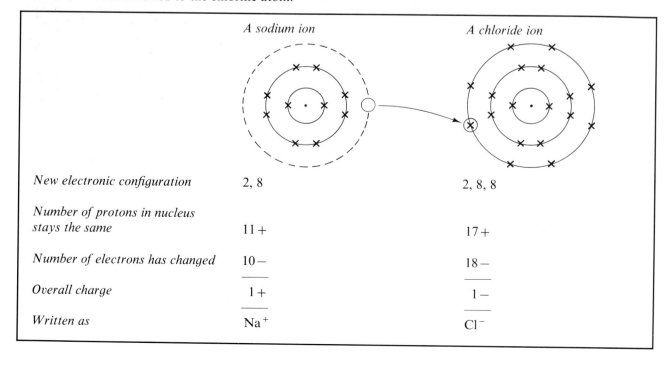

	A sodium ion	*A chloride ion*
New electronic configuration	2, 8	2, 8, 8
Number of protons in nucleus stays the same	11+	17+
Number of electrons has changed	10−	18−
Overall charge	1+	1−
Written as	Na$^+$	Cl$^-$

11 Ionic and Covalent Bonding

In this reaction, the sodium atom loses an electron. This gives it the same full shell of electrons as neon, a stable noble gas.

a sodium atom	becomes a sodium ion with a 1+ charge	and loses an electron
Na	$\longrightarrow$ Na$^+$	+ e$^-$

The chlorine atom gains an electron. This gives it the same full shell of electrons as argon, another stable noble gas.

a chlorine atom	gains an electron	to become a chloride ion with a 1− charge
Cl	+ e$^-$ $\longrightarrow$	Cl$^-$

When any atom or group of atoms becomes charged in this way, it is called an **ion**. When a chlorine atom becomes an ion, its name is changed to chlor**ide**. All non-metals change their name in this way when they become ions. For example, an oxygen atom becomes an ox**ide** ion.

Particles with opposite positive and negative charges attract each other. This is known as **electrostatic attraction**. The newly-formed Na$^+$ and Cl$^-$ ions attract each other very strongly. They join together in a regular pattern called a **giant structure** of ions. The same regular arrangement of ions is repeated throughout the whole structure. Sodium chloride is a typical ionic compound. Other ionic compounds will have similar physical properties.

Physical properties of sodium chloride

- hard, shiny crystals
- non-volatile: does not easily turn to a gas
- high melting point (801 °C) due to strong electrostatic forces between ions
- solid does not conduct electricity
- does conduct electricity when melted
- water-soluble
- aqueous solution does conduct electricity

A sodium chloride crystal

Sodium chloride crystals are cube-shaped. This is because the sodium and chloride ions are arranged in a cubic pattern.

The arrangement of ions in sodium chloride

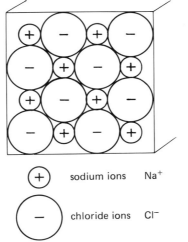

+ sodium ions Na$^+$

− chloride ions Cl$^-$

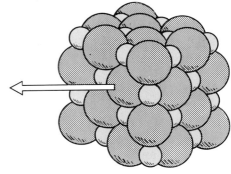

Which elements form ions?

To form an ion, an element has to lose or gain electrons and form the stable full shell of a noble gas. The following are the electronic structures of elements 3, 6 and 9.

Electronic configurations of lithium, carbon and fluorine

Lithium
Atomic number 3

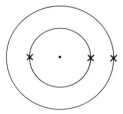

Electronic configuration:
2, 1

Lithium has one electron in its outer shell. It can easily lose one electron and form a 1+ ion:
$Li \rightarrow Li^+ + e^-$

All metals can lose electrons to form positively charged ions.

Carbon
Atomic number 6

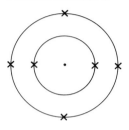

2, 4

The outer electron shell in carbon is half full. Carbon would need to lose or gain four electrons before it could form an ion. It is unable to do this.

Some non-metals with partly-filled electron shells do not form ions.

Fluorine
Atomic number 9

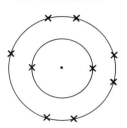

2, 7

Fluorine is one electron short of a full shell. Fluorine easily gains one electron and forms a 1− ion:
$F + e^- \rightarrow F^-$

Many non-metals can gain electrons to form negatively charged ions.

Ions of variable charge

As the atomic number gets higher, atoms get larger and have more electrons. Some metals have more complicated arrangements of electrons. The same metal atom can form more than one ion.

Copper for example can form both a Cu^+ and a Cu^{2+} ion:

A copper atom   forms a 1+ copper ion   and loses an electron
    Cu $\rightarrow$ Cu^+ + e^-

A copper atom   forms a 2+ copper ion   and loses two electrons
    Cu $\rightarrow$ Cu^{2+} + $2e^-$

In the same way, iron atoms can form ions with a 2+ charge (Fe^{2+}) and a 3+ charge (Fe^{3+}).

Naming compounds

The charge on an ion is often shown in the name of a compound, e.g.

copper(I) oxide means that this compound contains a copper ion with a **1+** charge

copper(II) oxide means that this compound contains a copper ion with a **2+** charge

iron(II) chloride contains an iron ion with a **2+** charge

iron(III) chloride contains an iron ion with a **3+** charge

11 Ionic and Covalent Bonding

Radicals

A radical is a group of atoms that carries a charge. Radicals can be positively or negatively charged ions. Here are some examples of radicals.

A nitrate ion

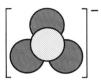

one nitrogen atom joined to three oxygen atoms

this group of four atoms carries a 1− charge

written:

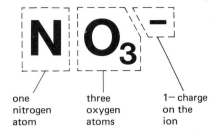

one nitrogen atom / three oxygen atoms / 1− charge on the ion

A carbonate ion

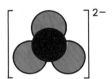

one carbon atom joined to three oxygen atoms

this group of four atoms carries a 2− charge

written:

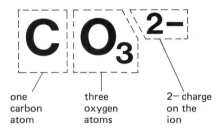

one carbon atom / three oxygen atoms / 2− charge on the ion

An ammonium ion

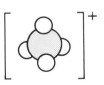

one nitrogen atom joined to four hydrogen atoms

this group of five atoms carries a 1+ charge

written:

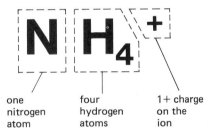

one nitrogen atom / four hydrogen atoms / 1+ charge on the ion

A sulphate ion

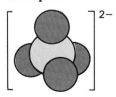

one sulphur atom joined to four oxygen atoms

this group of five atoms carries a 2− charge

written:

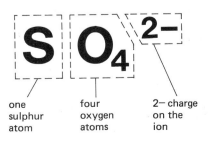

one sulphur atom / four oxygen atoms / 2− charge on the ion

Table of common ions

Positively charged ions
   (All metals together with H^+ and NH_4^+)

1+		2+		3+	
Lithium	Li^+	Magnesium	Mg^{2+}	Aluminium	Al^{3+}
Sodium	Na^+	Calcium	Ca^{2+}	Iron(III)	Fe^{3+}
Potassium	K^+	Barium	Ba^{2+}	Chromium	Cr^{3+}
Copper(I)	Cu^+	Copper(II)	Cu^{2+}		
Mercury(I)	Hg^+	Iron(II)	Fe^{2+}	3+ ions are quite rare and hard to form.	
Silver	Ag^+	Zinc	Zn^{2+}		
Hydrogen	H^+	Mercury(II)	Hg^{2+}		
Ammonium	NH_4^+	Lead	Pb^{2+}	A few 4+ ions exist, but they are even harder to form.	

Negatively charged ions
   (All non-metals and most radicals)

1−		2−		3−	
Fluoride	F^-	Oxide	O^{2-}	Phosphate	PO_4^{3-}
Chloride	Cl^-	Sulphide	S^{2-}	Nitride	N^{3-}
Bromide	Br^-	Carbonate	CO_3^{2-}		
Iodide	I^-	Sulphate	SO_4^{2-}	3− ions are rare and hard to form.	
Nitrate	NO_3^-				
Hydroxide	OH^-			4− ions are very hard to form.	
Hydrogen-carbonate	HCO_3^-				

Predicting the formula of an ionic compound

In an ionic compound, positive and negative ions join together. The number of + and − charges must always be equal. Here is an example:

when **one** silver ion	combines with	**one** chloride ion		silver chloride is formed
Ag^+	+	Cl^-	→	AgCl
1+ charge		1− charge		

The formula of silver chloride is AgCl. The 1+ charge on each silver ion is balanced by the 1− charge on each chloride ion.
   When magnesium chloride is formed, there is a difference in the formula:

one magnesium ion	needs	**two** chloride ions	to form	magnesium chloride
Mg^{2+}	+	$Cl^-\ Cl^-$	→	$MgCl_2$
2+ charge		total 2− charge		

In the last equation the formula of magnesium chloride is MgCl$_2$. The 2+ charge on each magnesium ion needs two chloride ions, each with a 1− charge, to balance it. Note that in the name and the formula, the positive ion always comes first and the negative ion second.

When one of the ions is a radical, a little care is needed to write the formula correctly:

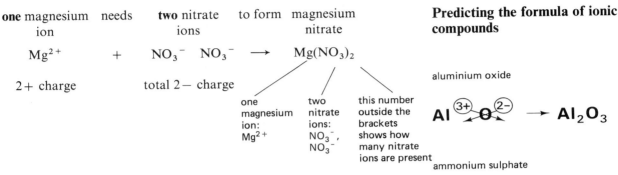

Predicting the formula of ionic compounds

Similarly, ammonium sulphate is written:

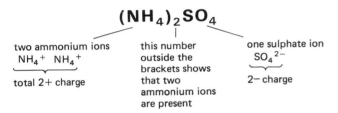

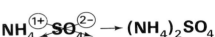

There is a short cut to predict the formula of an ionic compound. The two ions involved are written down side by side:

$$\text{magnesium ion} \quad \text{chloride ion}$$
$$Mg^{2+} \quad\quad Cl^{1-}$$

The number of the charge on the ion is then taken diagonally across to the other:

$$Mg \overset{2+}{} Cl \overset{1-}{} \rightarrow Mg_1Cl_2 \quad \text{or} \quad MgCl_2$$

Examples of some ionic compounds

Name	Formula	Melting point/°C	Boiling point/°C	State at room temperature (15°C)
Aluminium oxide	Al$_2$O$_3$	2047	3427	solid
Lead iodide	PbI$_2$	407	862	solid
Magnesium chloride	MgCl$_2$	714	1416	solid
Potassium bromide	KBr	734	1384	solid
Sodium fluoride	NaF	996	1827	solid

All these compounds are made from giant structures of ions. The ions are held together by strong electrostatic forces. This leads to the high melting and boiling points.

11 Ionic and Covalent Bonding

Covalent compounds: electron sharing

Another way that atoms join together is by **sharing electrons**. The two atoms in a molecule of chlorine are joined together in this way. The chlorine atom on its own is one electron short of a full outer shell. This makes chlorine very 'eager' to react and fill this gap. One way it can be filled is by gaining an electron from a metal atom and forming a Cl^- ion. Chlorine can also join with another chlorine atom, and share electrons.

Electronic configuration of a chlorine atom

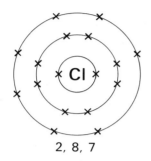

2, 8, 7

A chlorine molecule

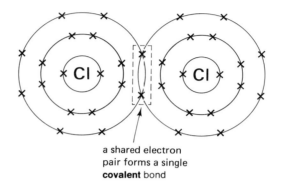

a shared electron pair forms a single **covalent** bond

Other ways of showing a chlorine molecule:

   $Cl-Cl$ Cl_2

A shared pair of electrons like this is called a **covalent bond**. This is the bond that joins the atoms together in a molecule of chlorine. By sharing electrons in this way, both atoms have a full outer shell of electrons. The element chlorine exists like this as Cl_2 molecules.

Another simple molecule is **hydrogen chloride**, HCl. Hydrogen and chlorine atoms on their own do not have full shells of electrons. By joining together and sharing electrons, both atoms gain a full shell.

Electronic configuration of a hydrogen atom

The first shell can only hold a maximum of two electrons. A hydrogen atom is one electron short of a full shell.

A hydrogen chloride molecule

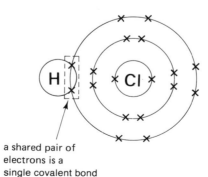

a shared pair of electrons is a single covalent bond

Other ways of showing a hydrogen chloride molecule:

   $H-Cl$ HCl

Methane, CH_4, is a molecule containing four hydrogen atoms joined to one carbon atom by covalent bonds.

A methane molecule

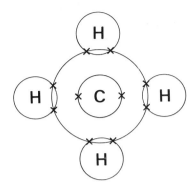

Other ways of showing a methane molecule:

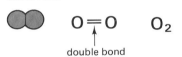

Electronic configuration of a carbon atom

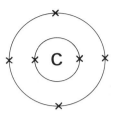

Carbon has **four** vacancies in its outer shell of electrons.

In an oxygen molecule, a **double bond** is formed by the sharing of two pairs of electrons.

An oxygen molecule

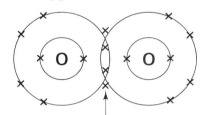

two shared electron pairs form a double covalent bond

Other ways of showing an oxygen molecule:

Electronic configuration of an oxygen atom

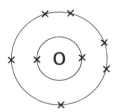

An oxygen atom is two electrons short of a full outer shell.

Electronic configuration of a nitrogen atom

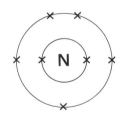

When two nitrogen atoms join together to form a molecule, a **triple bond** is formed. Three pairs of electrons are shared.

A nitrogen molecule

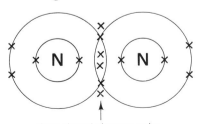

three shared electron pairs form a triple covalent bond

Other ways of showing a nitrogen molecule:

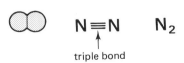

About four-fifths of the air we breathe is nitrogen. There is such a lot of it about because it is so unreactive. This is because the triple bond holding the nitrogen atoms together is very strong.

A nitrogen atom is three electrons short of a full outer shell.

Examples of small molecules

	Name	Formula	Shape	Melting point/°C	Boiling point/°C	State at room temp. (15°C)
Elements	Bromine	Br_2		−7	59	liquid
	Hydrogen	H_2		−259	−252	gas
	Iodine	I_2		114	184	solid
	Oxygen	O_2		−218	−183	gas
Compounds	Ammonia	NH_3		−77	−33	gas
	Ethanol	C_2H_6O		−117	79	liquid
	Methane	CH_4		−182	−161	gas
	Water	H_2O		0	100	liquid

Elements and compounds made from small molecules are gases or low-boiling-point and low-melting-point liquids and solids. This is because the forces between one molecule and the next are relatively weak.

Forces between molecules

Hydrogen
H_2

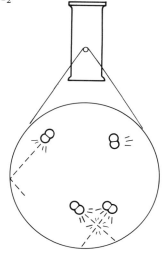

The forces between H_2 molecules are very weak. Hydrogen gas needs to be cooled to −252 °C before the molecules condense into a liquid.

Melting point   −259 °C
Boiling point   −252 °C

Water
H_2O

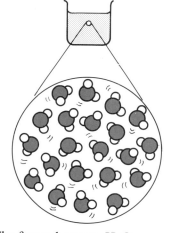

The forces between H_2O molecules are still quite weak. They are stronger than those between hydrogen molecules. Water therefore has a much higher melting and boiling point than hydrogen.

Melting point   0 °C
Boiling point   100 °C

Iodine
I_2

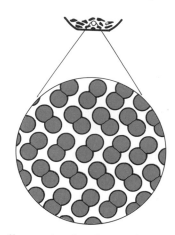

Iodine molecules, I_2, are large and heavy. The forces between iodine molecules are still quite weak. Iodine has a higher melting and boiling point than most small molecules.

Melting point   114 °C
Boiling point   184 °C

Large molecules

Molecules come in all shapes and sizes! Small molecules contain only a few atoms joined together by covalent bonds. A molecule of polyethene (polythene) is very large indeed. There may be thousands of atoms in a single molecule. Starch is another everyday substance made from very large molecules. The atoms in large molecules are joined together by covalent bonds in the same way that small molecules are. Atoms of the same element do not usually join together on their own to form large molecules. Nearly all large molecules are therefore **compounds**. They are always solids. They are often difficult to melt, and sometimes decompose when heated. Chapter 22 contains more information about large molecules.

Heating large molecules

All food contains many large molecules. When a slice of toast is overheated, it blackens to carbon and gives off a nasty smoke. The large molecules in the toast do not melt when heated. They have **decomposed**.

Polyethene is used to make most plastic bags. Unlike paper bags, polyethene does not rot when it is thrown away. Polyethene is said to be non-biodegradable. This means that careless disposal of plastic can cause problems.

Part of a polyethene molecule

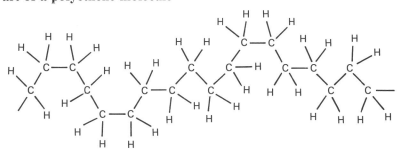

Polyethene molecules are very large. This diagram only shows a small part of one molecule. Even a small amount of polyethene contains millions of such long chains of carbon and hydrogen atoms.

Giant structures of atoms

Some non-metal atoms join together by covalent bonds to form giant structures. An example of this is silicon dioxide ('silica'), SiO_2. Sand and quartz are made from silicon dioxide. Silicon and oxygen atoms are joined together by covalent bonds throughout the whole structure. There are no individual molecules. The whole of each particle of silica is made from a giant structure of silicon and oxygen atoms. This is called a **macromolecule**.

A small part of the giant structure of silicon dioxide
Formula: SiO_2

Some watches and clocks contain a tiny crystal of quartz. This vibrates very fast at a regular rate when a small electric current is passed through it. The vibration of the crystal controls the clock and makes it keep very accurate time.

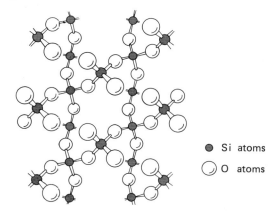

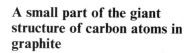

● Si atoms
◯ O atoms

Both elements and compounds can form giant atomic structures. The element carbon is another example of a macromolecule. Carbon atoms are joined to each other with covalent bonds, forming a giant structure. The carbon atoms can be joined in two different ways, either as diamond or as graphite.

A small part of the giant structure of carbon atoms in diamond

A small part of the giant structure of carbon atoms in graphite

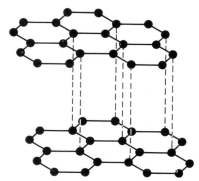

Diamond and graphite are both different forms of the element carbon. They are called **allotropes** of carbon. Allotropes are explained in more detail in Chapter 20.

The atoms in elements and compounds with this sort of structure are held together very strongly. They are very hard to melt. Silicon dioxide melts at 1610 °C and graphite at 3730 °C.

11 Ionic and Covalent Bonding

Which elements form covalent bonds?

To form a covalent bond, an element has to share electrons. Usually the stable full shell of a noble gas is formed.

Electronic configuration of sodium, silicon and chlorine

Sodium
Atomic number 11

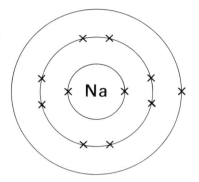

Silicon
Atomic number 14

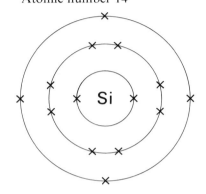

Chlorine
Atomic number 19

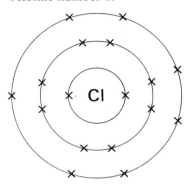

Electronic configuration:
2, 8, 1

2, 8, 4

2, 8, 7

Sodium has one electron in its outer shell. It easily loses this electron to form an ion.

Silicon has four electrons in its outer shell. It cannot lose or gain electrons to form an ion. It shares electrons, forming covalent bonds.

Chlorine is one electron short of a full shell of electrons.
  It can either gain an electron to form a 1− ion, or it can share electrons, forming a covalent bond.

All sodium compounds are ionic e.g. sodium chloride, Na^+Cl^-.

Silicon always forms covalent bonds
e.g. silane, SiH_4:

Chlorine can form ionic or covalent bonds, e.g.
  potassium chloride K^+Cl^- is an ionic compound,
  chlorine Cl_2, and hydrogen chloride HCl, are molecules containing covalently-bonded chlorine.

All metal atoms can form positively charged ions.
Only a few metals can share electrons and form covalent bonds.

Non-metal atoms with partly-filled electron shells usually form covalent bonds.

Non-metal atoms with nearly full electron shells can form either negatively charged ions or covalent bonds.

Metals

The atoms in metals are joined together with a special **metallic bond** to form a giant structure.

Part of the giant structure of atoms in aluminium

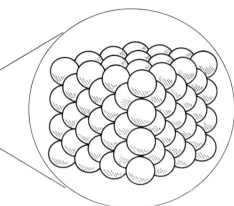

Aluminium is a strong, lightweight metal. It is used to build aircraft. Aluminium atoms join together into a three-dimensional giant structure. The atoms are held together by metallic bonds.

Metallic bonds are quite strong. The metal atoms are hard to pull apart. This means that most metals have high melting and boiling points.

Examples of some metals

Name	Symbol	Melting point/°C	Boiling point/°C	State at room temp. (15°C)
Aluminium	Al	660	2470	solid
Copper	Cu	1083	2595	solid
Mercury	Hg	−39*	357	liquid*
Sodium	Na	98	890	solid
Zinc	Zn	420	907	solid

* Mercury is the only metal that is a liquid at room temperature.

In metallic bonding, outer electrons of the metal atoms move freely from one atom to another. This allows all metals to conduct electricity when solid and when melted. An electric current consists of a flow of electrons along the metal.

What is an electric current?

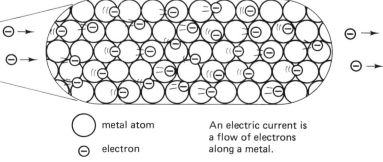

○ metal atom
⊖ electron

An electric current is a flow of electrons along a metal.

Summary

1. **Noble gases** are the only elements to remain as isolated single atoms. This is explained by their full electron shell.

2. All other atoms form various **chemical bonds** with each other.

3. A typical **ionic compound** may be formed by reacting a metal with a non-metal. The metal has only a few electrons in its outer shell. The non-metal has a nearly complete outer electron shell.
   - An **ion** is formed when an atom loses or gains electrons.
     Positive ions (+) are formed when atoms lose electrons.
     Negative ions (−) are formed when atoms gain electrons.
   - When two elements react together to form an ionic compound, there is an **electron transfer**. Only compounds can be made from ions.
   - An ionic compound contains ions of opposite charges. These are held together by strong **electrostatic forces** in a **giant structure of ions**.
   - A **radical** is a group of atoms with a charge, e.g. NO_3^- and NH_4^+. The **formula** of an ionic compound can be predicted if the charges on the ions are known, e.g.

two silver ions	combine with	one oxide ion	in silver oxide
Ag^+ Ag^+	+	O^{2-}	$\rightarrow Ag_2O$

   - **Properties of ionic compounds** include the following:

Property	Explanation
Hard shiny crystals.	Strong electrostatic forces hold ions together in a giant structure.
High melting and boiling points.	There are strong electrostatic forces between ions.
Solid does not conduct electricity.	Ions are held rigidly in a solid.
Ionic compounds *do* conduct electricity when melted or dissolved in water.	When melted or dissolved in water, ions are free to move and carry an electric current.

Summary continued overleaf

4
- A **covalent bond** is formed when atoms **share** electrons.
  - By sharing electrons, atoms usually gain a stable full shell of electrons.
  - Two fluorine atoms are joined together in a diatomic fluorine molecule:

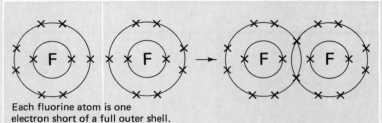

Each fluorine atom is one electron short of a full outer shell.

- A **shared pair of electrons** is a single covalent bond. Double and triple covalent bonds can also be formed.
- A **molecule** is formed when two or more atoms are joined together by covalent bonds.
- Elements and compounds made from **small molecules** are gases or liquids and solids with low melting and boiling points. This is because the forces between small molecules are very weak, e.g.

  oxygen O_2 water H_2O iodine I_2

- A single **large molecule** may contain hundreds or thousands of atoms. Starch and polyethene are examples of large molecules. They are solid compounds that are hard to melt. They often decompose on heating.
- Some non-metal atoms join together with covalent bonds to form giant atomic structures or **macromolecules**. They are all high-melting-point solids. This is because of the strong covalent bonds within the structure.
- Non-metal atoms usually join together by covalent bonds.

5 **Metal atoms** are joined to each other in a giant structure of atoms. The atoms are held together by metallic bonds. These allow the metal to conduct electricity. An electric current is a flow of electrons.

11 Ionic and Covalent Bonding

IONS ←— loss or gain of electrons —→ ATOMS

ATOMS branches into: Noble gases, Small molecules, Large molecules, Giant atomic structures (non-metals), Metals

	IONS	Noble gases	Small molecules	Large molecules	Giant atomic structures (non-metals)	Metals
Element or compound?	compounds	elements	elements or compounds	compounds	elements or compounds	elements
State at room temperature? (15° C)	solids	gases	gases or low melting and boiling point liquids and solids	solids	solids	solids (except mercury)
Conducts electricity?	no (when solid) yes (when dissolved in water or melted)	no	no	no	no (except graphite)	yes (when solid and liquid)
Structure	giant structure of ions	isolated single atoms	small groups of atoms	each molecule contains large numbers of atoms joined together	giant structure of atoms	giant structure of atoms
Bond type	ionic bonds	no bonds	covalent bonds			metallic bonds
Example	Sodium chloride	Neon	Ammonia	Polyethene	Silicon dioxide	Lead
Diagram						

11 Ionic and Covalent Bonding

Questions

1 ● The following diagrams show various arrangements of atoms:

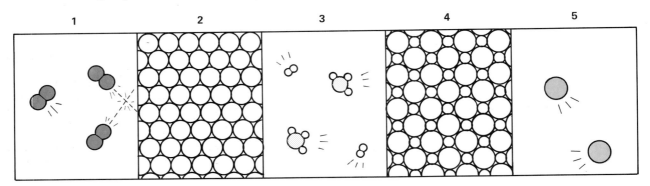

Which of these diagrams represent (a) a solid metal, (b) oxygen gas, (c) sodium chloride, (d) a mixture of two gases, (e) a noble gas? **R**

2 ● Use a periodic table to help you answer this question.
(a) Copy and complete the following table in which there are five spaces to fill in.

Compound	Formula	Type of bonding (ionic or covalent)
Water		covalent
Potassium chloride		ionic
Tetrachloromethane (carbon tetrachloride)	CCl_4	
Magnesium fluoride		

(b) By showing all the outer energy level electrons, draw a diagram to show the covalent bonds in a water molecule. (NWREB) **R**

3 ■ Describe the bonding in the following solids: (a) carbon (graphite), (b) iodine, (c) sodium chloride.
In your answer, describe clearly the particles that are present, what sort of forces hold them together, and the physical properties of each substance. **R**

4 ■ (a) The electronic structure of a sodium atom is 2,8,1 and that of a chlorine atom is 2,8,7. When they form an electrovalent (ionic) bond the sodium atom transfers one electron to the chlorine atom.
(i) Copy and complete the following diagrams of **an ion** of each element by drawing in the electrons.

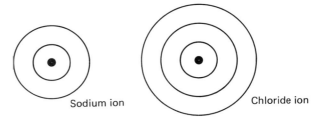

(ii) What holds the sodium ions and the chloride ions together in sodium chloride crystals?
(iii) Give the formula of sodium chloride.
(iv) Give one use of sodium chloride.
(b)
(i) Copy out the following diagrams and draw in the electrons to show the electronic structure of **an atom** of carbon (atomic number 6) and **an atom** of hydrogen (atomic number 1).

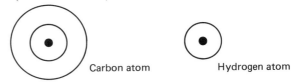

(ii) Draw a diagram to show the electronic arrangement in a molecule of methane (CH_4).
(iii) Name the type of bonding in a methane molecule. (NREB) **R**

5 ■ The following table provides some information about certain chemicals.

Substance	Melting point (°C)	Boiling point (°C)	Electrical conductivity of solid	of liquid	in water
A	1540	3000	good	good	insoluble
B	−114	−85	poor	poor	good
C	712	1418	poor	good	good
D	−68	57	poor	poor	good
E	−25	144	poor	poor	insoluble
F	−39	357	good	good	insoluble
G	1700	2776	poor	poor	insoluble
H	2045	3000	poor	good	insoluble

Answer the following questions by writing one of the letters **A** to **H**. Each letter may be used once, more than once or not at all.

From the substances shown, indicate:
  (i) the substance with the lowest melting point,
  (ii) **one** substance which is a liquid at room temperature,
  (iii) the substance which is a gas at room temperature,
  (iv) **one** substance which could be a metal,
  (v) **one** substance which is likely to be an ionic solid at room temperature,
  (vi) **one** substance which, at room temperature, is likely to consist of molecules containing covalent bonds,
  (vii) the substance which, at room temperature, is likely to have a covalently bonded macromolecular structure,
  (viii) **one** substance which is likely to consist of molecules containing covalent bonds, and which when added to water produces ions in solution,
  (ix) the substance which is likely to be an ionic solid at room temperature, and which is insoluble in water.
(NEA) **U**

6 ■ Sodium chloride is an ionic compound. It contains sodium ions (Na^+) and chloride ions (Cl^-).
  (i) Which is the larger ion, Na^+ or Cl^-? Give a reason for your choice.
  (ii) By means of a simple diagram show how these ions are arranged in a crystal of sodium chloride. (NEA) **R**

12 The Mole

When the tank of a car or motorbike is filled with petrol, the amount is measured in litres. When someone buys a bag of sugar, the amount is measured in kilograms or grams. A chemist may also measure out some petrol in litres – by **volume**. Sugar, or any substance, can be measured in the laboratory in grams – by **mass**.

A chemist may also measure the amount of a substance in **moles**. The following descriptions might be used:

'one mole of carbon atoms'
'one mole of sodium chloride crystals'
'half a mole of sugar'
'two moles of water molecules'
'three moles of ammonia gas'

This chapter explains what the mole is and why chemists find it so useful.

Relative atomic mass

There are 105 different sorts of atom known at present. These form the 105 known chemical elements. It is hard to find out how much each of these atoms weighs. They are very, very small. A single atom of carbon weighs about

$$0.000\,000\,000\,000\,000\,000\,000\,020\,09 \text{ g}$$

It is hard work writing down the actual mass of atoms. The numbers are very small. Because of this, chemists often compare masses of different atoms with each other.

We can compare all 105 elements with each other. To do this, the carbon atom is taken as a starting place. Carbon is given a **relative atomic mass** or A_r of 12.000 000. All other atoms are now compared to the mass of carbon.

The relative atomic mass is a number used to compare the masses of different atoms. It does not have any units. A full table of relative atomic masses may be found at the end of this book.

Comparing the masses of atoms

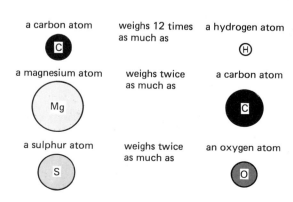

100

Relative atomic masses of the first ten elements

Atomic number	Name	Symbol	Relative atomic mass (A_r)
1	Hydrogen	H	1.0
2	Helium	He	4.0
3	Lithium	Li	6.9
4	Beryllium	Be	9.0
5	Boron	B	10.8
6	Carbon	C	12.0
7	Nitrogen	N	14.0
8	Oxygen	O	16.0
9	Fluorine	F	19.0
10	Neon	Ne	20.2

The relative atomic mass is not the same as the **atomic number**. The atomic number is the number of protons in the nucleus of each atom. The elements in the periodic table are arranged in order of increasing atomic numbers. Most relative atomic masses also increase throughout the periodic table. There are several exceptions to this. For example, look on a periodic table at elements 18 and 19, and at elements 52 and 53.

Why do chemists use the mole?

Chemists often need to know how many of one sort of particle react with another. This is vital before a chemical formula or equation can be written.

A formula

tells a chemist **how many** of each sort of atom are present in a substance.

The formula

CO_2

means that:

two oxygen atoms combine with each carbon atom in a molecule of carbon dioxide

An equation

tells a chemist **how many** particles of one substance react with another.

The equation

$$2Mg(s) + O_2(g) \longrightarrow 2MgO(s)$$

means that:

two magnesium atoms react with **one** oxygen molecule to give **two** magnesium oxides

Relative atomic masses

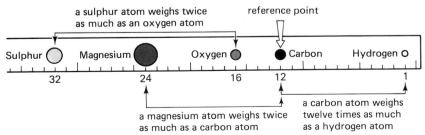

How do chemists find out how many particles of one sort react with another? Knowing only the mass of a substance is not enough. Someone may do an experiment and find out that

24 g	react	32 g	to	56 g
magnesium	with	oxygen	give	magnesium oxide

This information alone is not very helpful. To find out how many particles are reacting, **the mole** is essential.

What is the mole?

One mole of atoms of an element contains the relative atomic mass of that element in grams.

One mole of atoms of various elements

Element	A_r	Mass of one mole of atoms		
Carbon	12	12 g	12 g	1 mole carbon atoms
Magnesium	24	24 g	24 g	1 mole magnesium atoms
Sulphur	32	32 g	32 g	1 mole sulphur atoms
Copper	64	64 g	64 g	1 mole copper atoms

Chemists have calculated how many particles there are in one mole of any substance. Atoms are so small and lightweight that there are many millions of them in one mole.

The number of particles in one mole of any substance is

602 300 000 000 000 000 000 000.

That is just over six hundred thousand million million million! A shorthand way of writing this is 6.023×10^{23}. The '$\times 10^{23}$' means 'multiplied by ten, 23 times over'. This is called **Avogadro's number**, after an Italian chemist.

One mole of any substance contains the same number of particles as one mole of any other substance.

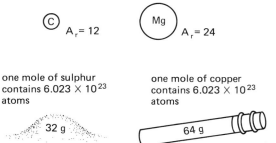

One mole of magnesium atoms weighs twice as much as one mole of carbon atoms. This is because each magnesium atom is twice as heavy as each carbon atom:

 $A_r = 12$ $A_r = 24$

One mole of copper atoms weighs twice as much as one mole of sulphur atoms, because each copper atom is twice as heavy as each sulphur atom:

(S) $A_r = 32$ (Cu) $A_r = 64$

Moles and structure

When thinking about moles, it is important to think also about the structure of a substance. For example, magnesium is a metal, so it has a giant structure of metal **atoms**. One mole of this element is called one mole of magnesium **atoms**.

Examples of moles and structure

Substance	Formula	Structure	How to describe one mole
Carbon	C	giant structure of **atoms**	one mole of carbon **atoms**
Chlorine	Cl_2	diatomic **molecules**	one mole of chlorine **molecules**
Hydrogen	H_2	diatomic **molecules**	one mole of hydrogen **molecules**
Magnesium	Mg	giant structure of **atoms**	one mole of magnesium **atoms**
Sodium chloride	NaCl	giant structure of **ions**	one mole of sodium and chloride (**ionic** compound)
Water	H_2O	**molecules**	one mole of water **molecules**

Moles of atoms

When an element is made of atoms, the mass of one mole is easy to find.

The relative atomic mass of carbon is 12: One mole of carbon atoms weighs 12 g

The A_r of magnesium is 24: One mole of magnesium atoms weighs 24 g

Often the mass of several moles is needed, or the mass of fractions of a mole.

one mole of carbon atoms weighs 12 g

two moles of carbon atoms so weigh 24 g

half a mole of carbon atoms weigh 6 g

It is generally easier to use this equation:

$$\text{number of moles} = \frac{\text{mass}}{A_r}$$
 – mass in grams
 – A_r relative atomic mass

This can be rearranged into another form as follows:

$$\text{mass} = \text{number of moles} \times A_r$$

These equations are used to turn:

moles ⟶ grams and grams ⟶ moles

They should be used any time the mass of a substance is quoted or required. The substance may be a solid, liquid or gas.

Rearranging equations

Here is an example of a mathematical equation:

$$a = \frac{b}{c}$$

⟶ the 'c' is taken across and multiplied by the 'a':

$$a = \frac{b}{c}$$

it can be rearranged to give:

$$b = a \times c$$ ⟵ the equation is reversed ⟵ $a \times c = b$

Examples

What is the mass of 2 moles of aluminium atoms? (Al = 27)

The question will always show the A_r when it is needed. The question says **'what is the mass'**, so the equation to use is

$$\begin{aligned}\text{mass} &= \text{moles} \times A_r \\ &= 2 \times 27 \\ &= \mathbf{54\,g}\end{aligned}$$

Remember to write 'g' or 'grams' after the answer.

What is the mass of 0.05 mole of carbon atoms? (C = 12)

$$\begin{aligned}\text{mass} &= \text{moles} \times A_r \\ &= 0.05 \times 12 \\ &= \mathbf{0.6\,g}\end{aligned}$$

How many moles of atoms are there in 36 g magnesium? (Mg = 24)

The question says **'how many moles'**, so the equation to use is

$$\begin{aligned}\text{number of moles} &= \frac{\text{mass}}{A_r} \\ &= \frac{36}{24} \\ &= \mathbf{1.5\ moles}\end{aligned}$$

Remember to write 'moles' after the answer.

How many moles of atoms are there in 1.0 g neon gas? (Ne = 20)

$$\begin{aligned}\text{number of moles} &= \frac{\text{mass}}{A_r} \\ &= \frac{1.0}{20} \\ &= \mathbf{0.05\ moles}\end{aligned}$$

Relative molecular mass

It is useful to be able to work out the mass of one mole of a compound. This is the **relative molecular mass** or **M_r**.

Examples
What is the mass of one mole of magnesium oxide MgO? (Mg = 24   O = 16)

Write down the formula: **Mg   O**

Remember this means   **one** magnesium and
                            one oxygen

Underneath each atom
write down the A_r: 24 + 16
Add them up: 40

One mole of magnesium oxide weighs **40 g**.

What is the mass of one mole of calcium carbonate, $CaCO_3$? (Ca = 40   C = 12   O = 16)

Formula: **Ca   C O_3**
Remember this means: **one** Ca, **one** C and **three** O

                                      3 × 16
A_r: 40 + 12 + 48

Add them up: 100

One mole of $CaCO_3$ weighs **100 g**.

What is the mass of one mole of ammonium sulphate, $(NH_4)_2SO_4$? (N = 14   H = 1   S = 32   O = 16)

Formula: **$(NH_4)_2$ S O_4**

           (14 + 4)
           (18 × 2) + 32 + (16 × 4)
             36   + 32 +   64
                       132

One mole of $(NH_4)_2SO_4$ weighs **132 g**.

In the formula: **$(NH_4)_2SO_4$**

NH_4 means **one** N and **four** H atoms

( )$_2$ means two of everything inside the bracket

Mole calculations I

1 • Find the mass of each of the following:
(a) 4 moles of aluminium atoms   (Al = 27)
(b) 2 moles of carbon atoms   (C = 12)
(c) 5 moles of magnesium atoms   (Mg = 24)
(d) 10 moles of sodium atoms   (Na = 23.3)
(e) 0.5 mole silicon atoms   (Si = 28)
(f) 0.1 mole helium atoms   (He = 4)
(g) 0.02 mole carbon atoms   (C = 12)
(h) 0.05 mole silicon atoms   (Si = 28)

2 • How many moles are in each of the following?
(a) 36 g carbon atoms   (C = 12)
(b) 112 g iron atoms   (Fe = 56)
(c) 60 g neon atoms   (Ne = 20)
(d) 96 g copper atoms   (Cu = 64)
(e) 3.5 g lithium atoms   (Li = 7)
(f) 3 g carbon atoms   (C = 12)
(g) 0.2 g helium atoms   (He = 4)
(h) 3.2 g copper atoms   (Cu = 64)

3 • What is the mass of one mole of each of the following compounds?
(a) carbon dioxide   (CO_2)   (C = 12   O = 16)
(b) silicon dioxide   (SiO_2)   (Si = 28   O = 16)
(c) methane   (CH_4)   (C = 12   H = 1)
(d) hydrogen chloride (HCl)   (H = 1   Cl = 35.5)
(e) sodium chloride   (NaCl)   (Na = 23.3 Cl = 35.5)
(f) aluminium oxide   (Al_2O_3) (Al = 27   O = 16)
(g) ethane   (C_2H_6)   (C = 12   H = 1)
(h) sulphur dioxide   (SO_2)   (S = 32   O = 16)

4 • What is the mass of one mole of each of the following compounds?
(a) potassium carbonate   (K_2CO_3)
    (K = 39   C = 12   O = 16)
(b) sulphuric acid   (H_2SO_4)
    (H = 1   S = 32   O = 16)
(c) nitric acid   (HNO_3)
    (H = 1   N = 14   O = 16)
(d) ammonium chloride   (NH_4Cl)
    (N = 14   H = 1   Cl = 35.5)
(e) calcium nitrate   ($Ca(NO_3)_2$)
    (Ca = 40   N = 14   O = 16)
(f) ammonium nitrate   (NH_4NO_3)
    (N = 14   H = 1   O = 16)
(g) calcium hydroxide   ($Ca(OH)_2$)
    (Ca = 40   O = 16   H = 1)
(h) aluminium sulphate   ($Al_2(SO_4)_3$)
    (Al = 27   S = 32   O = 16)

Moles of molecules

Many elements and compounds are made from molecules. The term '**mole of molecules**' is used to describe these.

Examples of moles of molecules

Substance	Formula	How to describe 1 mole
Bromine	Br_2	1 mole of bromine molecules
Carbon dioxide	CO_2	1 mole of carbon dioxide molecules
Chlorine	Cl_2	1 mole of chlorine molecules
Nitrogen	N_2	1 mole of nitrogen molecules
Sugar	$C_{12}H_{22}O_{11}$	1 mole of sugar molecules
Water	H_2O	1 mole of water molecules

One mole of molecules of a substance contains the same number of molecules as one mole of any other substance.

one mole of
chlorine molecules

one mole of
water molecules

one mole of
sugar molecules

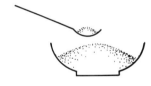

contains 6.023×10^{23} molecules

contains 6.023×10^{23} molecules

contains 6.023×10^{23} molecules

Cl_2

35.5 + 35.5

71 g

H_2 O

1 + 1 + 16

18 g

C_{12} H_{22} O_{11}

(12 × 12) + (22 × 1) + (11 × 16)
   144   +   22   +   176

342 g

Note that one mole of chlorine molecules weighs 71 g. The **element** chlorine exists as diatomic molecules Cl_2. When chlorine occurs in **compounds**, the relative molecular mass is added up as for any other substance.

Relative molecular mass of chlorine and its compounds

Formula: Cl_2 H   Cl   Ca Cl_2

           35.5 + 35.5   1 + 35.5   40 + 35.5 + 35.5

M_r: 71   36.5   111

Chemists do not usually use exactly one mole of a substance. It is useful to be able to find out about fractions of a mole of various compounds.

Examples

What is the mass of 0.05 mole of magnesium oxide (MgO)?
    (Mg = 24   O = 16)

Find the M_r of MgO: Mg   O
                                24 + 16
                                   40

The question asks '**what is the mass**', so the equation to use is:

    mass = moles × M_r
           = 0.05   × 40
           = **2.0 g**

In a similar way to previous calculations, use the formula:

$$\text{number of moles} = \frac{\text{mass}}{M_r}$$

This can be rearranged to find the mass:

    mass = number of moles × M_r.

How many moles are there in 20 g of iron(II) oxide (Fe_2O_3)?
    (Fe = 56   O = 16)

M_r of Fe_2O_3: Fe_2 O_3
                      (2 × 56) + (3 × 16)
                      112   +   48
                          160

The question asks '**how many moles**', so the equation to use is:

$$\text{number of moles} = \frac{\text{mass}}{M_r}$$

$$= \frac{20}{160}$$

= **0.125 mole**

For Mole calculations II, see overleaf.

Mole calculations II

5 ■ Find the mass of each of the following:

(a) 0.1 mole calcium carbonate (CaCO$_3$)
(Ca = 40   C = 12   O = 16)

(b) 0.2 mole sodium chloride (NaCl)
(Na = 23.3   Cl = 35.5)

(c) 0.01 mole magnesium oxide (MgO)
(Mg = 24   O = 16)

(d) 0.025 mole carbon dioxide (CO$_2$)
(C = 12   O = 16)

(e) 0.02 mole iron(III) oxide (Fe$_2$O$_3$)
(Fe = 56   O = 16)

(f) 4 moles water molecules (H$_2$O)
(H = 1   O = 16)

(g) 0.075 mole calcium nitrate (Ca(NO$_3$)$_2$)
(Ca = 40   N = 14   O = 16)

(h) 0.04 mole ammonium sulphate ((NH$_4$)$_2$SO$_4$)
(N = 14   H = 1   S = 32   O = 16)

6 ■ Find the number of moles in each of the following:

(a) 8 g methane (CH$_4$)
(C = 12   H = 1)

(b) 32 g sulphur dioxide (SO$_2$)
(S = 32   O = 16)

(c) 1.1 g carbon dioxide (CO$_2$)
(C = 12   O = 16)

(d) 12.25 g sulphuric acid (H$_2$SO$_4$)
(H = 1   S = 32   O = 16)

(e) 13.35 g aluminium chloride (AlCl$_3$)
(Al = 27   Cl = 35.5)

(f) 8 g copper(II) sulphate (CuSO$_4$)
(Cu = 64   S = 32   O = 16)

(g) 14.5 g magnesium hydroxide (Mg(OH)$_2$)
(Mg = 24   O = 16   H = 1)

(h) 12.8 g ammonium nitrate (NH$_4$NO$_3$)
(N = 14   H = 1   O = 16)

Finding the formula of a compound from reacting masses

Chemists often discover or make new compounds. One essential experiment that must then be done is to find the formula. The formula of magnesium oxide is known to be MgO. But why not Mg$_2$O or MgO$_3$ or some other formula? The amounts of magnesium and oxygen reacting together can be measured, and from this the formula worked out.

The crucible lid is carefully lifted from time to time. This lets in oxygen from the air to react with the magnesium. If the lid is left off for too long, some magnesium oxide smoke escapes. This leads to an error in the result.

The following reaction happens: magnesium + oxygen → magnesium oxide
                                                    (from the air)

Example of masses measured: [0.024 g] + [?] → [0.040 g]

mass of oxygen is found by subtraction: 0.040 − 0.024 = **0.016 g**

From these results the formula can be found:

Write down the symbols of the elements reacting (metal first):	Mg	O
Write down the masses:	0.024 g	0.016 g
Find the number of moles of atoms of each $\left(\text{number of moles} = \dfrac{\text{mass}}{A_r}\right)$: (Mg = 24 O = 16)	$\dfrac{0.024}{24}$	$\dfrac{0.016}{16}$
	0.001	0.001
Find the ratio:	1 :	1
Write the formula:	Mg$_1$O$_1$ or **MgO**	

The reaction between magnesium and oxygen

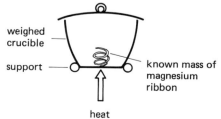

The experiment with copper(II) oxide described here is another example of finding the formula of a compound.

Reducing copper(II) oxide

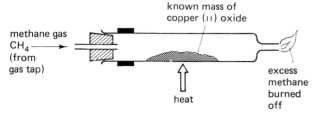

Copper(II) oxide is a black powder. The methane removes the oxygen from copper(II) oxide. Copper(II) oxide is **reduced** to copper. The methane has acted as a **reducing agent**.

The following reaction occurs:

copper(II) + methane → copper + carbon + water
oxide   dioxide

Examples of masses measured:

4.0 g →(reduction: loss of oxygen)→ 3.2 g

Mass of oxygen lost is found by subtraction:
4.0 − 3.2 = **0.8 g**

To find the formula:

Symbols:	Cu		O
Masses:	3.2 g		0.8 g
Moles:	$\dfrac{3.2}{64}$		$\dfrac{0.8}{16}$
	0.05		0.05
Ratio:	1	:	1
Simplest formula:		**CuO**	

A similar method must be used to find the formula of any compound from the reacting masses.

Examples

Find the simplest formula of an oxide of iron formed by reacting 2.24 g iron with 0.96 g oxygen.
(Fe = 56   O = 16)

Symbols:	Fe		O
Masses:	2.24		0.96
Moles:	$\dfrac{2.24}{56}$		$\dfrac{0.96}{16}$
	0.04		0.06
Ratio:	2	:	3
Simplest formula:		**Fe$_2$O$_3$**	

2.84 g of an oxide of phosphorus are formed when 1.24 g phosphorus react with excess oxygen. Find its simplest formula.
(P = 31   O = 16)

Symbols:	P		O
Masses:	1.24 g		1.60 g
			(found by subtraction)
Moles:	$\dfrac{1.24}{31}$		$\dfrac{1.60}{16}$
	0.04		0.10
Ratio:	2	:	5
Simplest formula:		**P$_2$O$_5$**	

An acid was analysed and found to contain 2.44% hydrogen, 39.02% sulphur and 58.54% oxygen by mass. Find its simplest formula.
(H = 1   S = 32   O = 16)

This question gives a '% by mass' for each element. Imagine there are 100 g of the substance. 2.44 g will be hydrogen, 39.02 g sulphur, and so on.

Symbols:	H	S	O
Masses:	2.44 g	39.02 g	58.54 g
Moles:	$\dfrac{2.44}{1}$	$\dfrac{39.02}{32}$	$\dfrac{58.54}{16}$
	2.44	1.22	3.66

Divide by the smallest number to get the ratio: (i.e. ÷1.22)   2 : 1 : 3

Simplest formula: **H$_2$SO$_3$**

Empirical and molecular formulae

The problems in the previous sections have all calculated the simplest ratio of elements in a compound. This is known as the **empirical formula**. The actual number of moles of each element in one mole of a compound gives the **molecular formula**. To find the molecular formula of a compound, the mass of one mole must be known:

Example

A hydrocarbon was found to contain 80% carbon and 20% hydrogen by mass. Its relative molecular mass was 30. Find the empirical formula and the molecular formula.
  (C = 12   H = 1)

	C	H
Symbols:	C	H
Masses:	80 g	20 g
Moles:	$\frac{80}{12}$	$\frac{20}{1}$
	6.67	20
Divide by the smaller number to get the ratio:	1	3

Empirical formula (simplest ratio): CH_3

Find mass of empirical formula: $\underbrace{12 + 3}$ = 15

Compare with M_r: 30 $\quad$ } M_r is **twice** mass of empirical formula

Molecular formula must be **twice** empirical formula: C_2H_6

Molecular formula is: C_2H_6.

Mole calculations III

7 These questions give practice in finding the formula of a compound from reacting masses.

- (a) Find the simplest formula of the carbon oxide formed when 0.24 g carbon react with 0.32 g oxygen.
  (C = 12   O = 16)

- (b) 0.20 g calcium reacted with fluorine to make 0.39 g calcium fluoride. Find the simplest formula of this compound.
  (Ca = 40   F = 19)

- (c) Find the simplest formula of the nitrogen fluoride formed when 7 g nitrogen react with 19 g fluorine.
  (N = 14   F = 19)

- (d) Find the simplest formula of the compound formed by 0.48 g carbon and 0.16 g hydrogen.
  (C = 12   H = 1)

- (e) A compound was found to contain 0.6 g magnesium, 0.8 g sulphur and 1.6 g oxygen. Find its simplest formula.
  (Mg = 24   S = 32   O = 16)

- (f) A compound was found to contain 40% carbon, 6.67% hydrogen and 53.33% oxygen by mass. Its relative molecular mass was 60. Find (i) its empirical formula, (ii) its molecular formula.
  (C = 12   H = 1   O = 16)

- (g) A hydrocarbon of relative molecular mass 78 was found to contain 92.31% carbon and 7.69% hydrogen by mass. Find its molecular formula.
  (C = 12   H = 1)

- (h) A sugar of M_r 180 was found to contain 40% carbon, 6.67% hydrogen and 53.33% oxygen by mass. Find its molecular formula.
  (C = 12   H = 1   O = 16)

12 The Mole

Moles of gases

When a reaction involves a gas, there are several ways to find the amount of gas involved.

Finding the amount of gas involved in a reaction
Find change in **mass**   OR   Find **gas volume**

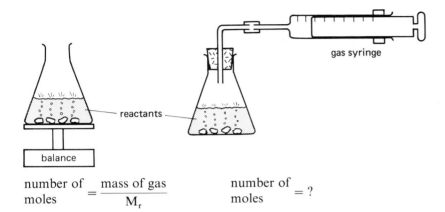

number of moles = $\dfrac{\text{mass of gas}}{M_r}$ number of moles = ?

It has been found that one mole of any gas occupies **24 litres** or **24 000 cm³** at room temperature and pressure. Room temperature is taken as about 20 °C.

A litre is sometimes written **1 dm³**, or one cubic decimetre.
One decimetre is 10 cm.

One mole of various gases at room temperature and pressure

1 mole of oxygen molecules   1 mole of ammonia molecules   1 mole of neon atoms

24 000 cm³ oxygen contains

6.023×10^{23} molecules of oxygen

24 000 cm³ ammonia contains

6.023×10^{23} molecules of ammonia

24 000 cm³ neon contains

6.023×10^{23} atoms of neon

Ways of describing one litre

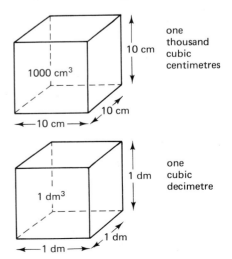

Particles in a gas

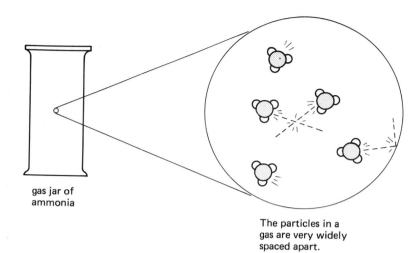

gas jar of ammonia

The particles in a gas are very widely spaced apart.

The effect of temperature on gases

As a gas gets hotter, the particles gain more energy. This means they move around faster. At constant pressure, the gas expands as it gets hotter:

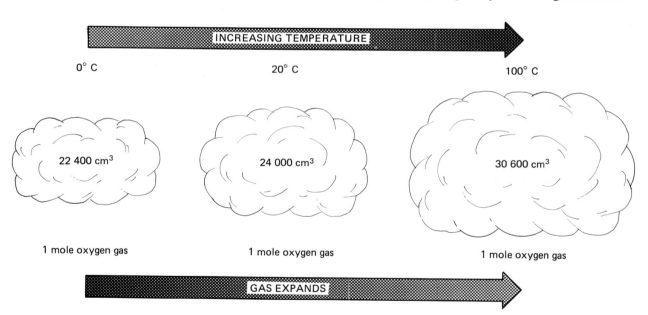

The following equation is useful to find the number of moles in a known volume of gas at room temperature and pressure.

$$\text{Number of moles of gas} = \frac{\text{volume of gas (in cm}^3)}{24\,000}$$

This can be rearranged to give:

$$\frac{\text{volume of gas}}{\text{(in cm}^3)} = \frac{\text{number of}}{\text{moles}} \times 24\,000$$

Gas volumes must all be measured at room temperature and pressure.

These equations are useful to turn:

moles ⟶ volumes of gas
or   volume of gas ⟶ moles

They should be used any time the **volume of a gas** is quoted or required.

Examples

How many moles are there in 480 cm³ ammonia gas, measured at room temperature and pressure?

The question asks '**how many moles**', so the equation to use is:

$$\textbf{number of moles of gas} = \frac{\text{volume}}{24\,000} = \frac{480}{24\,000}$$

$$= \textbf{0.02 mole}$$

Note that one mole of **any** gas occupies 24 000 cm³ at room temperature and pressure. It does not make any difference which gas is mentioned. In the previous example the gas was ammonia. There would be the same result though, using any other gas.

What is the volume of 0.006 mole chlorine gas, measured at room temperature and pressure?

The question asks '**what is the volume**', so the equation to use is:

volume of gas = number of moles × 24 000
= 0.006 × 24 000
= **144 cm³**

Mole calculations IV

These questions give examples of calculations involving gases. It is important to practise them until you are used to them.

8 ● Find the number of moles present in each of the following gases (all measured at room temperature and pressure):

(a) 240 cm³ ammonia
(b) 120 cm³ chlorine
(c) 600 cm³ oxygen
(d) 6000 cm³ hydrogen
(e) 6000 cm³ nitrogen
(f) 24 cm³ carbon dioxide
(g) 156 cm³ methane
(h) 48 dm³ helium

9 ■ Find the volume of each of the following numbers of moles of gases (all measured at room temperature and pressure).

(a) 0.1 mole fluorine
(b) 2 moles of neon
(c) 0.5 mole argon
(d) 0.025 mole hydrogen sulphide
(e) 0.25 mole sulphur dioxide
(f) 0.006 mole ethane
(g) 0.0045 mole krypton
(h) 5 moles carbon monoxide

The reaction of zinc and chlorine

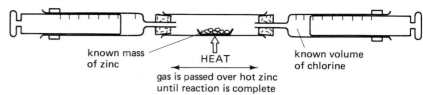

The **formula of a compound** can often be found from measuring gas volumes. For example zinc reacts with chlorine to make zinc chloride. The number of moles of chlorine reacting can be found by measuring the volume involved.

The following reaction occurs: zinc + chlorine ⟶ zinc chloride

Example: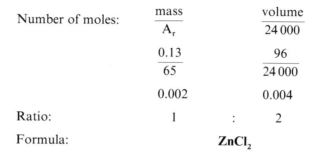

All gas volumes must be measured at room temperature and pressure.

	mass / A_r	volume / 24 000
Number of moles:	0.13 / 65	96 / 24 000
	0.002	0.004
Ratio:	1	: 2
Formula:	$ZnCl_2$	

Moles in solution

Chemists use many substances in solution in water, for example, hydrochloric acid is a solution of hydrogen chloride gas in water.

It is very important to know how concentrated a solution is. The **concentration** of a solution is often taken as the number of moles of a substance dissolved in each litre of water. One mole of any substance dissolved in one litre of water gives a 'one molar' solution.

The number of moles of a substance dissolved in a litre of water is called the **molarity** of a solution.

A one molar solution is written:

1.0 M

or

1.0 mol dm^{-3}

This means 'moles per litre'.

Making a one molar solution

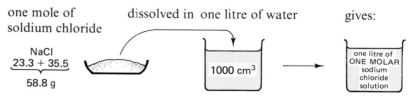

one mole of soldium chloride   dissolved in one litre of water   gives:

NaCl
23.3 + 35.5
58.8 g

1000 cm³

one litre of ONE MOLAR sodium chloride solution

Solutions of different molarities

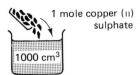
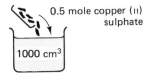
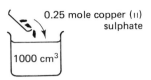

This solution contains 1 mole of copper(II) sulphate in 1 litre of water.
It is a 1.0 M solution.

This solution contains 0.5 mole copper(II) sulphate in 1 litre of water.
It has a molarity of 0.5 M.

This solution contains 0.25 mole copper(II) sulphate in 1 litre of water.
It has a concentration of 0.25 mol dm^{-3}.

SOLUTIONS GET LESS CONCENTRATED →

The following equation is useful:

$$\text{Number of moles in solution} = \frac{\text{volume of solution (cm}^3\text{)}}{1000} \times \text{molarity}$$

This can be rearranged to give:

$$\text{molarity} = \text{number of moles} \times \frac{1000}{\text{volume}}$$

$$\text{volume of solution} = \frac{\text{number of moles}}{\text{molarity}} \times 1000$$

These equations should be used any time information about moles, molarity or volume of a solution is quoted or required. Take care when a question refers to 'volume'. Look and see whether it is the volume of a **gas** or the volume of a **solution**.

Examples (continued on p.116)

How many moles are there in 500 cm³ 3.0 M sugar solution?
The question says '**how many moles**', so the equation to use is:

$$\textbf{number of moles} = \frac{\text{volume}}{1000} \times \text{molarity}$$

$$= \frac{500}{1000} \times 3$$

$$= \textbf{1.5 moles}$$

Examples

What is the molarity of 200 cm³ sodium chloride solution containing 0.1 mole?

The question says '**what is the molarity**', so the equation to use is:

$$\textbf{molarity} = \text{number of moles} \times \frac{1000}{\text{volume}}$$

$$= 0.1 \times \frac{1000}{200}$$

$$= \textbf{0.5 M}$$

What volume of 0.1 M copper(II) sulphate solution contains 0.025 moles of the salt?

The question says '**what volume**', so the equation to use is:

$$\textbf{volume} = \frac{\text{number of moles}}{\text{molarity}} \times 1000$$

$$= \frac{0.025}{0.1} \times 1000$$

$$= \textbf{250 cm}^3$$

What is the molarity of a solution containing 11.1 g of calcium chloride (CaCl₂) dissolved in 500 cm³ water?
(Ca = 40   Cl = 35.5)

Before the molarity of the solution can be found, the **mass** of the calcium chloride must be turned into **moles**:

M_r of CaCl₂: $\underbrace{\overset{\text{Ca}}{40} + \overset{\text{Cl}_2}{35.5 + 35.5}}_{111}$

Number of moles CaCl₂:

$$\text{number of moles} = \frac{\text{mass}}{M_r}$$

$$= \frac{11.1}{111}$$

$$= \textbf{0.1 mole}$$

The question asks '**what is the molarity**', so the equation to use is:

$$\textbf{molarity} = \text{number of moles} \times \frac{1000}{\text{volume}}$$

$$= 0.1 \times \frac{1000}{500}$$

$$= \textbf{0.2 M}$$

Mole calculations V

These calculations give practice in finding or using the number of moles of a substance in solution in water.

10 ■ How many moles are there in each of the following solutions?

(a) 1000 cm³ 0.5 M copper(II) sulphate solution.
(b) 2000 cm³ 2 M sodium chloride solution.
(c) 500 cm³ 0.1 M sulphuric acid.
(d) 100 cm³ 0.2 M sodium hydroxide solution.
(e) 2 dm³ 1 M ammonia solution.
(f) 10 cm³ 0.01 M copper(II) chloride solution.
(g) 100 cm³ 0.001 M copper(II) chloride solution.
(h) 5 dm³ 2 M nitric acid.

11 ■ What is the molarity of each of the following solutions?

(a) 1000 cm³ sodium chloride solution containing 2 moles.
(b) 500 cm³ sodium chloride solution containing 0.4 moles.
(c) 100 cm³ silver nitrate solution containing 0.08 moles.
(d) 250 cm³ ammonium chloride solution containing 0.1 mole.
(e) 200 cm³ potassium carbonate solution containing 0.02 mole.
(f) 2 dm³ citric acid solution containing 4 moles.
(g) 10 cm³ barium hydroxide solution containing 0.0001 mole.
(h) 50 cm³ potassium hydroxide solution containing 0.002 mole.

12 ▶ What is the molarity of each of the following solutions?

(a) 2.015 g sodium hydroxide (NaOH) dissolved in 200 cm³ water.
    (Na = 23.3   O = 16   H = 1)
(b) 0.147 g sodium chloride (NaCl) dissolved in 10 cm³ water.
    (Na = 23.3   Cl = 35.5)
(c) 6.37 g concentrated sulphuric acid (H_2SO_4) dissolved in 100 cm³ water.
    (H = 1   S = 32   O = 16)
(d) 5.055 g potassium nitrate (KNO_3) dissolved in 100 cm³ water.
    (K = 39.1   N = 14   O = 16)
(e) 6.4 g sulphur dioxide gas (SO_2) dissolved in 1000 cm³ water.
    (S = 32   O = 16)
(f) 0.85 g ammonia gas (NH_3) dissolved in 100 cm³ water.
    (N = 14   H = 1)
(g) 240 cm³ sulphur dioxide gas (measured at room temperature and pressure) dissolved in 200 cm³ water.
    (1 mole of a gas occupies 24 000 cm³ at room temperature and pressure)
(h) 480 cm³ ammonia gas (measured at room temperature and pressure) dissolved in 100 cm³ water.

Moles and structure

It is important to know the structure of an element or compound. This helps us to describe correctly and understand one mole of a substance.

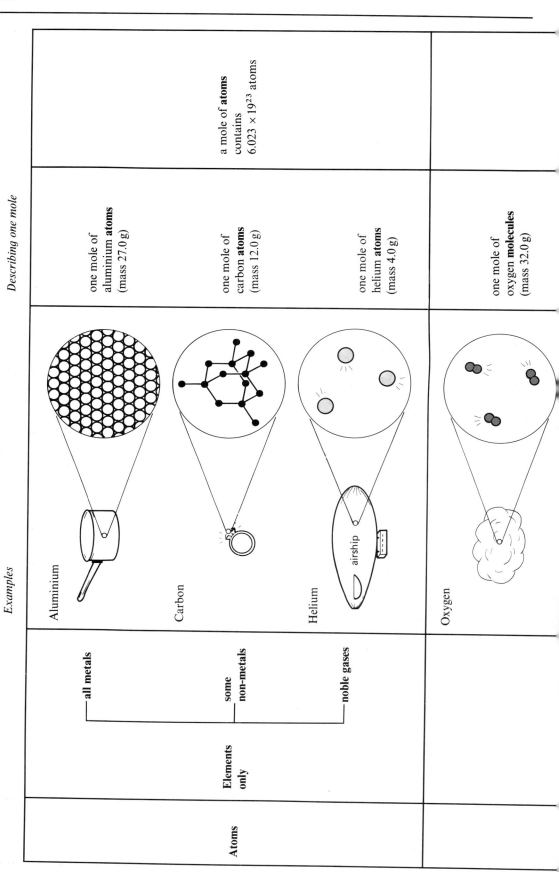

12 The Mole

Elements	Bromine	one mole of bromine **molecules** (mass 159.8 g)	1 mole of **molecules** contains 6.023 × 10²³ molecules
	Iodine	one mole of iodine **molecules** (mass 253.8 g)	
or			
Compounds	Ammonia	one mole of ammonia **molecules** (mass 17.0 g)	
	Water	one mole of water **molecules** (mass 18.0 g)	
Molecules			
Compounds only	Sodium chloride	one mole of sodium chloride	1 mole of sodium chloride contains: 6.023 × 10²³ sodium **ions** and 6.023 × 10²³ chloride **ions**.
Ions			

Summary

1. Chemists measure the amount of a substance in **moles**.

2. The **relative atomic mass** or A_r of an element is a number used to compare the masses of different elements.

3. **One mole** of atoms of an element contains the relative atomic mass in grams.

4. One mole of any substance always contains the same number of particles. This is called **Avogadro's number** and is 6.023×10^{23}.

5. The **relative molecular mass** or M_r is the mass of one mole of a compound.

6. The **formula** of a compound can be found by experiment. The relative number of moles of each element in the compound is measured.

7. One mole of any **gas** occupies **24 000 cm³** at room temperature and pressure.

8. A **one molar solution (1.0 M)** is made by dissolving one mole of a substance in one litre of water.

9. The **molarity** of a solution is the number of moles of a substance dissolved in each litre of water **(mol dm⁻³)**.

10. Calculations involving moles use one of the following three equations:

    - When **MASS** of a solid, liquid or gas is given or required:

    $$\text{number of moles} = \frac{\text{mass (g)}}{A_r} \quad \text{or} \quad \frac{\text{mass (g)}}{M_r}$$

    - When **GAS VOLUME** is given or required:

    $$\text{number of moles} = \frac{\text{volume (cm}^3\text{)}}{24\,000}$$

    - When a **SOLUTION** is involved:

    $$\text{number of moles} = \frac{\text{volume (cm}^3\text{)}}{1000} \times \text{molarity}$$

    These three equations may need to be rearranged.

12 The Mole

Questions

1. ● Find the mass in grams of one mole of:
   (a) water molecules, H_2O
   (b) oxygen molecules, O_2
   (c) calcium chloride, $CaCl_2$
   (d) sulphur dioxide molecules, SO_2
   (e) ammonium chloride, NH_4Cl
   (Relative atomic masses: $H = 1$ $N = 14$ $O = 16$
   $S = 32$ $Cl = 35.5$ $Ca = 40$) **H**

2. ■ A known mass of lead bromide was dissolved in water and heated with excess aluminium powder. After the reaction had finished and the excess aluminium removed, the remaining lead was washed, dried and weighed. The following results were obtained:
   Mass of lead bromide = 3.67 g
   Mass of lead remaining = 2.07 g
   (a) From these results, calculate the formula of lead bromide.
   (Relative atomic masses: $Pb = 207$ $Br = 80$)
   (b) Write a word equation for the reaction involved. **H**

3. ▶ A known volume of 0.1 M hydrochloric acid was added to an excess of zinc granules. The reaction produced 96 cm³ of hydrogen gas (measured at room temperature and pressure) as follows:
   $$Zn(s) + 2HCl(aq) \rightarrow ZnCl_2(aq) + H_2(g)$$
   (a) How many moles of hydrogen gas were produced?
   (b) (i) How many moles of hydrochloric acid must have been added?
       (ii) What volume of hydrochloric acid does this represent?
   (c) (i) How many moles of zinc reacted with the acid?
       (ii) What mass of zinc does this represent? ($Zn = 65$)
   (d) Sketch a graph of the volume of hydrogen collected against time during this experiment. Label this line 'zinc granules'.
   (e) Add to this sketch a line showing the effect of using the same amount of powdered zinc in place of the granules. Label this line 'zinc powder'. **U**

4. ▶ (a) Carbon dioxide is usually prepared by reacting calcium carbonate (marble chips) with dilute hydrochloric acid.
   (i) Copy out and complete the diagram below, so that the apparatus can be used to prepare and collect a sample of carbon dioxide. There are three errors which need correcting.

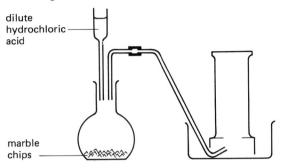

   (ii) Explain why carbon dioxide is **not** usually prepared by reacting calcium carbonate with dilute sulphuric acid.
   (b) 5 g of calcium carbonate are reacted with **excess** dilute hydrochloric acid. The equation for the reaction is
   $$CaCO_3 + 2HCl \rightarrow CaCl_2 + H_2O + CO_2$$
   (i) Explain the reason for using **excess** dilute hydrochloric acid.
   (ii) How many moles of carbon dioxide, CO_2, can be produced from 1 mole of calcium carbonate, $CaCO_3$?
   (iii) If the mass of 1 mole of $CaCO_3$ is 100 g, how many moles of $CaCO_3$ is 5 g?
   (iv) How many moles of CO_2 will be formed from 5 g of $CaCO_3$?
   (v) What mass, in grams, of CO_2 will be formed from 5 g of $CaCO_3$? (Mass of 1 mole of CO_2 is 44 g.)
   (vi) What volume, in litres, of CO_2 will be produced from 5 g of $CaCO_3$ at room temperature and pressure? (Molar volume of any gas at room temperature and pressure is 24 litres.) (NEA) **H**

13 Chemical Equations

Chemists from different countries can communicate with each other by chemical equations.

Communication is an important word in today's world. Usually people talk to each other in words. But there are many other ways of communicating. Messages may be transmitted in morse code. Computers can 'talk' to each other in their own languages. One way chemists can communicate information about a reaction is by writing a chemical equation. Chemical equations form an international language. Chemists from different countries can communicate with each other by equations.

What does an equation show?

Sodium reacts with chlorine to make sodium chloride. The chemical equation for this reaction shows two important things:

Equation: $2Na(s) + Cl_2(g) \rightarrow 2NaCl(s)$

1 Which chemicals are reacting?

sodium + chlorine ⟶ sodium chloride

2 How many moles of each substance are reacting?

2 moles sodium atoms + 1 mole chlorine molecules ⟶ 2 moles sodium chloride

Many equations also show state symbols. These will indicate whether a substance is a solid (s), liquid (l), gas (g), or dissolved in water (aq).

Investigating chemical reactions

A chemical equation is a summary of what is happening in a reaction. To study a chemical reaction many **experiments** need to be done. Equations sum up the results of those experiments. Of course, the experiments do not need to be done every time an equation is written. But at some time, experiments will have been done to work out every equation.

The following examples show experiments that may be done to work out equations.

Breaking down calcium carbonate (marble chips)

When calcium carbonate (marble chips) are heated, they decompose. Experiments can be done to show that the calcium carbonate breaks down into calcium oxide and carbon dioxide. This information can be used to write a word equation:

calcium carbonate(s) ⟶ calcium oxide(s) + carbon dioxide(g)

A symbol equation shows **how many moles** of each substance are involved. To find this, some measurements need to be made:

Decomposing calcium carbonate

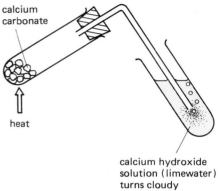

When calcium carbonate is heated, carbon dioxide gas is given off.

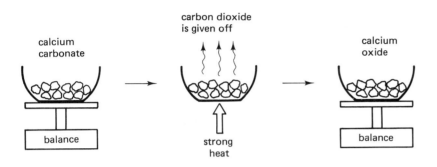

Mass: 2.00 g   1.12 g

Mass of carbon dioxide given off:
= 2.00 − 1.12
= 0.88 g

Information needed: 1 mole of gas occupies 24 000 cm³ at room temperature and pressure.
Relative atomic masses: Ca = 40   O = 16   C = 12

Calculation

Find M_r values:	$Ca \; C \; O_3$ $\underbrace{40 + 12 + 48}$ 100		$Ca \; O$ $\underbrace{40 + 16}$ 56	$C \; O_2$ $\underbrace{12 + 32}$ 44
Word equation:	calcium carbonate	⟶	calcium oxide +	carbon dioxide
Masses measured in experiment:	2.00 g		1.12 g	0.88 g
Number of moles, $\frac{mass}{M_r}$:	$\frac{2.00}{100}$ 0.02		$\frac{1.12}{56}$ 0.02	$\frac{0.88}{44}$ 0.02
Ratio:	1	:	1 :	1
Equation:	$CaCO_3(s)$	⟶	$CaO(s)$ +	$CO_2(g)$
Thus, this experiment shows that:	1 mole of calcium carbonate (s = solid)	⟶	1 mole of calcium oxide + (s = solid)	1 mole of carbon dioxide molecules (g = gas)

Reacting hydrochloric acid with magnesium

All metals react with at least one acid. Experiments can be done to show that magnesium reacts with hydrochloric acid as follows:

magnesium(s) + hydrochloric acid(aq) ⟶ magnesium chloride(aq) + hydrogen(g)

To find out how many moles of each substance are involved, several experiments must be done.

Experiment 1

Experiment 2

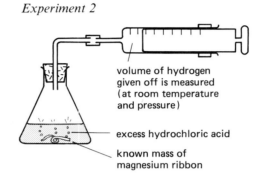

Example of results

mass of magnesium ribbon	= 0.096 g
volume 1.0 M acid needed	= 8.0 cm^3
volume 0.5 M magnesium chloride solution formed	= 8.0 cm^3
volume of hydrogen gas	= 96 cm^3

Extra information needed:

1 mole gas occupies 24 000 cm^3 at room temperature and pressure.
A_r of Mg = 24.

Calculation

Word equation:	magnesium +	hydrochloric acid	⟶	magnesium chloride +	hydrogen
Amount measured in experiment:	0.096 g	8 cm^3 of 1.0 M solution		8.0 cm^3 of 0.5 M solution	96 cm^3 of gas
Number of moles:	$\dfrac{\text{mass}}{A_r}$	$\dfrac{\text{volume}}{1000} \times \text{molarity}$		$\dfrac{\text{volume}}{1000} \times \text{molarity}$	$\dfrac{\text{volume}}{24\,000}$
	$\dfrac{0.096}{24}$	$\dfrac{8}{1000} \times 1$		$\dfrac{8}{1000} \times 0.5$	$\dfrac{96}{24\,000}$
	0.004	0.008		0.004	0.004
Ratio:	1 :	2	:	1 :	1
Equation:	Mg(s) +	2HCl(aq)	⟶	MgCl$_2$(aq) +	H$_2$(g)
This experiment shows that:	**1 mole** magnesium atoms (s = solid) +	**2 moles** hydrochloric acid (aq = aqueous solution)	⟶	**1 mole** magnesium chloride (aq = aqueous solution) +	**1 mole** hydrogen molecules (g = gas)

Making predictions from equations

These examples have shown how an equation may be written from the results of various experiments. Sometimes it is necessary to work the other way round. Once the equation is known, then it is possible for various things to be predicted. For example, you may be given the equation for the reaction of magnesium and hydrochloric acid. You may then need to predict how much acid to add in order to react exactly with a certain amount of magnesium. This can be worked out as follows.

Example
What volume of 0.4 M hydrochloric acid is needed to react completely with 0.48 g of magnesium?
(Mg = 24)

Write down the equation: $Mg(s) + 2HCl(aq) \rightarrow MgCl_2(aq) + H_2(g)$

Note how many moles of each substance are mentioned in the question.
1 mole Mg atoms   **2 moles** HCl

Turn mass of Mg into moles: $\dfrac{mass}{A_r} = \dfrac{0.48}{24}$

0.02 moles magnesium ↔ ? moles acid

Look at ratio in equation: 1 : 2
Find number of moles of acid: 0.02 → **0.04 moles HCl**

Question says '**what volume of acid**' so the equation to use is:

$$volume = \dfrac{number\ of\ moles}{molarity} \times 1000$$

$$= \dfrac{0.04}{0.4} \times 1000$$

$$= \mathbf{100\ cm^3}$$

Examples

Silver carbonate breaks down on heating as follows:

$$2Ag_2CO_3(s) \rightarrow 4Ag(s) + 2CO_2(g) + O_2(g)$$

Find the mass of silver formed when 5.52 g of silver carbonate are heated. (Ag = 108   C = 12   O = 16   1 mole of a gas = 24 000 cm³ at room temperature and pressure.

Extra information needed: Find M_r of Ag_2 C O_3
$(2 \times 108) + 12 + (3 \times 16)$
$216 + 12 + 48$
276

Equation: $2Ag_2CO_3(s) \rightarrow 4Ag(s) + 2CO_2(g) + O_2(g)$

Number of moles of relevant substances: $2Ag_2CO_3$: $4Ag$

Turn mass of Ag_2CO_3 into moles: $\dfrac{mass}{M_r} = \dfrac{5.52}{276}$

0.02 moles $\rightarrow$? moles silver

Ratio: 2   :   4

Number of moles silver: 0.02 $\rightarrow$ **0.04 moles Ag**

The question says **find mass of silver**:   mass = moles × A_r = 0.04 × 108
= **4.32 g**

Find the volume of ammonia gas formed when 1.605 g of ammonium chloride is heated as in the equation: $NH_4Cl(s) \rightarrow NH_3(g) + HCl(g)$
(N = 14   H = 1   Cl = 35.5
1 mole gas = 24 000 cm³ at room temperature and pressure.)

Extra information needed: M_r N H_4 Cl
14 + 4 + 35.5   = 53.5

Equation: $NH_4Cl(s) \rightarrow NH_3(g) + HCl(g)$

Number of moles of relevant substances: NH_4Cl : NH_3

Turn mass of NH_4Cl into moles: $\dfrac{mass}{M_r} = \dfrac{1.605}{53.5}$

0.03 moles $\rightarrow$? moles ammonia

Ratio: 1   :   1

No. of moles ammonia: 0.03 $\rightarrow$ **0.03 moles NH_3**

The question says '**find the volume of ammonia**':

volume = moles × 24 000 = 0.03 × 24 000
= **720 cm³**

13 Chemical Equations

Writing balanced equations

It is very useful to be able to 'balance' an equation. A balanced equation is one which has the same number of atoms of each element on either side of the equation.

Antoine Lavoisier was a famous French chemist who did a number of experiments that led him to suggest the **law of conservation of mass**. This states that matter can neither be created nor destroyed in a chemical reaction. The mass of the products of a reaction must equal the mass of the reactants. This law is the basis for writing a balanced equation. There must always be the same number of atoms on each side of the equation.

In balancing an equation, the number of moles of one or more of the substances may need to be changed. This may mean changing:

H_2O	into	$2H_2O$	or	$3H_2O$
1 mole water molecule		2 moles water molecules		3 moles water molecules

An equation is never balanced by changing the actual formula. For example, the formula of water H_2O should never be changed into H_3O or HO_2 simply to balance the equation.

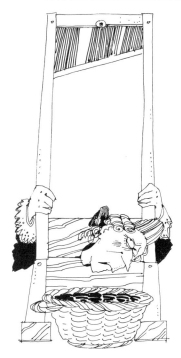

Antoine Lavoisier was a famous French chemist who was executed in the French Revolution. Someone said of him that it took one second to cut off his head and a hundred years to get another one like it.

Example

Methane (CH_4) burns in oxygen to give carbon dioxide and water. Write a balanced equation for this reaction.

Write down the formulae of each of the substances:

	Reactants	Products
Unbalanced equation:	$CH_4 + O_2 \longrightarrow$	$CO_2 + H_2O$
See where it is not balanced:	1 C atom 4 H atoms 2 O atoms	1 C atom 2 H atoms 3 O atoms
To balance H atoms, write **$2H_2O$**:	$CH_4 + O_2 \longrightarrow$ ↑ 4 H atoms	$CO_2 + \mathbf{2H_2O}$ ↑ 4 H atoms
To balance O atoms, write $2O_2$:	$CH_4 + 2O_2 \longrightarrow$ ↑ 4 O atoms	$CO_2 + 2H_2O$ 4 O atoms
Balanced equation:	$CH_4 + 2O_2 \longrightarrow$	$CO_2 + 2H_2O$
	1 C atom 4 H atoms 4 O atoms	1 C atom 4 H atoms 4 O atoms
	Number of atoms in reactants =	Number of atoms in products

13 Chemical Equations

Example

Solid iron(III) oxide (Fe_2O_3) is reduced by hydrogen gas to iron metal and steam. Write a balanced equation, including state symbols, for this reaction.

Unbalanced equation:	$Fe_2O_3 + H_2 \longrightarrow$	$Fe + H_2O$
See where it is not balanced:	2 Fe atoms 3 O atoms 2 H atoms	1 Fe atom 1 O atom 2 H atoms
To balance Fe atoms, write **2Fe**:	$Fe_2O_3 + H_2 \longrightarrow$ ↑ 2 Fe atoms	**2**$Fe + H_2O$ ↑ 2 Fe atoms
To balance O atoms, write **3H$_2$O**:	$Fe_2O_3 + H_2 \longrightarrow$ ↑ 3 O atoms	$2Fe + $ **3**H_2O ↑ 3 O atoms
To balance H atoms, write **3H$_2$**:	$Fe_2O_3 + $ **3**$H_2 \longrightarrow$ ↑ 6 H atoms	$2Fe + 3H_2O$ ↑ 6 H atoms
Balanced equation:	$Fe_2O_3 + 3H_2 \longrightarrow$	$2Fe + 3H_2O$
	2 Fe atoms 3 O atoms 6 H atoms	2 Fe atoms 3 O atoms 6 H atoms
Look at question for information about state symbols:	$Fe_2O_3(s) + 3H_2(g) \longrightarrow$	$2Fe(s) + 3H_2O(g)$

Summary

1. A chemical equation shows **which chemicals** are present and **how many moles** of each substance are reacting. It may also show state symbols.

2. An equation is the result of **experiments** done to find out about a reaction.

3. Calculations on equations are
   either **from** information about a reaction (gas volume, masses etc.), to write an equation,
   or **given** the equation for a reaction, to find out about amounts of substances reacting.

4. The **law of conservation of mass** states that matter cannot be created or destroyed in a chemical reaction. The mass of products must always equal the mass of reactants.

5. In getting an equation to **balance**, the number of moles of each substance is changed, until there are the same number of atoms on each side of the equation:

Unbalanced equation: $C_3H_8 + O_2 \rightarrow CO_2 + H_2O$

Balanced equation: $C_3H_8 + 5O_2 \rightarrow 3CO_2 + 4H_2O$

13 Chemical Equations

Questions

1 ● $CaCO_3 \longrightarrow CaO + CO_2$
(Relative atomic masses: C = 12 O = 16 Ca = 40)

Copy out the following sentences, filling in the four spaces.

100 g of calcium carbonate when heated will produce _____ g of calcium oxide and _____ g of carbon dioxide.
Therefore 10 g of calcium carbonate when heated will produce _____ g of calcium oxide and _____ g of carbon dioxide.   (NWREB)   **H**

2 ■ (a) An experiment to change copper(II) oxide to copper was carried out in the apparatus below.

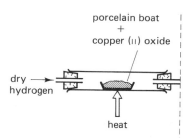

(i) Copy and complete the diagram by drawing beyond the dotted line a suitable apparatus to show how the unreacted hydrogen may be collected by the downward displacement of water.
(ii) What is the chemical term used to describe what has happened to the copper(II) oxide?
(b) The masses of the porcelain boat and its contents were recorded.
(i) Copy out and complete the table.

Mass of boat + copper(II) oxide	= 3.26 g
Mass of boat	= 2.46 g
Mass of copper(II) oxide	=
Mass of boat + copper	= 3.10 g
Mass of boat	= 2.46 g
Mass of copper	=
Mass of oxygen in copper(II) oxide	=

(Relative atomic masses: Cu = 64   O = 16)

(ii) How many moles of copper(II) oxide were used?
(iii) How many moles of copper were produced?
(iv) What is the relative molecular mass of copper(II) oxide?
(v) Copy out and complete the word equation and symbol equation for the reaction.
Word equation:
copper(II) oxide + hydrogen ⟶ copper + _____
Symbol equation:
_____ + _____ ⟶ _____ + _____
                                                           (WMEB)   **H**

3 ▶ The following questions give the chemical equation for various reactions. Use the equations to calculate the information required.
All gas volumes are measured at room temperature and pressure. (1 mole gas = 24 000 cm³ at room temperature and pressure)

(a) What mass or iron could be obtained by reducing 1.8 g iron(II) oxide (FeO)?
(Fe = 56   O = 16)
$$FeO(s) + H_2(g) \longrightarrow Fe(s) + H_2O(l)$$

(b) Calculate what volume of carbon dioxide gas could be obtained by heating 1.55 g copper carbonate as follows:
(Cu = 64   C = 12   O = 16)
$$CuCO_3(s) \longrightarrow CuO(s) + CO_2(g)$$

(c) What volume of 0.1 M hydrochloric acid is needed to react exactly with 0.5 g calcium carbonate?
(Ca = 40   C = 12   O = 16)
$$CaCO_3(s) + 2HCl(aq) \longrightarrow CaCl_2(aq) + H_2O(l) + CO_2(g)$$

(d) Find the mass of copper metal formed by reducing 2.0 g copper oxide with methane:
(Cu = 64   O = 16)
$$4CuO(s) + CH_4(g) \longrightarrow 4Cu(s) + CO_2(g) + 2H_2O(l)$$

(e) Find the volume of nitrogen gas formed when 100 cm³ ammonia gas reduce copper oxide as follows:
$$3CuO(s) + 2NH_3(g) \longrightarrow 3Cu(s) + N_2(g) + 3H_2O(l)$$

(f) What volume of 0.2 M sulphuric acid is needed to react with 25 cm³ 0.2 M sodium hydroxide solution?
$$2NaOH(aq) + H_2SO_4(aq) \longrightarrow Na_2SO_4(aq) + 2H_2O(l)$$

(g) What mass of sodium chloride could be obtained from the solution formed when 25 cm³ 0.5 M barium chloride solution reacts with 25 cm³ 0.5 M sodium sulphate solution?
(Na = 23.3   Cl = 35.5)
$$BaCl_2(aq) + Na_2SO_4(aq) \longrightarrow 2NaCl(aq) + BaSO_4(s)$$

(h) What volume of sulphur dioxide gas could be obtained from burning 1 g sulphur in oxygen?
(S = 32)
$$S(s) + O_2(g) \longrightarrow SO_2(g) \qquad \textbf{H}$$

4 ▶ Sodium nitrate can be prepared by neutralising nitric acid with sodium hydroxide solution. The equation for the reaction is:
$$HNO_3 + NaOH \longrightarrow NaNO_3 + H_2O$$
(Relative atomic masses: H = 1   N = 14   O = 16   Na = 23)

(a) State the mass of 1 mole of sodium hydroxide, NaOH.
(b) What mass of sodium nitrate would be formed when one mole of sodium hydroxide reacts completely with nitric acid?
(c) Hence calculate the mass of sodium nitrate produced when 10.0 g of sodium hydroxide reacts completely with nitric acid.   (NEA)   **H**

5 ▸ The following questions give information about the amount of various substances involved in a reaction. Calculate the number of moles of each substance, and use this information to write balanced chemical equations, including state symbols.
(Assume 1 mole gas = 24 000 cm³ at room temperature and pressure.)

(a) 2.45 g concentrated sulphuric acid (H_2SO_4) reacted with 2.94 g sodium chloride (NaCl) to give 3.565 g sodium sulphate (Na_2SO_4) and 1200 cm³ hydrogen chloride gas (HCl).
(H = 1   O = 16   Na = 23.3   S = 32   Cl = 35.5)

(b) 0.13 g zinc metal reacted with 40 cm³ 0.1 M nitric acid (HNO_3) to give 48 cm³ hydrogen gas and a solution containing 0.378 g zinc nitrate ($Zn(NO_3)_2$).
(Zn = 65   N = 14   O = 16)

(c) 0.533 g sodium carbonate (Na_2CO_3) reacted with 20 cm³ 0.5 M hydrochloric acid (HCl) to make 20 cm³ 0.5 M sodium chloride solution, 0.09 g water and 120 cm³ carbon dioxide gas.
(Na = 23.3   C = 12   O = 16   H = 1)

(d) 0.16 g copper metal reacted with 50 cm³ 0.1 M silver nitrate solution ($AgNO_3$). 0.54 g silver metal was displaced and 50 cm³ 0.05 M copper(II) nitrate solution ($Cu(NO_3)_2$) was produced.
(Cu = 64   Ag = 108)

(e) 48 cm³ ammonia gas (NH_3) was broken down on heating to give 24 cm³ nitrogen gas (N_2) and 72 cm³ hydrogen gas (H_2).

(f) 1.436 g lead dioxide (PbO_2) were reduced by 288 cm³ hydrogen gas (H_2) to give 1.242 g of lead metal and 0.216 g water.
(Pb = 207   O = 16   H = 1)

(g) 0.508 g iodine crystals (I_2) reacted with 48 cm³ chlorine gas (Cl_2) to make 0.65 g liquid iodine monochloride (ICl).
(I = 127   Cl = 35.5).

(h) 0.843 g sodium hydrogencarbonate ($NaHCO_3$) broke down on heating to give 0.533 g sodium carbonate (Na_2CO_3), 0.09 g water and 120 cm³ carbon dioxide gas.
(H = 1   C = 12   O = 16   Na = 23.3)   **H**

6 ▸ 2.5 cm³ of 1.0 M lead nitrate solution were placed in a test-tube. When 0.5 cm³ of 1.0 M potassium iodide solution was added, a bright yellow precipitate formed. After centrifuging, the height of the precipitate was measured.
Successive 0.5 cm³ volumes of 1.0 M potassium iodide solution were added, and the height of the precipitate measured in a similar way.
The results were as follows:

Volume of 1.0 M potassium iodide solution added/cm³	0	0.5	1.0	1.5	2.0	2.5	3.0	3.5	4.0
Height of precipitate/mm	0	2.4	5.2	8.0	11.0	14.0	14.0	14.0	14.0

(a) Plot a graph of height of precipitate (vertical axis) against volume of potassium iodide added (horizontal axis).
(b) Why did the height of the precipitate not change between 2.5 cm³ and 4.0 cm³?
(c) How many moles are there in 2.5 cm³ of 1.0 M lead nitrate solution?
(d) This is the equation for the reaction:
$$Pb(NO_3)_2(aq) + 2KI(aq) \rightarrow PbI_2(s) + 2KNO_3(aq)$$
How many moles of potassium iodide reacted with 2.5 cm³ of 1.0 M lead nitrate solution?
(e) How would you obtain a pure dry sample of the lead iodide formed in the experiment?   **H**

14 Acids, Alkalis and Salts

Acids suggest danger to most people. Some concentrated acids can be very dangerous. They must be handled with great care. Other acids are part of our everyday lives. Vinegar and orange juice both contain acids.

Alkalis are also part of everyday life. Some alkalis are very dangerous. A splash of sodium hydroxide solution in the eye can blind someone. Others – soaps and detergents – are examples of everyday alkalis. When acids and alkalis meet, they react with each other. A new substance called a **salt** is formed.

The pH scale

acidic						neutral	alkaline						
very acidic → → → slightly acidic							slightly alkaline → → → very alkaline						
1	2	3	4	5	6	7	8	9	10	11	12	13	14

The **pH** of a solution shows whether it is acidic, alkaline or neutral. The pH scale is a set of numbers from 1 to 14. The pH of a solution is usually measured by an **indicator**. This is a chemical that changes colour when the pH changes. The pH of a substance is measured when it is dissolved in water.

Colour changes of some indicators

Indicator   *pH of colour change*

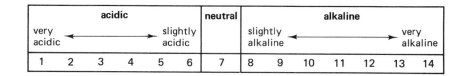

Methyl orange — pH 3.7 — red | yellow

Litmus — pH 7 — red | blue

Phenolphthalein — pH 9.3 — colourless | red

Universal indicator (a mixture of indicators) — pH: 1 2 3 4 5 6 7 8 9 10 11 12 13 14 — red, orange, yellow, green, blue, violet

14 Acids, Alkalis and Salts

Acids

Examples of some acids

Where is acid found?	Name of acid	Formula
vinegar	Ethanoic acid (acetic acid)	$C_2H_4O_2$
citrus fruits	Citric acid	$C_6H_8O_7$
stomach	Hydrochloric acid	HCl
artificially made acids	Sulphuric acid	H_2SO_4
	Hydrochloric acid	HCl
	Nitric acid	HNO_3

Reactions of acids

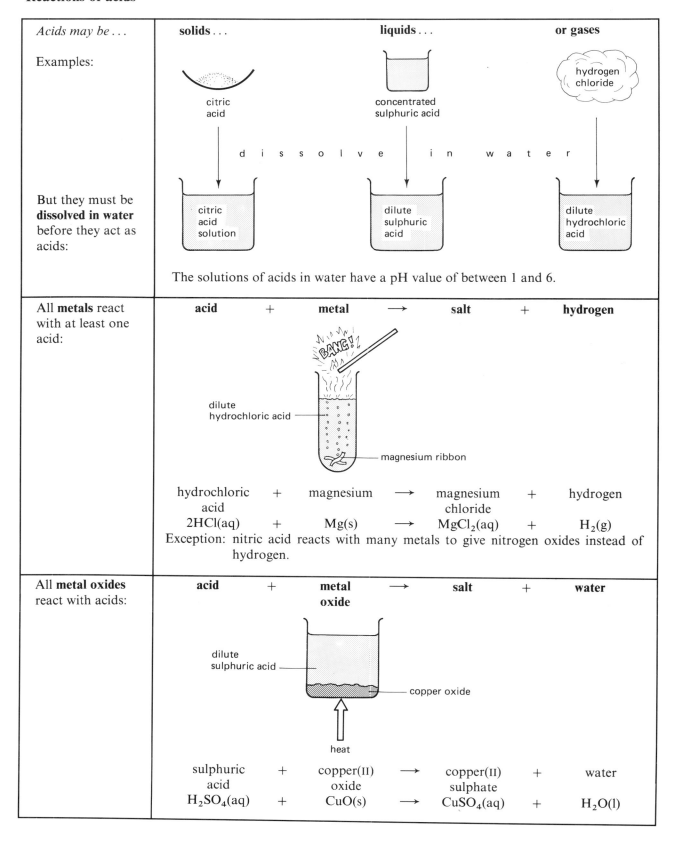

Acids may be...	**solids...**	**liquids...**	**or gases**
Examples:	citric acid	concentrated sulphuric acid	hydrogen chloride
But they must be **dissolved in water** before they act as acids:	citric acid solution	dilute sulphuric acid	dilute hydrochloric acid

The solutions of acids in water have a pH value of between 1 and 6.

All **metals** react with at least one acid:

acid + metal → salt + hydrogen

hydrochloric acid + magnesium → magnesium chloride + hydrogen

$2HCl(aq) + Mg(s) \rightarrow MgCl_2(aq) + H_2(g)$

Exception: nitric acid reacts with many metals to give nitrogen oxides instead of hydrogen.

All **metal oxides** react with acids:

acid + metal oxide → salt + water

sulphuric acid + copper(II) oxide → copper(II) sulphate + water

$H_2SO_4(aq) + CuO(s) \rightarrow CuSO_4(aq) + H_2O(l)$

All **carbonates** react with acids	**acid** + **carbonate** → **salt** + **water** + **carbon dioxide**
	hydrochloric + calcium → calcium + water + carbon acid carbonate chloride dioxide $2HCl(aq)$ + $CaCO_3(s)$ → $CaCl_2(aq)$ + $H_2O(l)$ + $CO_2(g)$
Solutions of an acid in water always **conduct electricity**:	Solutions of acids in water always contain **ions**. It is the ions that carry the electric current through the water. The **hydrogen ion, H^+**, is present in all solutions of acids in water. When H^+ ions are dissolved in water, the pH will be between 1 and 6. The H^+ ion gives acids their special properties.

It is important to understand the difference between the concentration and the strength of an acid.

The **concentration** simply means how many moles of the acid are dissolved in each litre of water. Here are some sentences that refer to concentration:

'The 0.001 M hydrochloric acid was of a low concentration.'
'This 4 M ethanoic acid is quite concentrated.'

The concentration can be increased by adding more acid, or decreased by diluting with water.

The **strength** of an acidic solution refers to how well the acid is split up into ions. An acid is said to be either strong or weak. Its strength cannot be changed. Here are some sentences that refer to acid strength:

'0.1 M hydrochloric acid is a strong acid because it splits up almost completely into $H^+(aq)$ and $Cl^-(aq)$ ions.'

'0.1 M ethanoic acid is a weak acid, as only some of the acid molecules have split up into ions.'

Acids may be divided into:

	Strong acids	*Weak acids*
Example:	hydrochloric acid	ethanoic acid (acetic acid)
Formula:	HCl	$C_2H_4O_2$
Electrical conductivity of aqueous solution:	very good	poor
pH of 0.1 M solution:	pH 1	pH 5
Explanation:	The HCl has split up almost completely into H^+ and Cl^- ions.	The $C_2H_4O_2$ forms only a few ions, and most of it stays as molecules.

Bases and alkalis

A **base** is a substance that reacts with an acid and neutralises it. A new substance called a salt is formed. Some bases are water soluble and others are not. Bases that dissolve in water are called alkalis.

Bases and alkalis

```
              bases
           ┌─────┴─────┐
       insoluble     water       = an alkali
       in water     soluble

e.g:   copper(II)   sodium
       oxide        hydroxide
       CuO          NaOH
```

Examples of some everyday alkalis

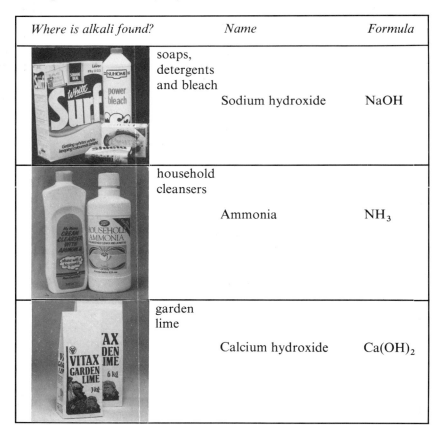

Where is alkali found?	Name	Formula
soaps, detergents and bleach	Sodium hydroxide	NaOH
household cleansers	Ammonia	NH_3
garden lime	Calcium hydroxide	$Ca(OH)_2$

Examples of some bases used in the laboratory

Name	Formula	Does the base dissolve in water?	pH of aqueous solution	
Copper(II) oxide	CuO	no	—	These bases do not dissolve in water. This means their pH cannot be measured.
Magnesium oxide	MgO	no	—	
Iron(II) oxide	FeO	no	—	
Ammonia	NH_3	yes	10	These water-soluble bases are called **alkalis**. The solutions of alkalis in water have a pH between 8 and 14.
Calcium hydroxide	$Ca(OH)_2$	yes	12	
Potassium hydroxide	KOH	yes	14	
Sodium hydroxide	NaOH	yes	14	

14 Acids, Alkalis and Salts

Reactions of bases

Bases are usually...	metal oxides...	and hydroxides and ammonia	
Examples: If the base does dissolve in water, it is called an **alkali**:	magnesium oxide — insoluble in water pH cannot be measured, as magnesium oxide does not dissolve.	sodium hydroxide → DISSOLVE IN WATER → sodium hydroxide solution ammonia → ammonia solution Solutions of alkalis in water have a pH between 8 and 14.	
All bases react with **acids**. The acid and base **neutralise** each other:	*Insoluble base*: BASE + ACID → SALT + WATER (magnesium oxide + dilute sulphuric acid, heat) magnesium oxide + sulphuric acid → magnesium sulphate + water MgO(s) + H$_2$SO$_4$(aq) → MgSO$_4$(aq) + H$_2$O(l)		
	Alkali: ALKALI + ACID → SALT + WATER (sodium hydroxide solution + dilute hydrochloric acid → sodium chloride solution) sodium hydroxide + hydrochloric acid → sodium chloride + water NaOH(aq) + HCl(aq) → NaCl(aq) + H$_2$O(l)		
Solutions of alkalis in water always **conduct electricity**:	battery — bulb — solution of alkali in water	The hydroxide ion, OH$^-$, is present in all solutions of alkalis in water. When OH$^-$ ions are dissolved in water, the pH will be between 8 and 14. The OH$^-$ ion gives alkalis their special properties.	

Alkalis may be divided into:	Strong alkalis	Weak alkalis
Example:	Sodium hydroxide	Ammonia solution
Formula:	NaOH	NH$_3$
Electrical conductivity of aqueous solution:	very good	poor
pH of 0.1 M solution:	pH 14	pH 10
Explanation:	The NaOH has split up almost completely into Na$^+$ and OH$^-$ ions.	The NH$_3$ forms only a few ions. Most of it stays as molecules.

Salts

When an acid and a base react together, they neutralise each other. A new substance called a **salt** is formed. It is possible to make thousands of different salts. Which salt is made depends on the acid and base used.

Here is an example:

General reaction: **base + acid ⟶ salt + water**

Word equation: sodium hydroxide + hydrochloric acid ⟶ sodium chloride + water

Symbol equation: $NaOH(aq) + HCl(aq) \rightarrow NaCl(aq) + H_2O(l)$

The salt formed here is sodium chloride (NaCl). The 'sodium' part of this salt comes from the base, sodium hydroxide. The 'chloride' part comes from the hydrochloric acid. Nearly all salts have two parts like this. All salts are in fact made from ions.

All salts contain...

Everyday neutralisation

Shampoo contains a mild alkali. When hair is shampooed, the small scales on each hair open out.

Hair **conditioner** contains a mild acid. The alkali in shampoo is neutralised and the scales on the hairs shut down. This leaves the hair shiny. Any weak acid such as vinegar or lemon juice has the same effect.

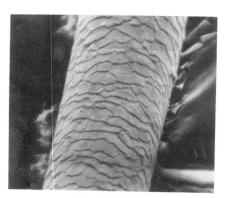

+IONS from a base   and   −IONS from an acid

e.g: copper(II) oxide + sulphuric acid
CuO H_2SO_4
↓contains   ↓contains
Cu^{2+} SO_4^{2-}
salt formed is $CuSO_4$
copper(II) sulphate

sulphuric acid forms salts called **sulphates**

e.g: sodium hydroxide + hydrochloric acid
NaOH   HCl
↓contains   ↓contains
Na^+ Cl^-
salt formed is NaCl
sodium chloride

hydrochloric acid form salts called **chlorides**

e.g: calcium hydroxide + nitric acid
$Ca(OH)_2$ $2HNO_3$
↓contains   ↓contains
Ca^{2+} $NO_3^- + NO_3^-$
salt formed is $Ca(NO_3)_2$
calcium nitrate

nitric acid forms salts called **nitrates**

This photograph of a hair was taken with the help of an electron microscope. It shows the scales that coat the surface of the hair.

Making salts in the laboratory

There are several different ways to make salts. The two 'parts' of the salt have to be chosen from suitable substances. These are then reacted together.

Method 1 Reacting a metal and an acid

All metals react with at least one acid. This method can therefore be used on a number of metals. Some unreactive metals need very strong, concentrated acids and only react very slowly. Other very reactive metals explode dangerously with acids. It is best then to use this method with moderately reactive metals.

Testing for saturation

A small amount of solution is removed on the end of a cold, dry stirring rod. If crystals form on the rod, then the rest of the solution will also form crystals when cooled.

Example: Making magnesium sulphate $MgSO_4$

1

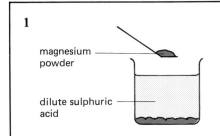

Magnesium powder is added to cold dilute acid until the reaction stops. There is then excess magnesium powder.

General reaction: **metal + acid → salt + hydrogen**
Word equation: magnesium + sulphuric acid → magnesium sulphate + hydrogen
Symbol equation: $Mg(s) + H_2SO_4(aq) \rightarrow MgSO_4(aq) + H_2(g)$

2

Excess magnesium is removed by filtering.

3

Magnesium sulphate solution is heated to evaporate off excess water. Solution is heated until it is **saturated**.

4

When cooled, the solution will crystallise.

5

Remaining solution is poured off and crystals pressed dry between sheets of filter paper.

Method 2 Reacting a base with an acid

When a metal is either very reactive or very unreactive, it is useful to react the metal oxide or hydroxide with an acid.

Examples:

Sodium metal Na	is dangerously reactive...	so it is better to use...	Sodium hydroxide NaOH
Copper metal Cu	is rather unreactive...	so it is better to use...	Copper(II) oxide CuO

Example
Making copper(II) sulphate $CuSO_4$

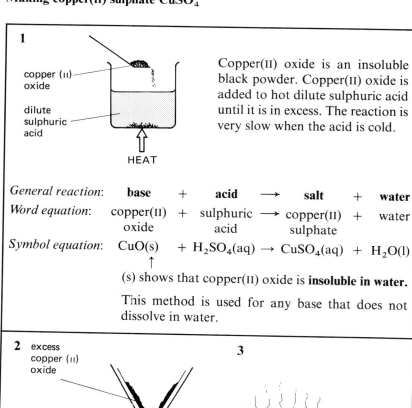

Copper(II) oxide is an insoluble black powder. Copper(II) oxide is added to hot dilute sulphuric acid until it is in excess. The reaction is very slow when the acid is cold.

General reaction: **base + acid → salt + water**

Word equation: copper(II) oxide + sulphuric acid → copper(II) sulphate + water

Symbol equation: $CuO(s) + H_2SO_4(aq) \rightarrow CuSO_4(aq) + H_2O(l)$

(s) shows that copper(II) oxide is **insoluble in water.**

This method is used for any base that does not dissolve in water.

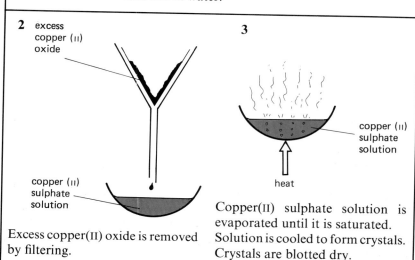

Excess copper(II) oxide is removed by filtering.

Copper(II) sulphate solution is evaporated until it is saturated. Solution is cooled to form crystals. Crystals are blotted dry.

Example
Making sodium nitrate NaNO$_3$

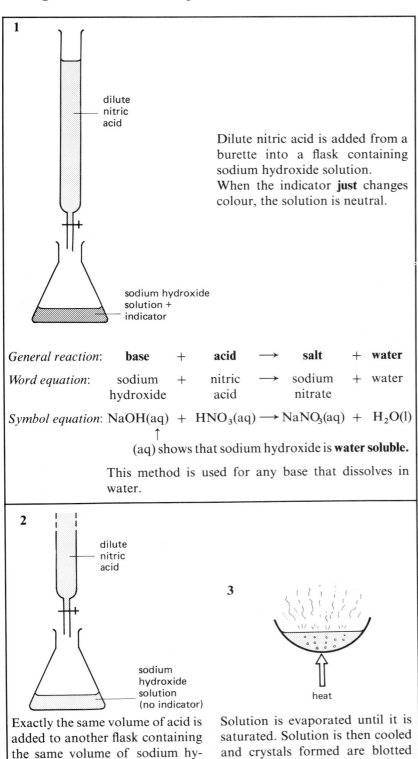

1 Dilute nitric acid is added from a burette into a flask containing sodium hydroxide solution.
When the indicator **just** changes colour, the solution is neutral.

General reaction: **base + acid ⟶ salt + water**

Word equation: sodium hydroxide + nitric acid ⟶ sodium nitrate + water

Symbol equation: NaOH(aq) + HNO$_3$(aq) ⟶ NaNO$_3$(aq) + H$_2$O(l)

(aq) shows that sodium hydroxide is **water soluble.**

This method is used for any base that dissolves in water.

2 Exactly the same volume of acid is added to another flask containing the same volume of sodium hydroxide solution. No indicator is used this time.

3 Solution is evaporated until it is saturated. Solution is then cooled and crystals formed are blotted dry.

Method 3 Reacting a carbonate with an acid
All carbonates react with acids to make a salt.

Example

Making copper(II) chloride CuCl$_2$

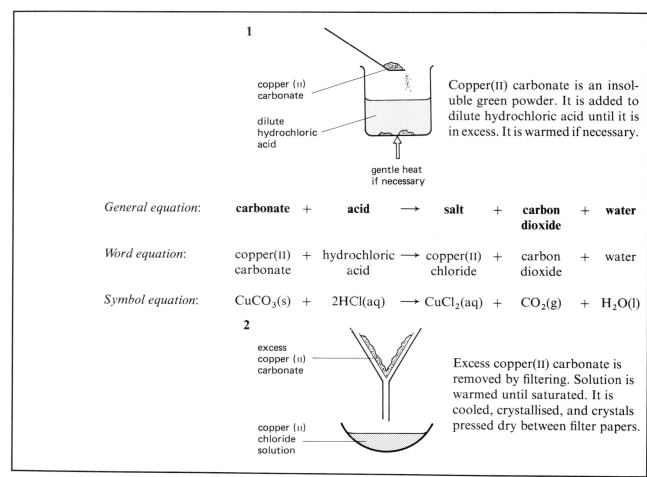

General equation: **carbonate + acid → salt + carbon dioxide + water**

Word equation: copper(II) carbonate + hydrochloric acid → copper(II) chloride + carbon dioxide + water

Symbol equation: CuCO$_3$(s) + 2HCl(aq) → CuCl$_2$(aq) + CO$_2$(g) + H$_2$O(l)

Copper(II) carbonate is an insoluble green powder. It is added to dilute hydrochloric acid until it is in excess. It is warmed if necessary.

Excess copper(II) carbonate is removed by filtering. Solution is warmed until saturated. It is cooled, crystallised, and crystals pressed dry between filter papers.

Which compounds are soluble in water?
Soluble compounds

All nitrates

All salts of sodium, potassium and ammonium

All chlorides *except*
    silver chloride
    lead chloride (which only dissolves in hot water)

All sulphates *except*
    barium sulphate
    lead sulphate

Insoluble compounds

All carbonates *except*
    sodium, potassium and ammonium carbonates

All hydroxides *except*
    sodium, potassium and ammonium hydroxides

Method 4 Making an insoluble salt
All the examples so far have involved making salts that dissolve in water. To make an insoluble salt, a **precipitation reaction** is needed.

Example

Making lead sulphate PbSO$_4$

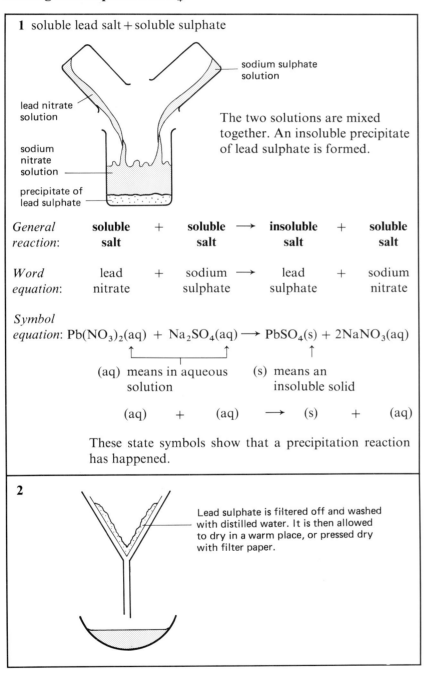

1 soluble lead salt + soluble sulphate

The two solutions are mixed together. An insoluble precipitate of lead sulphate is formed.

General reaction: **soluble salt** + **soluble salt** ⟶ **insoluble salt** + **soluble salt**

Word equation: lead nitrate + sodium sulphate ⟶ lead sulphate + sodium nitrate

Symbol equation: Pb(NO$_3$)$_2$(aq) + Na$_2$SO$_4$(aq) ⟶ PbSO$_4$(s) + 2NaNO$_3$(aq)

(aq) means in aqueous solution

(s) means an insoluble solid

(aq) + (aq) ⟶ (s) + (aq)

These state symbols show that a precipitation reaction has happened.

2 Lead sulphate is filtered off and washed with distilled water. It is then allowed to dry in a warm place, or pressed dry with filter paper.

Summary

1. Acids and alkalis **neutralise** each other to make new substances called salts.

2. The **pH scale** measures whether a solution is acidic, neutral or alkaline. pH 1–6 is acidic; pH 7 is neutral; pH 8–14 is alkaline.

3. **An indicator** is a chemical that changes colour as the pH changes.

4. Acids may be solids, liquids or gases, but they must be **dissolved in water** before they act as acids.

5. Acids react with **metals, metal oxides** and **carbonates** to make salts.

6. A **base** is a substance that reacts with an acid and neutralises it. An **alkali** is a water-soluble base.

7. - Solutions of **acids** in water contain the **hydrogen ion, H^+**.
   - Solutions of **alkalis** in water contain the **hydroxide ion, OH^-**.
   These ions allow the solutions to conduct electricity. They also give rise to the special properties of acids and alkalis.

8. - **Strong acids and alkalis** in aqueous solution are almost completely split up into ions. e.g:
     nitric acid HNO_3, potassium hydroxide KOH.
   - **Weak acids and alkalis** form only a few ions and most of the particles stay as molecules. e.g:
     citric acid $C_6H_8O_7$, ammonia NH_3.

9. All **salts** are made from ions, and can be prepared in various ways:
   - **Soluble salts** can be made from:
     a metal + an acid
     a metal oxide or hydroxide + an acid
     a carbonate + an acid
   - **Insoluble salts** are made by a precipitation reaction, from two soluble salts.

Questions

1. ● (a) Give the names of one acid and one alkali.
   (b) Name an indicator you could use to test for the presence of an acid.
   (c) What colour would the indicator you have chosen in (b) become, when placed in an acid solution?
   (d) Give the name of the acid which is used in car batteries.
   (e) Name one substance you could use to neutralise some battery acid. **R**

2. ● The pH scale is used to show how acid or alkaline a solution is. Here are some numbers on this scale:
   pH: 1 5 7 10 14
   (a) What sort of solution would have a pH of 14?
   (b) What sort of solution would have a pH of 1?
   (c) Which pH from the above table would be measured in: (i) dilute ethanoic acid solution, (ii) ammonia solution?
   (d) Which number is the pH of pure water? **R**

3. ■ Copper(II) sulphate crystals ($CuSO_4 \cdot 5H_2O$) can be made by adding an excess of copper(II) oxide to warm dilute sulphuric acid. The excess copper(II) oxide which is insoluble in water needs to be removed.
   (a) Why is excess copper(II) oxide used in this experiment?
   (b) How could the excess copper(II) oxide be removed?
   (c) How could a sample of pure dry copper(II) sulphate crystals be obtained from this solution? **U**

4. ■ The following is a list of salts and the chemicals used to prepare them:
   calcium carbonate
   calcium chloride
   copper(II) oxide
   hydrochloric acid
   magnesium metal
   sodium hydroxide
   sulphuric acid
   (a) Which of these substances would react with hydrochloric acid to give off: (i) hydrogen gas, (ii) carbon dioxide gas?
   (b) Which of these substances would dissolve in water to give a solution that would neutralise dilute nitric acid?
   (c) Write a word equation and a symbol equation for the reaction of copper(II) oxide with hydrochloric acid.
   (d) Which acid would you use to prepare a sample of magnesium sulphate from magnesium metal?
   (e) Write a symbol equation for the reaction in (d). **R**

5. ► (a) Describe in detail how you would prepare a pure, dry sample of magnesium sulphate crystals ($MgSO_4 \cdot 7H_2O$).
   (b) Calculate the maximum mass of magnesium sulphate crystals, $MgSO_4 \cdot 7H_2O$, that could be prepared from 8.0 g of magnesium oxide (MgO). Explain why, in practice, a smaller mass than this would be obtained. (Relative atomic masses: H = 1 O = 16 Mg = 24 S = 32) **H**

6. ► Sulphuric acid forms two sodium salts, which are called sodium sulphate and sodium hydrogensulphate.

Name of salt	Formula	Ions from the salts present in aqueous solution
Sodium sulphate	Na_2SO_4	$Na^+(aq)$, $SO_4^{2-}(aq)$
Sodium hydrogensulphate	$NaHSO_4$	$Na^+(aq)$, $H^+(aq)$, $SO_4^{2-}(aq)$

(a) What would you expect the pH values of these solutions to be: (i) sodium sulphate, (ii) sodium hydrogensulphate?
(b) Barium nitrate solution was added to separate portions of these solutions. Describe what you would observe for the solution of: (i) sodium sulphate, (ii) sodium hydrogensulphate.
(c) Name a reagent that will change sodium hydrogensulphate solution into sodium sulphate solution.
(NEA) **U**

7. ► The four substances listed in the table below are all used in the home. The table shows the results expected for each substance in each of three simple tests.

Substance	Add water then indicator	Action of gentle heat on sample	Action of acid on substance
sodium carbonate	alkaline	no reaction	odourless gas
sodium hydrogencarbonate	alkaline	gas evolved	odourless gas
tartaric acid	acidic	no reaction	no reaction
calcium hypochlorite	alkaline	no reaction	gas with a strong smell

(a) Devise an identification key which will show how this information could be used to identify an unknown solid as one of these substances.
(b) One type of fire extinguisher produces carbon dioxide by reacting a metal carbonate with an acid. Copy out and complete the balanced equation for the reaction between sodium carbonate and hydrochloric acid.
$Na_2CO_3 + 2HCl = $ _____ + _____ + _____
Given that the relative atomic masses of Na = 23 C = 12 O = 16:
(i) What is the relative mass of CO_2?
(ii) What is the relative mass of Na_2CO_3?
(iii) What mass of CO_2 would be formed by reacting 212 g of sodium carbonate with excess acid? (MEG) **H**

15 Introduction to the Periodic Table

There are over a hundred different chemical elements. Each one has its own properties and reactions. Chemists need to find a way of sorting out elements.

Over the last 150 years, chemists have found a way to classify the elements. A Russian chemist called Mendeleev proposed his first **Periodic Table of Elements** in 1869. From this, our present periodic table has been developed.

Writing elements in the periodic table

In the periodic table information about each element can be written in a box like this:

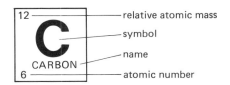

Classifying elements

The periodic table **classifies** elements. The elements are arranged in order of increasing atomic number as follows:

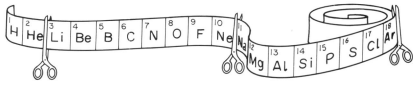

105 elements would make a very long line. This line has been 'cut' at various places, and arranged in a table.

Imagine you are starting to collect stamps. Someone had given you a box of several hundred loose stamps.

They need to be sorted out in some way. Most people sort stamps into countries. These are then put into alphabetical order.

146

15 Introduction to the Periodic Table

Periodic table of the elements

Groups	I	II												III	IV	V	VI	VII	VIII
Periods																			
1	1 **H** hydrogen 1																		4 **He** helium 2
2	7 **Li** lithium 3	9 **Be** beryllium 4												11 **B** boron 5	12 **C** carbon 6	14 **N** nitrogen 7	16 **O** oxygen 8	19 **F** fluorine 9	20 **Ne** neon 10
3	23 **Na** sodium 11	24 **Mg** magnesium 12												27 **Al** aluminium 13	28 **Si** silicon 14	31 **P** phosphorus 15	32 **S** sulphur 16	35.5 **Cl** chlorine 17	40 **Ar** argon 18
4	39 **K** potassium 19	40 **Ca** calcium 20	45 **Sc** scandium 21	48 **Ti** titanium 22	51 **V** vanadium 23	52 **Cr** chromium 24	55 **Mn** manganese 25	56 **Fe** iron 26	59 **Co** cobalt 27	59 **Ni** nickel 28	64 **Cu** copper 29	65 **Zn** zinc 30	70 **Ga** gallium 31	73 **Ge** germanium 32	75 **As** arsenic 33	79 **Se** selenium 34	80 **Br** bromine 35	84 **Kr** krypton 36
5	85.5 **Rb** rubidium 37	88 **Sr** strontium 38	89 **Y** yttrium 39	91 **Zr** zirconium 40	93 **Nb** niobium 41	96 **Mo** molybdenum 42	98 **Tc** technetium 43	101 **Ru** ruthenium 44	103 **Rh** rhodium 45	106 **Pd** palladium 46	108 **Ag** silver 47	112 **Cd** cadmium 48	115 **In** indium 49	119 **Sn** tin 50	122 **Sb** antimony 51	128 **Te** tellurium 52	127 **I** iodine 53	131 **Xe** xenon 54
6	133 **Cs** caesium 55	137 **Ba** barium 56	139 **La** lanthanum 57	178.5 **Hf** hafnium 72	181 **Ta** tantalum 73	184 **W** tungsten 74	186 **Re** rhenium 75	190 **Os** osmium 76	192 **Ir** iridium 77	195 **Pt** platinum 78	197 **Au** gold 79	201 **Hg** mercury 80	204 **Tl** thallium 81	207 **Pb** lead 82	209 **Bi** bismuth 83	210 **Po** polonium 84	210 **At** astatine 85	222 **Rn** radon 86
7	223 **Fr** francium 87	226 **Ra** radium 88	227 **Ac** actinium 89	261 **Unq** unnilquadium 104	262 **Unp** unnilpentium 105													

140 **Ce** cerium 58	141 **Pr** praseodymium 59	144 **Nd** neodymium 60	147 **Pm** promethium 61	150 **Sm** samarium 62	152 **Eu** europium 63	157 **Gd** gadolinium 64	159 **Tb** terbium 65	162.5 **Dy** dysprosium 66	165 **Ho** holmium 67	167 **Er** erbium 68	169 **Tm** thulium 69	173 **Yb** ytterbium 70	175 **Lu** lutetium 71
232 **Th** thorium 90	231 **Pa** protactinium 91	238 **U** uranium 92	237 **Np** neptunium 93	242 **Pu** plutonium 94	243 **Am** americium 95	247 **Cm** curium 96	247 **Bk** berkelium 97	251 **Cf** californium 98	254 **Es** einsteinium 99	253 **Fm** fermium 100	256 **Md** mendelevium 101	254 **No** nobelium 102	257 **Lw** lawrencium 103

non-metal

metal

The columns of elements going down are called **groups**.
Elements in the same group usually have similar properties.

The lines of elements going across are called **periods**.
There are seven periods in the table.

15 Introduction to the Periodic Table

Metals and non-metals

The periodic table divides elements into metals and non-metals. There are only 22 non-metals.

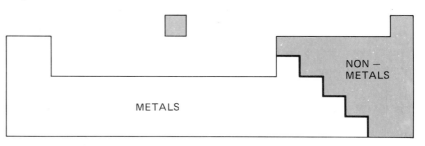

Chemical bonding in the periodic table

Most elements react to form compounds. The type of chemical bond formed can be predicted from the position of an element in the periodic table.

Most **metals** form ionic compounds with non-metals. Some examples are picked out:

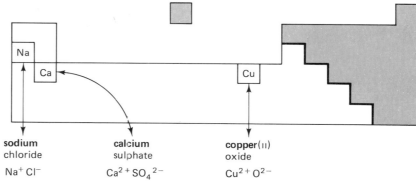

sodium chloride
$Na^+ Cl^-$

calcium sulphate
$Ca^{2+} SO_4^{2-}$

copper(II) oxide
$Cu^{2+} O^{2-}$

Non-metals in Groups III, IV and V do not usually form ions. They form compounds joined with covalent bonds. Some examples are picked out:

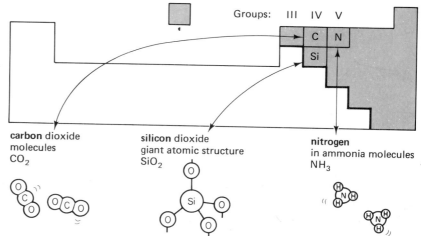

carbon dioxide molecules
CO_2

silicon dioxide giant atomic structure
SiO_2

nitrogen in ammonia molecules
NH_3

Elements in the same group have similar properties. They behave like a chemical family.

Each member of a family is different, but there are always family likenesses. Each element in a group has its own properties but there are always 'family likenesses' within the group.

Non-metals in Groups VI and VII:
either form **molecules** with other non-metal atoms
   or   form **ions** with metals

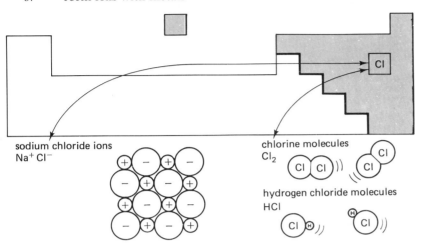

The **noble gases** in Group VIII are very unreactive.
They do not usually form compounds and stay as isolated single atoms.

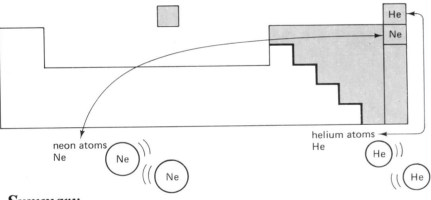

Summary

> 1 The periodic table of elements is a way of **classifying** chemical elements. Elements are arranged in order of increasing atomic number.
>
> 2 Lines of elements going across are called **periods**.
>   Columns of elements going down are called **groups**.
>
> 3 Elements in the **same group** are like a chemical 'family'.
>   Each element in the group has its own properties, but there are 'family likenesses' between elements in the group.
>
> 4 **Metals** are on the left and bottom of the periodic table.
>   **Non-metals** are to the top and right.
>
> 5 **Metals** react with non-metals to form **ionic compounds**.
>   **Non-metals either** join with other non-metals to make **covalent compounds or** with metals to make **ionic compounds**.

16 Group I and II Metals

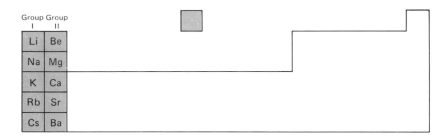

Groups I and II contain the most reactive metals in the periodic table. These metals are not found by themselves in nature. They are so reactive that they quickly combine with other elements to form compounds.

Group I elements: the 'alkali metals'

Name	Symbol	Melting point /°C	Boiling point /°C	Density /g cm^{-3}
Lithium	Li	180	1330	0.53
Sodium	Na	98	890	0.97
Potassium	K	64	774	0.86
Rubidium	Rb	39	688	1.53
Caesium	Cs	29	690	1.90

Group I elements are sometimes called the alkali metals. This is because they react with water to form alkaline solutions.

Where are Group I metals found?

The *elements* themselves do not occur in nature. They are too reactive.
There are very many **compounds** of Group I metals:
Sodium chloride, NaCl, is the most common Group I compound.

Every tonne of ordinary seawater contains about 30 kg of sodium chloride.
The Dead Sea contains about ten times as much sodium chloride dissolved in it as ordinary seawater. This makes it very dense, which allows bathers like this one to float high in the water.

Some parts of the world contain huge underground 'rock salt' deposits like this one in Cheshire.

Properties of Group I elements

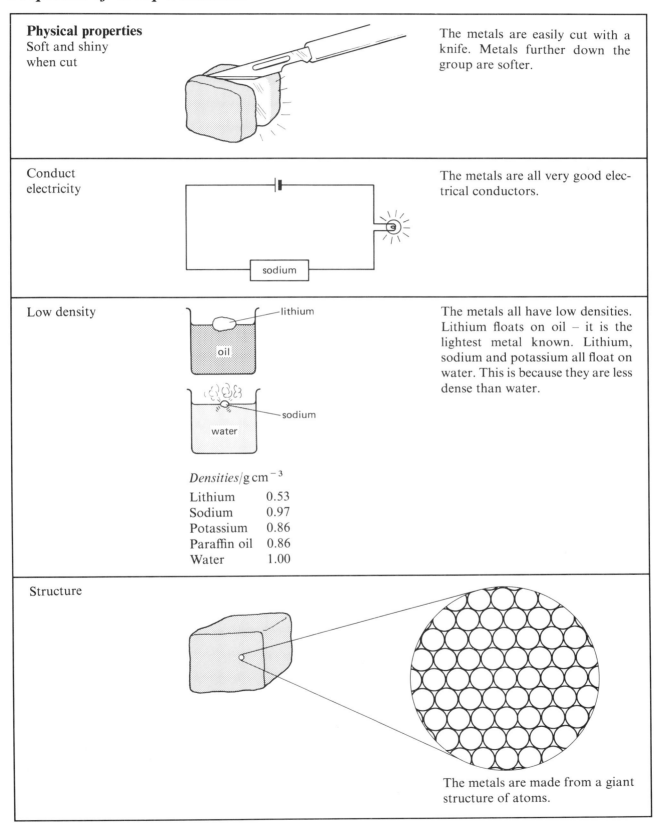

Physical properties Soft and shiny when cut		The metals are easily cut with a knife. Metals further down the group are softer.
Conduct electricity		The metals are all very good electrical conductors.
Low density	*Densities*/g cm^{-3} Lithium 0.53 Sodium 0.97 Potassium 0.86 Paraffin oil 0.86 Water 1.00	The metals all have low densities. Lithium floats on oil – it is the lightest metal known. Lithium, sodium and potassium all float on water. This is because they are less dense than water.
Structure		The metals are made from a giant structure of atoms.

16 Group I and II Metals

Chemical properties

Reaction with air:

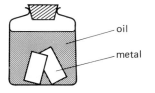

The metals are stored under oil. This is because they react with air.

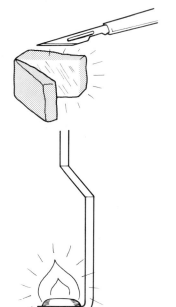

The metals are only shiny when freshly cut. They quickly tarnish as they react with air.

Metals all burn easily in air, with coloured flames, e.g:

sodium + oxygen $\xrightarrow{\text{orange flame}}$ sodium oxide

$4Na(s) + O_2(g) \longrightarrow 2Na_2O(s)$

potassium + oxygen $\xrightarrow{\text{lilac flame}}$ potassium oxide

Reaction with water

Metals all react easily with cold water. The heat from the reaction melts the metal as it reacts:

sodium	+	water	→	sodium hydroxide	+	hydrogen	reacts well
$2Na(l)$	+	$2H_2O(l)$	→	$2NaOH(aq)$	+	$H_2(g)$	
potassium	+	water	→	potassium hydroxide	+	hydrogen	reacts so well that the hydrogen produced catches fire
$2K(l)$	+	$2H_2O(l)$	→	$2KOH(aq)$	+	$H_2(g)$	

The melted metals move over the surface of the water like a hovercraft. They float on a cushion of hydrogen gas and steam.

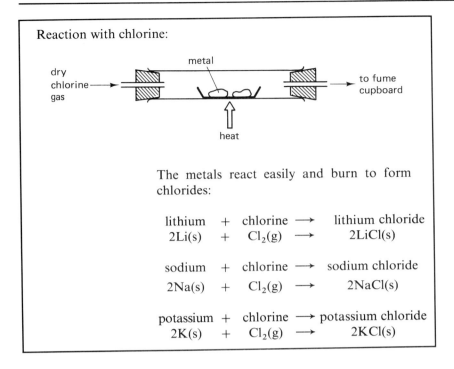

Reaction with chlorine:

The metals react easily and burn to form chlorides:

lithium + chlorine ⟶ lithium chloride
2Li(s) + Cl$_2$(g) ⟶ 2LiCl(s)

sodium + chlorine ⟶ sodium chloride
2Na(s) + Cl$_2$(g) ⟶ 2NaCl(s)

potassium + chlorine ⟶ potassium chloride
2K(s) + Cl$_2$(g) ⟶ 2KCl(s)

Group I ions

Lithium ion	Li$^+$
Sodium ion	Na$^+$
Potassium ion	K$^+$
Rubidium ion	Rb$^+$
Caesium ion	Cs$^+$

The elements in a group in the periodic table behave like a family. There are many 'family likenesses' between elements in the group. But each element has its own character.

The properties of the alkali metals are very similar. The compounds they form have similar formulae:

Group I compounds

Metal	Chloride	Bromide	Nitrate	Sulphate	Carbonate
Lithium	LiCl	LiBr	LiNO$_3$	Li$_2$SO$_4$	Li$_2$CO$_3$
Sodium	NaCl	NaBr	NaNO$_3$	Na$_2$SO$_4$	Na$_2$CO$_3$
Potassium	KCl	KBr	KNO$_3$	K$_2$SO$_4$	K$_2$CO$_3$

Group I compounds are made from **ions**. All the alkali metals form ions with a 1+ charge.

As we have seen, alkali metals and their compounds are very **similar** in many ways. However, there is also a **trend** within the group. The further down the group, the more reactive the element.

Reactivity of Group I metals

Lithium
Sodium   metals get more reactive
Potassium

The reaction of alkali metals with cold water is an example of this trend. Lithium reacts quite gently, sodium is more reactive, and potassium is so reactive that the hydrogen produced catches fire.

Uses of alkali metals and compounds

Salting roads
Rock salt is spread on roads in winter. The salt melts the ice, and the grit makes the road less slippery.

Street lamps
Sodium vapour in street lamps gives them an orange glow.

Seasoning food
Salt is used to season food.

Making glass
Glass is made by melting sodium carbonate (Na_2CO_3) with sand and calcium carbonate.

Burglar alarms
Sodium is used in the photo-electric cells of burglar alarms.

Group II metals

Name	Symbol	Melting point/°C	Boiling point/°C	Density /g cm^{-3}
Beryllium	Be	1280	2477	1.85
Magnesium	Mg	650	1110	1.74
Calcium	Ca	850	1487	1.54
Strontium	Sr	768	1380	2.62
Barium	Ba	714	1640	3.51

The metals in Group II are similar in many ways to those in Group I. They are less reactive than Group I metals.

Where are Group II metals found?

The **elements** of Group II do not occur in nature. They are too reactive. There are very many **compounds** of Group II metals:

Magnesium chloride
MgCl$_2$

Every tonne of seawater contains about 5 kg of magnesium chloride.

Calcium carbonate
CaCO$_3$

These limestone cliffs are made from calcium carbonate. Other forms of calcium carbonate are marble, chalk and coral.

Calcium phosphate
Ca$_3$(PO$_4$)$_2$

Calcium phosphate is an essential part of bones and teeth. Enough calcium compounds in the diet are essential to good health.

Michelangelo created this famous statue called the Pietà in 1564. It is made from marble mined in Carrara in Italy. Marble is a form of calcium carbonate, CaCO$_3$.

Properties of Group II elements

Physical properties	The metals are silvery and shiny when kept away from air. They are good conductors of electricity. They are made from a giant structure of atoms.

Chemical properties

Reaction with air:

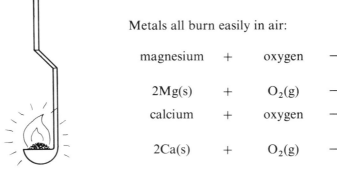

Metals all burn easily in air:

magnesium + oxygen → magnesium oxide
$2Mg(s)$ + $O_2(g)$ → $2MgO(s)$
calcium + oxygen → calcium oxide
$2Ca(s)$ + $O_2(g)$ → $2CaO(s)$

The metals are not as reactive as those in Group I. They do not need to be stored under oil.

Reaction with water:

Magnesium reacts very slowly with liquid water. It reacts more rapidly with steam:

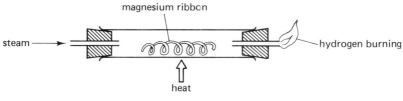

magnesium + steam → magnesium oxide + hydrogen
$Mg(s)$ + $H_2O(g)$ → $MgO(s)$ + $H_2(g)$

Note that the product is magnesium oxide. Magnesium does not form the hydroxide.

Calcium reacts easily with cold water. Hydrogen gas is formed:

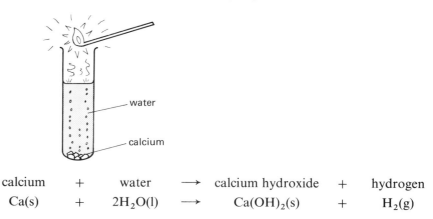

calcium + water → calcium hydroxide + hydrogen
$Ca(s)$ + $2H_2O(l)$ → $Ca(OH)_2(s)$ + $H_2(g)$

The metal oxides and hydroxides produced in these reactions are all bases. They can neutralise acids to make salts (Chapter 14).

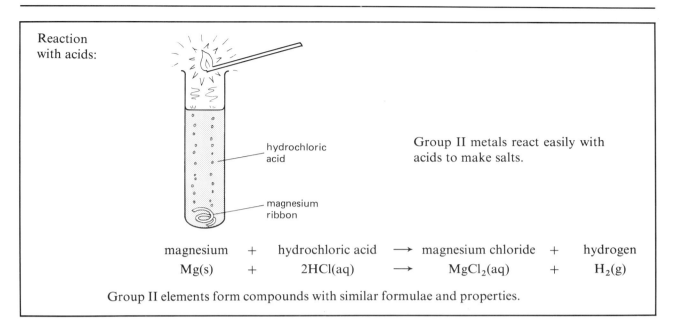

Group II compounds

Metal	Chloride	Bromide	Nitrate	Sulphate	Carbonate
Magnesium	$MgCl_2$	$MgBr_2$	$Mg(NO_3)_2$	$MgSO_4$	$MgCO_3$
Calcium	$CaCl_2$	$CaBr_2$	$Ca(NO_3)_2$	$CaSO_4$	$CaCO_3$

Group II ions
Beryllium ion	Be^{2+}
Magnesium ion	Mg^{2+}
Calcium ion	Ca^{2+}
Strontium ion	Sr^{2+}
Barium ion	Ba^{2+}

All Group II compounds are made from ions. All these metals form ions with a 2+ charge.

Group II metals and their compounds are very **similar** in many ways. There is also a **trend** within the group. The further down the group, the more reactive the element.

Reactivity of metals of Groups I and II

Group I   Group II
Lithium   Beryllium
Sodium   Magnesium
Potassium   Calcium

Metals in both groups get more reactive down the group.

Group II metals are similar to Group I metals, but they are not as reactive.

Some reactions of calcium and its compounds

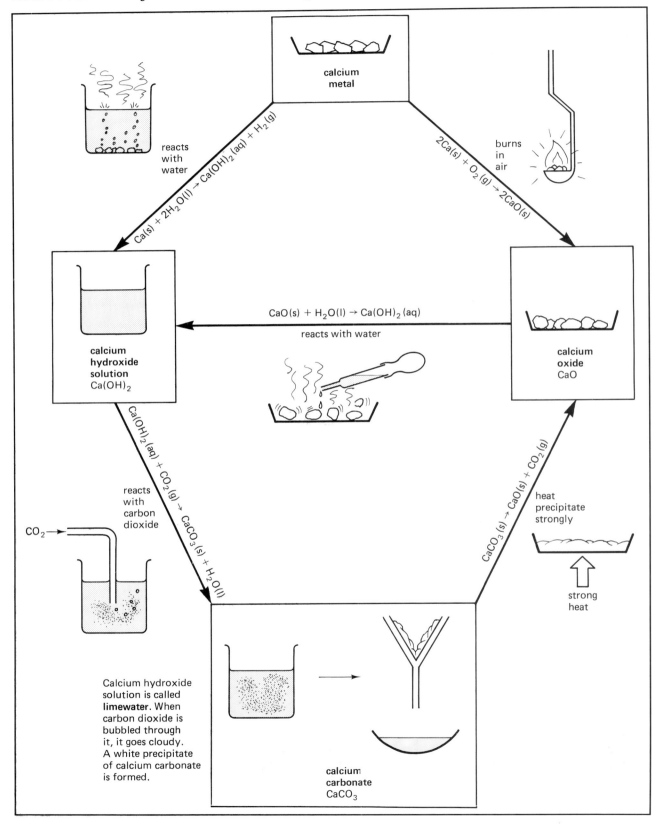

Hardness in water

When some Group II compounds dissolve in rainwater, they make the water 'hard'. Hard-water areas usually occur where rain has fallen on limestone hills. Rainwater is acidic due to dissolved carbon dioxide. It can also contain other acid gases like sulphur dioxide. This comes from burning fuels in factories and power stations.

How does water become hard?

Rainwater dissolves acid gases from the air:

$$CO_2(g) + H_2O(l) \longrightarrow \underset{\text{('H}_2\text{CO}_3\text{')}}{\overset{\text{carbonic acid}}{HCO_3^-(aq) + H^+(aq)}}$$

Acid rain reacts with limestone:

limestone + carbonic acid $\longrightarrow$ calcium hydrogencarbonate + water + carbon dioxide

$$CaCO_3(s) + H_2CO_3(aq) \longrightarrow Ca(HCO_3)_2(aq) + H_2O(l) + CO_2(g)$$

Hard water contains dissolved calcium salts.

Some calcium compounds in rocks are slightly soluble in water, and simply dissolve. For example:

calcium sulphate $\xrightarrow{\text{dissolves in water}}$ calcium sulphate solution

$$CaSO_4(s) \longrightarrow CaSO_4(aq)$$

Like compounds of calcium, magnesium compounds dissolve into water and make it hard.

Hardness in water is caused mainly by the presence of dissolved salts of calcium and magnesium. These dissolved minerals are important for good health. People living in hard-water areas tend to be healthier than those in areas where water is said to be 'soft'. Soft water contains only small amounts of dissolved calcium and magnesium compounds.

Removing hardness from water

Stalactites and stalagmites

When hard water evaporates, the calcium hydrogencarbonate breaks down into limestone:

$$Ca(HCO_3)_2(aq) \longrightarrow CaCO_3(s) + H_2O(l) + CO_2(g)$$

Over millions of years this process leads to the shapes in limestone caves.

Soap

When soap is used in hard water, scum is formed. This is a nuisance because it wastes soap, sticks in clothes being washed and leaves a mess in the washbasin and bath.

calcium ions in hard water + octadecanoate (stearate ions) in soap ⟶ calcium octadecanoate (calcium stearate) 'scum'

Boiling

When water is boiled, the calcium hydrogencarbonate breaks down leaving a 'scale' or 'fur' in kettles, pipes and boilers. The 'fur' is calcium carbonate.

$$Ca(HCO_3)(aq) \longrightarrow CaCO_3(s) + CO_2(g) + H_2O(l)$$

When this 'fur' builds up, it can block pipes and waste heating fuel in boilers.

Ion exchange

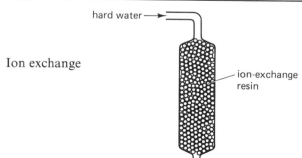

Certain chemicals called ion-exchange resins can remove hardness from water. The ions causing hardness, like calcium (Ca^{2+}), are exchanged for other ions such as sodium (Na^+) which do not cause hardness.

Uses of Group II metals and compounds

Flashlights and flares

The bright light from burning magnesium is used in flash cubes for cameras and in distress flares at sea (see page 230).

Talcum powder

Talc is made from magnesium silicate.

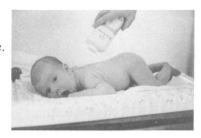

Plaster of paris

Plaster of paris is a form of calcium sulphate. When mixed with water, it expands and sets hard in 5 minutes. It is used to protect broken bones.

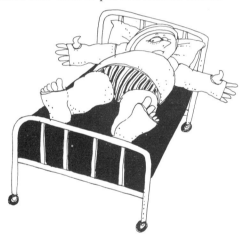

Fireworks

The brilliant red colour of some fireworks is caused by strontium compounds.

Upset stomachs

Magnesium oxide MgO is called 'magnesia'. Because this is a base, it neutralises stomach acid.

Cement

Cement is made by heating a mixture of clay and calcium carbonate, $CaCO_3$ (limestone). When mixed with sand and water, it makes mortar, which is used to bind bricks together.

Plaster

Walls are plastered with calcium sulphate (gypsum) mixed with water.

Lime

Calcium hydroxide $Ca(OH)_2$ is added to the soil as 'lime'. It neutralises acids in the soil.

X-rays

To take an X-ray picture of a person's intestines, they are given a 'barium meal'. This contains barium sulphate, $BaSO_4$, which shows up on X-ray photos. Most barium compounds are poisonous, but barium sulphate is insoluble in water and is safe to eat in this way.

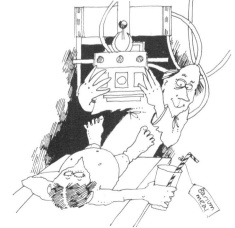

Summary

1. Group I elements are called the **alkali metals** because of the alkaline solution formed when they react with water.

2. Elements of Groups I and II are so **reactive** that they do not occur naturally. Compounds of these metals are very common, e.g. salt, limestone.

3. Elements in the same group have **similar properties**. Group I metals have very similar physical and chemical properties. Group II metals are similar to these in Group I, but they are less reactive.

4. **Group I metals** form ions with a 1+ charge, e.g. Li^+, Na^+, K^+. They therefore form **ionic compounds** with formulae similar to one another, e.g. LiCl, NaCl, KCl.

5. **Group II metals** form ions with a 2+ charge, e.g. Mg^{2+}, Ca^{2+}, Ba^{2+}. They therefore form **ionic compounds** with similar formulae, e.g. $MgCl_2$, $CaCl_2$, $BaCl_2$.

6. There is a **trend** of properties within Groups I and II. The metals get more reactive further down the group.

7. When some Group II compounds dissolve in rainwater, they make the water **hard**. Hardness in water leads to pipes and boilers being lined with 'scale'. Soap forms scum with hard water. Hardness may be removed by boiling or by ion exchange.

8. Compounds for Groups I and II have many **uses**, e.g. sodium chloride for food and icy roads, calcium carbonate for cement.

Questions

1. • Use a periodic table of the elements to answer the following questions:
   (a) Name or give the symbols of **two** metals in Group III.
   (b) Name or give the symbols of **two** non-metals in Group VI.
   (c) Name or give the symbols of **two** gases at room temperature in the halogens group.
   (d) Name or give the symbols of **two** metals in the alkali metals group.
   (e) Give the symbol of a metal element that is liquid at room temperature.
   (f) Give the symbol of a non-metal element that is a black shining solid at room temperature. (WMEB) R

2. • Sodium reacts with water to produce hydrogen. This may be shown using the apparatus below.

   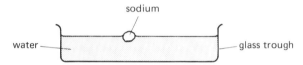

   (a) Why is the sodium floating on the water?
   (b) Hydrogen is produced in the reaction of sodium with water. Describe the test for hydrogen.
   (c) How is sodium normally stored in the laboratory?
   (d) Copy out and complete the word equation for the reaction of sodium with water.

   sodium + water ⟶ _____ + _____

   (e) Why is it especially dangerous if sodium is allowed to come into contact with water?
   Sodium is an alkali metal.
   (f) Name two other elements in this 'family' of elements.
   (g) How would you expect this 'family' of elements to react with chlorine? Describe and name the product formed by one of these elements. (SEREB) U

3. ■ (a) The diagram below represents an apparatus which can be used to pass hydrogen over heated copper(II) oxide and collect the products.

   Answer the following questions about the experiment.
   (i) Before the hydrogen was lit at the jet, some of it was collected in a test-tube and ignited well away from the apparatus. This was repeated until the sample burned quietly. The jet was then lit. Explain why it was necessary to do this.
   (ii) Name **one** substance which could be used to dry the hydrogen.
   (iii) State the colour of copper(II) oxide.
   (iv) State the colour of the residue in the combustion tube after the reaction.
   (v) Describe a test you would carry out to show that the residue was a metal.
   (vi) Name the type of reaction the copper(II) oxide has undergone.
   (vii) Name liquid **A** which turns anhydrous copper(II) sulphate blue and has a boiling point of 100 °C at a pressure of one atmosphere.
   (viii) Explain why the U-tube is immersed in a beaker of cold water.
   (ix) Write a symbol equation for the reaction between copper(II) oxide and hydrogen.
   (x) At the end of the experiment the heat was removed and hydrogen passed through until the residue was cold. The hydrogen supply was then disconnected and the residue removed. Explain why this procedure was necessary.

   (b) Rubidium is a Group I metal which is more reactive than sodium. Note the position of rubidium in the periodic table. When rubidium reacts with water, a gas **P** is given off and a colourless solution **Q** is formed which is a strong alkali. Use this information to help you answer the following questions.
   (i) Name the group of metals of which rubidium is a member.
   (ii) Rubidium reacts readily with some gases in the air. State how it would be stored in the laboratory.
   (iii) Describe **one** observation you would make when rubidium reacts with water.
   (iv) State the approximate pH value of solution **Q**.
   (v) Name gas **P**.
   (vi) Name solution **Q**.
   (vii) Solution **Q** can be neutralised by dilute hydrochloric acid forming a salt **S** and water only. Write the formula of salt **S**.
   (viii) Describe briefly how you would obtain a sample of salt **S** from the reaction mixture used in part (vii).
   (ix) State what you would see if you added solution **Q** to copper(II) sulphate solution. (NEA) U

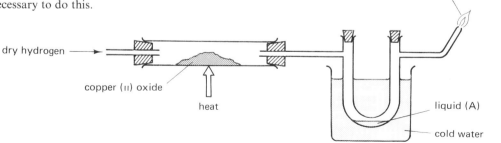

17 Group VII Elements: the Halogens

Halogen compounds found in the sea

Name	Formula	
Sodium chloride	NaCl	
Sodium bromide	NaBr	
Magnesium bromide	$MgBr_2$	
Sodium iodide	NaI	these are found in seaweed
Potassium iodide	KI	

Group VII contains some of the most reactive non-metals in the periodic table. Like Groups I and II, these elements are so reactive that they do not occur in nature. Group VII elements are called the 'halogens'. This comes from a Greek word, meaning 'salt-makers'. Halogens react with most metals to make salts.

Group VII elements

The halogens

Name	Symbol	Melting point/°C	Boiling point/°C	State at room temperature (15°C)
Fluorine	F	−220	−188	gas
Chlorine	Cl	−101	−35	gas
Bromine	Br	−7	59	liquid
Iodine	I	114	184	solid

Certain sorts of seaweed have the ability to extract iodine compounds from seawater. This seaweed contains quite a lot of iodine compounds.

Where are the halogens found?

The elements themselves are not found in nature. They are too reactive. There are very many compounds of the halogens, mostly found in seawater.

17 Group VII Elements: The Halogens

Making chlorine in the laboratory

Chlorine is made by adding concentrated hydrochloric acid to manganese(IV) oxide and warming.

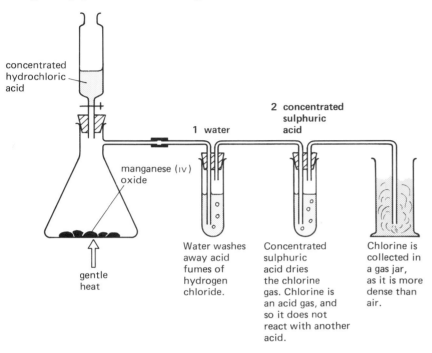

Chlorine was used as a poisonous gas by both sides in World War I. As it is very dense, it easily filled the trenches, killing or injuring unprotected people and animals. Gas masks contained canisters of activated charcoal which filtered out the chlorine.

The experiment is carried out in a fume cupboard, because chlorine is very poisonous.

Equation:

Manganese(IV) + hydrochloric → manganese(II) + water + chlorine
oxide   acid   chloride

$MnO_2(s) + 4HCl(aq) \rightarrow MnCl_2(aq) + 2H_2O(l) + Cl_2(g)$

Potassium manganate(VII) (potassium permanganate), $KMnO_4$, can be used instead of manganese(IV) oxide. It does not need to be heated to react. Chlorine is manufactured by the electrolysis of brine (see Chapter 25).

Properties of the halogens — Physical properties

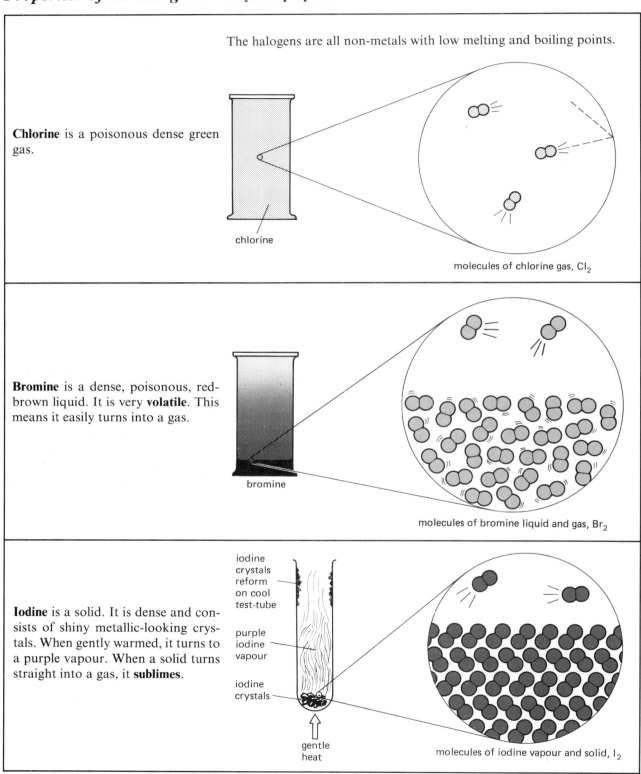

The halogens are all non-metals with low melting and boiling points.

Chlorine is a poisonous dense green gas.

Bromine is a dense, poisonous, red-brown liquid. It is very **volatile**. This means it easily turns into a gas.

Iodine is a solid. It is dense and consists of shiny metallic-looking crystals. When gently warmed, it turns to a purple vapour. When a solid turns straight into a gas, it **sublimes**.

The halogens all exist as diatomic molecules. The two atoms in the molecule are joined by a **covalent bond**.

Chemical properties

Reaction with metals:	Halogens react with most metals to make salts: 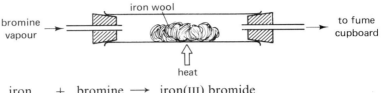 iron + bromine → iron(III) bromide $2Fe(s) + 3Br_2(g) \rightarrow 2FeBr_3(s)$ sodium + chlorine → sodium chloride $2Na(s) + Cl_2(g) \rightarrow 2NaCl(s)$
Reaction with hydrogen:	A hydrogen flame continues to burn in a gas jar of chlorine, making hydrogen chloride gas: 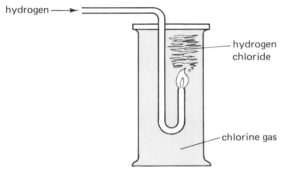 hydrogen + chlorine → hydrogen chloride $H_2(g) + Cl_2(g) \rightarrow 2HCl(g)$ The hydrogen chloride may form steamy fumes in moist air.
Reaction with indicators:	Chlorine gas dissolves in water to make a powerful bleach. Damp indicator paper shows an acid reaction with chlorine, then it is quickly bleached.
Displacement reactions:	Chlorine can **displace** bromine and iodine from a solution of their salts: 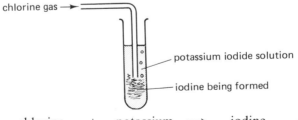 chlorine + potassium iodide → iodine + potassium chloride $Cl_2(g) + 2KI(aq) \rightarrow I_2(aq) + 2KCl(aq)$ chlorine + potassium bromide → bromine + potassium chloride $Cl_2(g) + 2KBr(aq) \rightarrow Br_2(aq) + 2KCl(aq)$ Chlorine is more reactive than bromine and iodine. This is why it can displace them in this way. Bromine is more reactive than iodine. Bromine can displace iodine from a solution of potassium iodide.

When halogens react with metals they form ionic compounds, e.g. Na^+Cl^-. Halogens always form ions with a 1− charge. When halogens react with non-metals they form covalent molecules, e.g. HCl. All the halogens have very similar chemical properties.

There is also a trend in properties. The further down the group, the less reactive the element. This is the opposite of the behaviour shown by metals of Groups I and II.

Group VII elements form compounds with similar formulae and properties.

Reactivity of the halogens

Group VII

Fluorine
Chlorine
Bromine
Iodine

Elements get **less** reactive down the group.

Some Group VII compounds

Halogens	Sodium	Magnesium	Hydrogen
Fluoride	NaF	MgF_2	HF
Chloride	NaCl	$MgCl_2$	HCl
Bromide	NaBr	$MgBr_2$	HBr
Iodide	NaI	MgI_2	HI

Group VII Ions

Fluoride ion	F^-
Chloride ion	Cl^-
Bromide ion	Br^-
Iodide ion	I^-

Hydrogen chloride and hydrochloric acid

Hydrogen chloride gas is a useful compound of chlorine. It dissolves in water to produce hydrochloric acid.

Making hydrogen chloride in the laboratory

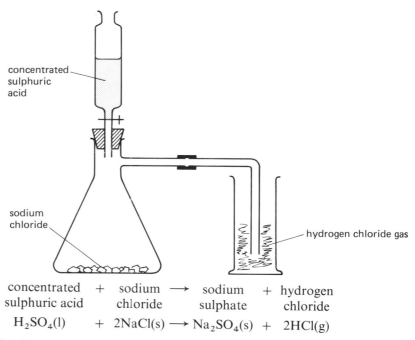

concentrated + sodium → sodium + hydrogen
sulphuric acid   chloride   sulphate   chloride

$H_2SO_4(l)$ + $2NaCl(s)$ → $Na_2SO_4(s)$ + $2HCl(g)$

Hydrogen chloride is more dense than air, so it can be collected in a gas jar.
Hydrogen chloride cannot be collected over water because it is very soluble.

Physical properties of hydrogen chloride

Structure:	Hydrogen chloride is a dense colourless gas with a choking smell. It forms cloudy fumes in moist air. 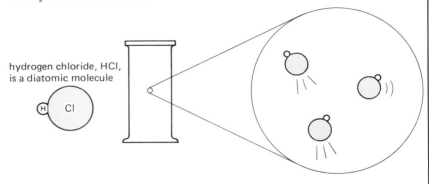

Chemical properties of hydrogen chloride

Reaction of hydrogen chloride with ammonia:	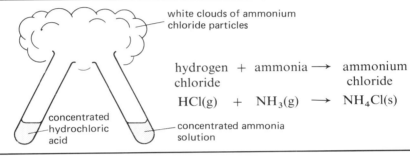 hydrogen + ammonia → ammonium chloride chloride $HCl(g) + NH_3(g) \rightarrow NH_4Cl(s)$
Reaction of hydrogen chloride with water:	Hydrogen chloride reacts very easily with water. About 500 cm³ hydrogen chloride will dissolve into 1 cm³ water. 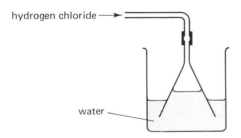 The solution formed is called **hydrochloric acid**: hydrogen + water → hydrochloric acid chloride $HCl(g) + H_2O(l) \rightarrow H_3O^+(aq) + Cl^-(aq)$ hydrochloric acid contains: chloride ions, Cl^- hydroxonium ions, H_3O^+ H_3O^+ ions are present in all solutions of acids
Reactions of hydrochloric acid:	Hydrochloric acid shows all the reactions of an acid. It reacts with metals, bases and carbonates (see Chapter 14).

Uses of halogens and their compounds

Swimming pools and water
Chlorine is used to kill harmful bacteria in swimming pools and in the water supply.

Non-stick surfaces
'Teflon' is a fluorine compound that forms the non-stick coating on pans and the base of skis.

Bleach
Bleach contains chlorine dissolved in sodium hydroxide solution.

Photography
Silver bromide is sensitive to light and is coated onto photographic films.

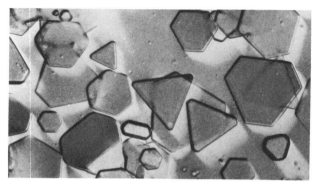

The grains of silver bromide on the camera film look like the picture above when magnified 6000 times.

Dental health
Small amounts of fluorine compounds can protect teeth from decay. These are included in 'fluoride' toothpastes and added to some water supplies.

17 Group VII Elements: The Halogens

Summary

1 Group VII elements are called the **halogens**.

2 All of the halogens are so **reactive** that they do not occur naturally. Compounds of the halogens are found in seawater, e.g. sodium chloride.

3 **Chlorine** is made in the laboratory by the action of concentrated hydrochloric acid on heated manganese(IV) oxide:
$MnO_2(s) + 4HCl(aq) \rightarrow MnCl_2(aq) + 2H_2O(l) + Cl_2(g)$

4 The halogens all have **similar physical and chemical properties**.

5 *Either*
halogens react with metals to form **ions** with a 1− charge, e.g. Cl^-, Br^-, I^-. These ionic compounds have similar formulae e.g. NaCl, NaBr, NaI.
Or
halogens react with non-metals to form **molecules**, e.g. HCl.

6 There is a **trend** of physical and chemical properties within the group. The elements get less reactive further down the group.

7 **Hydrogen chloride** is made in the laboratory by reacting sodium chloride with concentrated sulphuric acid:
$H_2SO_4(l) + 2NaCl(s) \rightarrow Na_2SO_4(s) + 2HCl(g)$

8 Hydrogen chloride dissolves in water to make **hydrochloric acid**.

9 Elements and compounds of Group VII have many **uses**, e.g. fluoride compounds in toothpaste, chlorine to sterilise water.

Questions

1 ● (a) (i) Name the reagents that can be used to prepare the gas hydrogen chloride.
  (ii) By means of a simple diagram show how hydrogen chloride is usually collected.
(b) Hydrochloric acid is prepared by dissolving hydrogen chloride in water.

Diagram 1   Diagram 2

Explain why the apparatus in diagram 1 is unsuitable for this preparation, and why it can be done using the apparatus in diagram 2. (NEA) **R**

2 ■ The table opposite shows the symbols of some elements in the periodic table:

(a) Using only the symbols shown below, give the symbols of:
  (i) a metal,
  (ii) a non-metal,
  (iii) a metal that reacts vigorously with cold water,
  (iv) a magnetic element,
  (v) a very unreactive metal,
  (vi) a gas that does not form compounds.

(b) What is the name of the block of elements that includes iron, copper and gold?
(c) Give the names of the two allotropes of carbon.
(d) (i) What name is given to the group of elements with symbols F, Cl, Br, and I?
  (ii) How do the melting and boiling points of these elements change as you go down the group?
  (iii) How does the reactivity of these elements change as you go down the group? **R**

18 Group VIII Elements: the Noble Gases

Electronic configuration of a neon atom

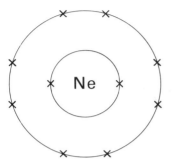

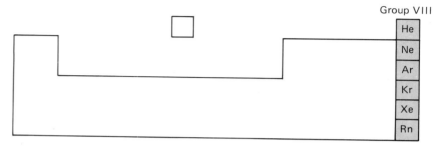

Neon has a full outer shell of electrons. This makes it very stable as it is. The noble gases all have full outer electron shells.

Group VIII contains the least reactive elements in the periodic table. They are called the **noble gases**. They are all gases with low melting and boiling points.

Group VIII elements

Name	Symbol	Melting point/°C	Boiling point/°C
Helium	He	−270	−269
Neon	Ne	−249	−246
Argon	Ar	−189	−186
Krypton	Kr	−157	−152
Xenon	Xe	−112	−108
Radon	Rn	−71	−62

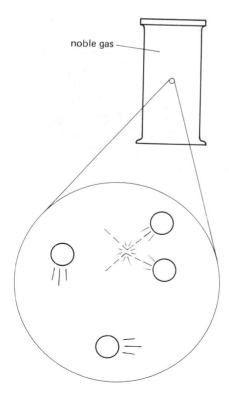

Where are the noble gases found?

Noble gases are found in the atmosphere. Just under 1% of the air is made of these gases, mostly argon. They are obtained by fractionally distilling liquid air (see Chapter 14).

Properties of the noble gases

The noble gases consist of isolated single atoms:

Atoms of most elements react to form compounds. The compounds are generally more stable than the elements. Atoms of noble gases, however, are very stable as they are. Most noble gases do not react to form compounds at all.

18 Group VIII Elements: The Noble Gases   173

Uses of the noble gases

Airships

Helium has a low density and is used to fill airships and weather balloons.

Diving

Divers breathe a mixture of oxygen and helium. If a diver breathes air, nitrogen dissolves into the bloodstream and can cause the 'bends'. Helium does not dissolve into the blood in this way.

Light bulbs

Light bulbs are filled with argon gas. It is very unreactive and helps protect the filament.

Neon lights

When an electric current is passed through neon gas, it gives out a bright light.

Summary

1 Group VIII elements are called the **noble gases**.

2 All noble gases are very **unreactive** and consist of single isolated atoms. Noble gases make up about 1% of the atmosphere.

3 Noble gases have many **uses**, e.g. argon in light bulbs, helium in airships.

19 The Transition Metals

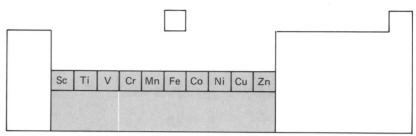

Copper is a fairly unreactive metal. For this reason, it is sometimes found as 'native copper' in the earth.

The **transition metals** are found in the centre block of the periodic table. They have very similar properties to each other, even though they are not a group like the halogens or alkali metals. Since they are so alike, they are studied together. They are sometimes called the **heavy metals** because of their high density. There are three rows of transition metals in the periodic table. Only the first row is studied here.

The first row of transition metals

Name	Symbol	Melting point/°C	Boiling point/°C	Density/g cm^{-3}
Scandium	Sc	1540	2730	3.0
Titanium	Ti	1675	3260	4.5
Vandium	V	1900	3000	6.0
Chromium	Cr	1890	2482	7.2
Manganese	Mn	1240	2100	7.2
Iron	Fe	1535	3000	7.9
Cobalt	Co	1492	2900	8.9
Nickel	Ni	1453	2730	8.9
Copper	Cu	1083	2595	8.9
Zinc	Zn	420	907	7.1

Where are the transition metals found?

Transition metals are not as reactive as metals in Groups I and II. A few transition metals like copper can occur naturally, but mostly they exist as compounds. A compound from which a metal can be extracted is called an ore. Ores of transition metals often have strange-sounding names, e.g. haematite which is an oxide of iron, Fe_2O_3.

19 The Transition Metals

Properties of transition metals

Physical properties
Transition metals are all dense, strong metals with high melting points. They conduct heat and electricity very easily.

Structure
Transition metals, like all metals, are made from a giant structure of metal atoms:

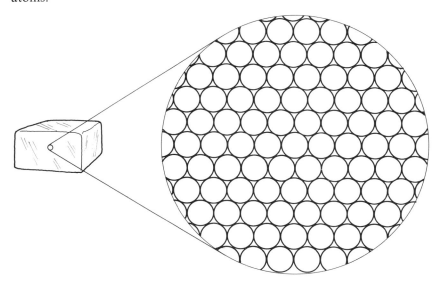

The densities of the first 36 elements

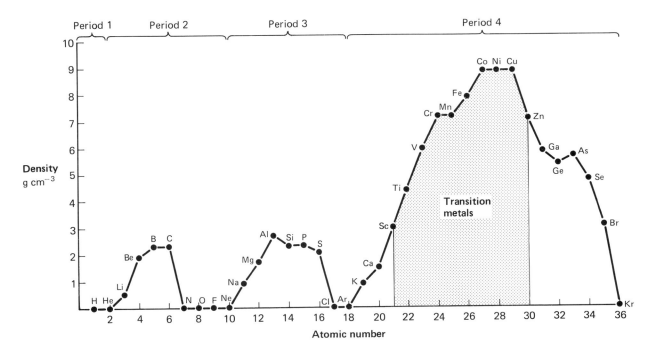

This graph shows the high density of transition metals compared to other elements.

19 The Transition Metals

The different colours of people's hair is due to the presence of transition metal compounds. Blonde hair contains titanium compounds, red hair contains molybdenum compounds and brown hair contains compounds of iron, copper and cobalt.

Transition metals cause the colours in jewels such as emeralds, sapphires, and amethysts. The gold and silver used to make the settings for the jewels are also transition metals.

Colours of some transition metal compounds

Name	Formula	Colour
Potassium **chrom**ate	K_2CrO_4	yellow
Potassium **mangan**ate(VII)	$KMnO_4$	purple
Iron(II) chloride	$FeCl_2$	green
Copper(II) sulphate	$CuSO_4$	blue

Some transition metal ions
Chromium ions: Cr^{2+} and Cr^{3+}
Iron ions: Fe^{2+} and Fe^{3+}
Copper ions: Cu^+ and Cu^{2+}

Chemical properties
Transition metals are not very reactive.

Reaction with water:	Some transition metals, like chromium and copper, do not react with water. Iron reacts slowly with water in the presence of oxygen from the air. Rust is produced, which is a form of iron oxide.
Catalysts:	Many transition metals and their compounds are good catalysts. **Iron** is a catalyst when ammonia is made by the Haber process: $$N_2(g) + 3H_2(g) \xrightarrow[\text{catalyst}]{\text{iron}} 2NH_3(g)$$ **Manganese**(IV) oxide acts as a catalyst when hydrogen peroxide solution breaks down: 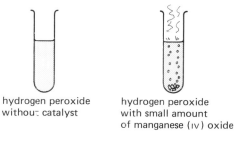 $$2H_2O_2(aq) \rightarrow 2H_2O(l) + O_2(g)$$
Reaction with acids:	All transition metals react with at least one acid, provided it is concentrated enough. Some transition metals react with dilute acids: 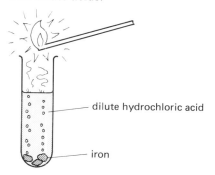 iron + hydrochloric acid → iron(II) chloride + hydrogen $$Fe(s) + 2HCl(aq) \rightarrow FeCl_2(aq) + H_2(g)$$ The iron(II) chloride formed in this reaction is a pale green solution. Nearly all transition metal compounds are **coloured**.

Like all metals, transition elements form **positive ions**. The charge on these ions can vary. The same metal can have ions with **different charges**.

Making iron from its ores

It is unlikely that we shall ever run out of iron. It is the second most abundant metal after aluminium. Nearly 5% of the earth's crust is made from iron compounds. The centre of the earth is thought to contain iron at very high temperatures and pressures. Since iron is a magnetic metal, this causes the earth to have a magnetic field.

Iron is extracted from one of its ores, such as haematite, Fe_2O_3. The iron(III) oxide is **reduced** to iron metal in a blast furnace. These furnaces are very large and are worked 24 hours a day. They can make over 1000 tonnes of iron a day.

A blast furnace

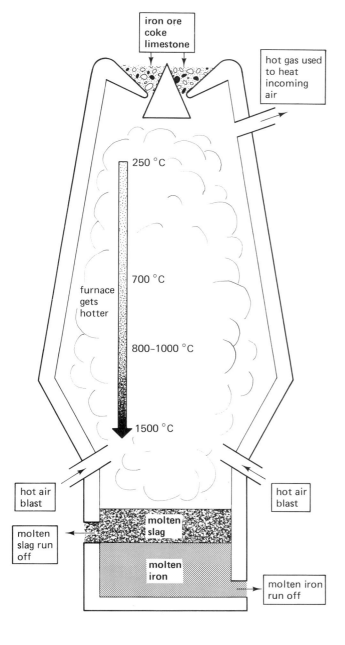

Reactions in a blast furnace

1. Iron ore, limestone and coke are fed into the top of the blast furnace.

2. Hot air is blasted up the furnace from the bottom.

3. Oxygen from the air reacts with coke to form carbon dioxide:

    $$C(s) + O_2(g) \longrightarrow CO_2(g)$$

4. Carbon dioxide reacts with more coke to form carbon monoxide:

    $$CO_2(g) + C(s) \longrightarrow 2CO(g)$$

5. Carbon monoxide is a reducing agent. Iron(III) oxide is reduced to iron:

    reduction = loss of oxygen
    $$Fe_2O_3(s) + 3CO(g) \longrightarrow 2Fe(l) + 3CO_2(g)$$

6. Dense molten iron falls to the bottom of the furnace and is run off.

    There are many impurities in iron ore. The limestone helps remove these as follows:

7. Limestone is broken down on heating to calcium oxide:

    $$CaCO_3(s) \longrightarrow CaO(s) + CO_2(g)$$

8. Calcium oxide reacts with impurities like sand (silicon dioxide) to form a liquid called 'slag':

    $$CaO(s) + SiO_2(s) \longrightarrow CaSiO_3(l)$$
    impurity   slag

    The liquid slag falls to the bottom of the furnace and is tapped off.

19 The Transition Metals

Making steel

The iron produced in a blast furnace is called **cast iron**. It is brittle and impure. Most cast iron is changed into steel. This is done by removing impurities and adding carbon and small amounts of metals.

The impurities are removed from the cast iron with a blast of oxygen. Calcium oxide (lime) is also added, to remove impurities as slag.

Making steel from cast iron

A sample of a patient's blood is being tested for the amount of iron it contains. If the iron level is too low, the patient may be suffering from anaemia.

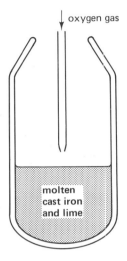

Various metals and amounts of carbon are then added to the pure iron. This makes different types of steel.

When the protective layer of paint on a car becomes scratched, the steel underneath rusts when it comes into contact with water and air.

Molten iron being poured into a converter in which it is made into steel.

Uses of transition metals

Transition metals are dense, strong and not very reactive. This makes them useful materials for many everyday objects.

Electrical
Copper is an excellent conductor of electricity and is used in wires.

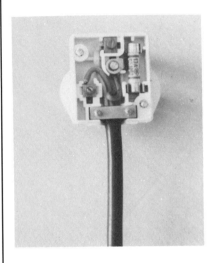

Cooking
Many kettles and pans are made from copper, steel or cast iron. This is because they conduct heat well.

Plumbing
Copper does not react with water and is used in water pipes.

Construction
When iron contains small amounts of carbon, it forms steel. Steel is widely used in buildings, vehicles, tanks, etc.

Chrome plating
Chromium does not react with water. A thin layer of chromium on steel provides a shiny surface for trims, hub caps, etc.

Catalysts
Nickel is used as a catalyst to turn vegetable oil into margarine.

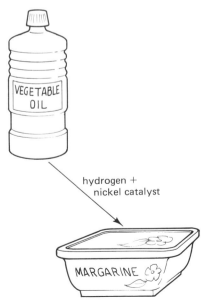

19 The Transition Metals

Summary

1 Elements in the central block of the periodic table are called the **transition metals**. Because of their similar properties, they are studied together.

2 Some transition metals like copper are **found in nature**. Many compounds or **ores** of these metals also occur.

3 **The metals** are all dense, strong and have high melting points. They conduct heat and electricity well.

4 Transition metals are not very reactive. When they do react, they form **coloured compounds**.

5 **Iron** is the most widely used transition metal. It is extracted from its ores in a blast furnace:

$$\underset{\text{iron ore}}{Fe_2O_3(s)} + 3CO(g) \underset{\text{reduction}}{\longrightarrow} \underset{\text{iron}}{2Fe(l)} + 3CO_2(g)$$

6 The properties of transition metals make them very **useful**, e.g. steel in construction, copper in pipes.

Questions

1 ● Read the passage below, then answer the questions on it.

'3000 years ago it was known that when iron oxide was heated in a charcoal fire, a spongy solid mass of iron was obtained that could be beaten into shape and used for tools and weapons. Eventually primitive furnaces were built into the hillsides, facing the prevailing wind. The furnace with its charge of charcoal and iron ore was left to burn for 3 or 4 days. After the fire had gone out, solid lumps of iron were removed and the process was started up again. These were known as 'batch furnaces'. It was during the 1300s and 1400s that the crude furnaces were converted to take a constant blast of air by using bellows. This forced air blast allowed higher temperatures in the furnaces causing the iron to melt and by this time the iron founders had learned how to handle and cast the molten iron into moulds. Up until the 1600s the fuel used in the furnaces was charcoal. Dud Dudley pioneered the use of coal and coke as a fuel but it was not until the 1700s that coke alone was used. Through the 1800s the blast furnaces grew in size and complexity. A Shropshire furnace in the eighteenth century made about 20 tonnes of iron each week. A modern blast furnace can produce up to 10 000 tonnes of iron in a day!'

(a) Describe how a 'batch furnace' worked.
(b) Why were 'batch furnaces' built to face the previling wind?
(c) What fuel is used in modern blast furnaces?
(d) What could primitive iron makers **not** do to iron that the iron makers in the 1400s could do?
(e) Man has been able to make iron from iron oxide for roughly: 200 years, 300 years, 600 years, 3000 years. Choose the correct answer. (SEB) **H**

2 ■ Chromium is a hard bluish-white metal with a very high melting point (1903 °C). One of its naturally occurring ores is chrome ironstone, which is a mixture of iron(II) oxide and chromium(III) oxide. Pure chromium is obtained from this ore by heating it with powdered aluminium. The metal is relatively unreactive and keeps a shiny surface in air. Chromium containing added carbon is almost as hard as diamond.

The word 'chromium' comes from the Greek word for 'colour'. Most chromium compounds are coloured. The green of emeralds and the red of rubies are due to the presence of small amounts of chromium compounds.

(a) Write down the formula of the two compounds found in chrome ironstone.
(b) Write a symbol equation for the reaction between aluminium and chromium(III) oxide. What type of reaction is this?
(c) Suggest a use for the metal chromium. Give a reason for your choice.
(d) Where would you expect to find chromium in the periodic table? Give a reason for your answer. **H**

3 ■ Nickel, a transition element, reacts with dilute hydrochloric acid to form a green solution **A** and hydrogen. When sodium carbonate solution is added to solution **A**, a green precipitate of nickel carbonate ($NiCO_3$) and a colourless solution **B** are formed.

Heating nickel carbonate produces a solid **C** and carbon dioxide is given off. When solid **C** is mixed with a black solid **D** and the mixture is heated, nickel is reformed and a gas is given off.

(a) Give the name or formula of: (i) solution **A**, (ii) solution **B**, (iii) solid **C**, (iv) solid **D**.
(b) State **two** physical properties of the element nickel.
(c) State **one** property of nickel compounds which is characteristic of transition element compounds.
(d) Write the formula for the nickel ions present in nickel carbonate. (NEA) **U**

4 ■ (a) Iron rusts in the presence of air and water.
(i) Copy out, complete and label the diagrams below to demonstrate experiments you would carry out to confirm that **both** of these substances are necessary for rusting to occur.

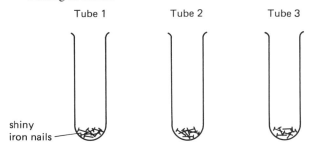

(ii) State the appearance of the nails in each of the three test-tubes at the end of the experiment.
(iii) Name one substance which, when dissolved in water, increases the rate at which iron rusts.
(iv) Write the chemical name for rust.
(b) Objects made of iron or steel can be protected from rusting by covering them with a layer of zinc.
(i) Name the zinc-plating process.
(ii) Explain why zinc protects the iron from rusting even if the zinc surface layer is broken and the iron is exposed.
(c) Study the following reaction scheme.

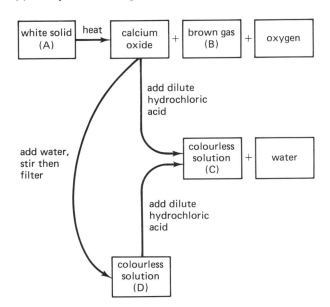

(i) Give the name or formula of: solid **A**; gas **B**; solution **C**; solution **D**.
(ii) Write a symbol equation for the reaction between calcium oxide and dilute hydrochloric acid.
(iii) Name the type of reaction taking place when calcium oxide reacts with dilute hydrochloric acid.
(iv) Name another compound which would give off brown gas **B** when heated.
(v) Describe one test you would carry out to identify solution **D**. Give the result of the test. (NEA) **R**

5 ■ Part of the periodic table is shown on the following diagram:

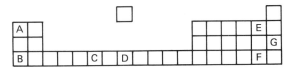

(a) Give the letters of two elements in the same period.
(b) Give the letters of two elements in the same group.
(c) Give the letters of two transition metals.
(d) Give one physical property and one chemical property in which alkali metals are different from transition metals.
(e) Give the letter of the element which exists as isolated single atoms.
(f) Give the letter of the most reactive metal on the table. **R**

6 ▶ The blast furnace is used to convert iron ore into impure iron. The following diagram shows a simple outline of the furnace:

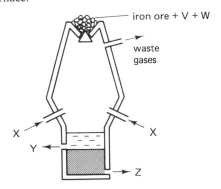

(a) Give the names of the three raw materials V, W and X.
(b) Give the names of the two products Y and Z.
(c) The chemical that reacts with iron ore to produce iron is carbon monoxide. What sort of a reagent is carbon monoxide in this reaction?
(d) Write an equation for the reaction between carbon monoxide and iron(II) oxide.
(e) What is the relative molecular mass of iron(III) oxide? (Fe = 56   O = 16)
(f) How many tonnes of iron could be obtained from 80 tonnes of iron(III) oxide? **R**

20 Group IV Elements

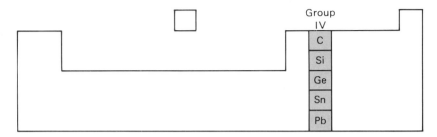

Group IV is in the centre of the periodic table. It is between the metals on the left side and the non-metals on the right. Group IV contains both non-metals like carbon and silicon and metals like tin and lead in the same group. Germanium has properties of both metals and non-metals.

Group IV elements

Name	Symbol	Melting point/°C	Boiling point/°C	Density/g cm^{-3}
Carbon	C	sublimes at 3730	4830	graphite 2.3 diamond 3.5
Silicon	Si	1410	2360	2.3
Germanium	Ge	937	2830	5.4
Tin	Sn	232	2270	7.3
Lead	Pb	327	1744	11.3

Where are Group IV elements found?

You are made of carbon compounds. Carbon compounds are found in all living things – both plants and animals. When food is overcooked, as in burned toast or meat, black carbon remains.

Silicon compounds are found in rocks and minerals. Sand is silicon dioxide, SiO_2. 26% of the earth's crust is made of silicon compounds.

Tin and lead occur as various ores, found in rocks.

Carbon allotropes

The element carbon exists in two forms – diamond and graphite. Although they seem to be very different, both of these are forms of the same element. The cause of the difference is in the arrangement of the atoms. These two forms of carbon are known as **allotropes**. Allotropes are different physical forms of the same element.

Diamond

The 3-dimensional structure of carbon atoms in diamond makes it the hardest substance known:

Density 3.5 g cm^{-3}

Graphite

The layered structure of carbon atoms in graphite makes it very slippery, as the layers slide over each other:

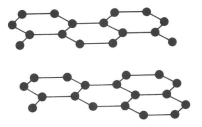

Density 2.3 g cm^{-3}

This bit is used to drill through layers of rock in search of oil. It is studded with tiny artificially made diamonds. Diamonds are harder than any rock and help the bit cut through the ground.

The 'lead' in pencils is made from graphite and clay. A very 'soft' pencil contains a lot of graphite. When a key is stiff in a lock, it can often be loosened by rubbing it with a soft pencil lead. The graphite acts as a lubricant.

Diamond is more dense than graphite, since the carbon atoms in diamond are packed together more tightly.

Clear and shiny when polished.	Dull grey and opaque.
Does not conduct electricity.	Graphite does conduct electricity. It is the only non-metal that does this.

Allotropes are made of the same sort of atom. Because of this, they often have the same chemical properties. Coal is a very impure form of carbon that burns well in a fire. A shovel full of diamonds would burn to give out just as much heat, but the fire would be very expensive!

Uses of Group IV elements

Coal

Coal and coke are impure forms of carbon. Millions of tonnes are burned every year. Coal is a **fossil fuel** and is being used up very quickly without being replaced.

Silicon chips

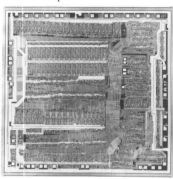

Very small thin slices of pure silicon can be treated and coated with various chemicals to leave complex electrical circuits on the surface. Silicon chips are widely used in calculators and computers.

'Tin' cans

Steel cans are coated on the inside with a thin layer of tin. This stops the cans rusting and spoiling the food inside.

Soldering

Soft solder is used to join electrical connections and central heating pipes. It is a mixture of tin and lead.

Petrol

Lead tetraethyl is added to petrol in many countries to prevent the petrol 'knocking' in the engine. The fumes released into the air contain lead compounds. If there is a lot of traffic, the amount becomes harmful to health.

Summary

1 **Group IV** is in the centre of the periodic table. It contains both non-metals and metals in the same group.

2 **Carbon** compounds are found in all living things. **Silicon** is the second most abundant element in the earth's crust. It is found in many rocks and minerals.

3 Carbon exists in two physical forms or **allotropes**. Diamond and graphite have very different physical properties. The differences are caused by the different arrangement of atoms in each form.

4 Group IV elements are very **useful**, e.g. coal as a fuel and silicon for micro-circuits.

Questions

1 ● Carbon is able to exist in two different forms, known as allotropes, the structures of which are shown.

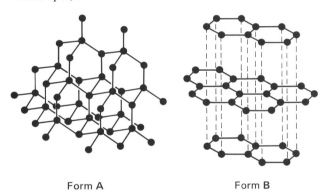

Form A   Form B

(a) Name form **A** and **B** of carbon.
(b) Give **one** important use for each form.
(c) Name the gas produced when each form completely burns in oxygen.
(d) Explain why form **B** is relatively soft. (NREB) **R**

2 ● The following diagrams show the arrangements of four different sorts of particles:

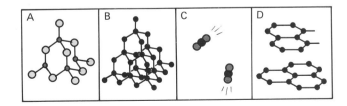

(a) Which diagram shows the structure of: (i) graphite, (ii) diamond, (iii) carbon dioxide, (iv) silicon dioxide?
(b) Graphite is a soft slippery solid. How does the diagram show this property?
(c) Diamond and silicon dioxide are very hard solids. How do the diagrams show this property? **R**

3 ■ (a) Carbon can exist in two forms in the same physical state. One form can be represented by the structure:

Form X

(i) What is the name given to different forms of the same element in the same physical state?
(ii) Name the form **X** of carbon above.
(iii) Name the other form, **Y**, of carbon and draw its structure.
(iv) Give a property for each form of carbon and a use that depends on this property.

(b) Both carbon and carbon monoxide can be used to convert copper(II) oxide to copper.

$$C + 2CuO \longrightarrow 2Cu + CO_2$$
$$CO + CuO \longrightarrow Cu + CO_2$$

(i) How are carbon and carbon monoxide acting in these two reactions?
(ii) Name another metal oxide that can be converted to its metal in the laboratory by using either carbon or carbon monoxide.
(iii) Name a metal oxide that cannot be converted to its metal in the laboratory by using either carbon or carbon monoxide.

(c) Copy out the sentences below and use them to calculate how much carbon is needed to convert 8.0 g of copper(II) oxide to copper as follows:

$$C + 2CuO \longrightarrow 2Cu + CO_2$$

(Relative atomic masses: C = 12   Cu = 64
O = 16)

_____ mole/s copper(II) oxide react with _____ mole/s carbon.
Therefore _____ g of copper(II) oxide react with 12 g carbon. Therefore 8.0 g copper(II) oxide react with _____ g carbon. (WMEB) **U**

21 Organic Chemistry

The oil in chip pans is an organic chemical. When heated too strongly, the oil catches fire.

Turning on a gas tap at school or at home releases the simplest of all organic chemicals: it is called methane. Camping gas stoves burn another organic chemical: it is called butane. The engine of a motor bike or a car is powered by petrol: this is a mixture of several organic chemicals. In all these examples, organic chemicals are useful because they burn.

Sometimes burning can be a nuisance and very dangerous. If a racing car crashes, the petrol may escape and catch fire. Racing drivers can be very badly injured by fire. The oil in chip pans can suddenly catch fire on a stove if heated too strongly. Whole houses have been burned down because of chip-pan fires. These organic chemicals are only safe if handled with great care.

The bodies of animals, including humans, also use organic chemicals as fuels to keep them alive and healthy. The fuel needed is found in the plants and animals eaten as food. All living things contain many organic chemicals. All organic chemicals contain the element **carbon**. There are over two million compounds containing carbon. For convenience, chemists study these compounds in a separate branch of chemistry called **organic chemistry**.

Coal, oil and natural gas

These three substances are useful to us as fuels. They are also the raw materials from which we get nearly all our organic chemicals. They are called **fossil fuels** because they were formed from living things – either trees or animals.

Most of the coal we use today was formed about 250 million years ago. Much of the world was then covered with sub-tropical swamps and forests. As the vegetation died, it was covered with layers of mud and sand. Over millions of years, this turned into coal. Most coal can be used with little further processing. Much of it is burned in power stations to produce electricity and to make iron from its ores.

Oil and natural gas are often found together in underground deposits. They were formed when very small sea animals died and their remains fell to the sea bed. This was about 150 million years ago, when dinosaurs roamed the earth. The remains of these too were covered with layers of sand and mud. Eventually they formed deposits of oil and gas, now found far below the earth's surface, e.g. under the North Sea. The oil and gas are not found in underground pools or caves. They are soaked into the porous rock, rather like water soaks into a sponge. The deposits are under great pressure, and if a hole is drilled into the rock, the gas or oil comes shooting out.

Natural gas (mostly methane) is also used in industry and the home as a fuel. Oil comes out of the ground as a dark brown liquid with an unpleasant smell, called **crude oil**. Crude oil consists of a mixture of hundreds of **hydrocarbons.** A hydrocarbon is a compound of **hydro**gen and **carbon**. The hydrocarbon molecules in this mixture vary from those containing only a few carbon and hydrogen atoms, to those containing over a hundred. Before the oil can be useful to us, the hydrocarbons in it need to be separated out from each other. This is done by **fractional distillation**. When the crude oil is brought to a refinery, it is separated into **fractions** by boiling. Each fraction contains a mixture of molecules which distil off between two boiling points. This works because each hydrocarbon in the mixture has its own boiling point. The smaller, lighter molecules have low boiling points. The large heavy molecules have higher boiling points. The most useful fraction boils off between 25 °C and 190 °C. This is used for petrol for cars and contains molecules with 5 to 10 carbon atoms. The whole process is carried out in a **fractionating column**.

Many sea birds are covered in crude oil when oil tankers run aground or illegally wash out their tanks at sea.

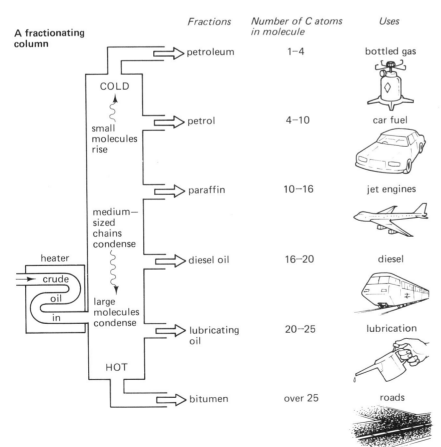

A fractionating column

Fractions	Number of C atoms in molecule	Uses
petroleum	1–4	bottled gas
petrol	4–10	car fuel
paraffin	10–16	jet engines
diesel oil	16–20	diesel
lubricating oil	20–25	lubrication
bitumen	over 25	roads

Electronic structure of methane

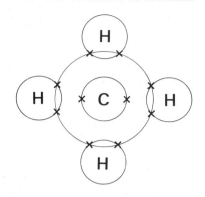

Structural formula of methane

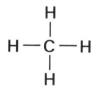

Naming organic compounds

Name of molecule starts with	Number of carbon atoms in molecule
meth-	1
eth-	3
prop-	3
but-	4

Firstly, the crude oil is heated to turn it into a gas. This is then pumped into the column. The column itself is hot at the bottom and cool at the top. As the hot gases rise up the column they begin to cool down. The molecules with the longer chains of carbon atoms soon condense to a liquid. The molecules with shorter chains of carbon atoms rise higher up the column before they condense. The molecules with very short chains of carbon atoms escape from the top of the column as gases.

The different fractions from the column have different properties and uses. The hydrocarbons from the top of the column are gases. Petrol is a thin, runny liquid, and lubricating oil is much thicker. Tar or bitumen is a thick black solid. The difference between all of these hydrocarbons is the length of the chain of carbon and hydrogen atoms in the molecule. Very long chains of atoms in the molecules make thick liquids or solids. Short chains of atoms make thin liquids or gases. Think of spaghetti! It is much easier to stir a bowl of spaghetti pieces than a bowl of long strands – but not as much fun to eat!

Some simple hydrocarbons

Methane is the simplest and most common hydrocarbon. A carbon atom has four electrons in its outer shell, so it forms four covalent bonds. When it forms bonds with hydrogen atoms, the compound is called methane. Methane is only the first of a 'family' of similar molecules called **alkanes**.

The first four alkanes

Name	Molecular formula	Structural formula	Boiling point/°C
Methane	CH_4	H–C(H)(H)–H	−164
Ethane	C_2H_6	H–C(H)(H)–C(H)(H)–H	−87
Propane	C_3H_8	H–C(H)(H)–C(H)(H)–C(H)(H)–H	−42
Butane	C_4H_{10}	H–C(H)(H)–C(H)(H)–C(H)(H)–C(H)(H)–H	0

In these compounds, carbon is forming covalent bonds with other carbon atoms to form chains of atoms. It is the only element which commonly behaves in this way.

In going from one alkane to the next, an extra —C(H)(H)— group is added.

Any family of organic chemicals which gets bigger in this way is called a **homologous series**. All the names of the alkanes end with the letters –**ane**. The first part of the name tells us how many carbon atoms there are in the molecule.

Butane is therefore a member of the alkane family with four carbon atoms. You may have heard of the octane rating of petrol. Octane is an alkane present in petrol that contains eight carbon atoms. In all these molecules the carbon atom is joined to four other atoms. This is the greatest number of other atoms to which carbon can be joined. When this happens, the compound is said to be **saturated**.

Like any homologous series, alkanes have similar chemical properties. They are not very reactive, but the smaller molecules burn very easily. When anything burns, heat energy is given out, so alkanes are useful as fuels. They burn with a clean, blue-yellow flame to produce carbon dioxide and water, e.g:

methane + oxygen ⟶ carbon dioxide + water
$CH_4(g) + 2O_2(g) \longrightarrow CO_2(g) + 2H_2O(g)$

propane + oxygen ⟶ carbon dioxide + water
$C_3H_8(g) + 5O_2(g) \longrightarrow 3CO_2(g) + 4H_2O(g)$

Portable gas cookers burn either propane or butane gas as fuels.

Alkenes

Another important homologous series is called the **alkenes**. These are compounds of carbon and hydrogen only, so they too are hydrocarbons. All alkenes have a **double bond** between two carbon atoms. The simplest alkene has only two carbon atoms. It is called **ethene**.

The first three alkenes

Name	Molecular formula	Structural formula	Boiling point/°C
Ethene	C_2H_4	H₂C=CH₂	−104
Propene	C_3H_6	H₂C=CH—CH₃	−48
Butene	C_4H_8	H₂C=CH—CH₂—CH₃	−6

Saturated and unsaturated molecules

H—C(H)(H)—C(H)(H)—H ethane

Ethane is **saturated** as each carbon atom is joined to **four** other atoms.

H₂C=CH₂ ethene

Ethene is **unsaturated,** as each carbon atom is only joined to **three** other atoms.

Look at the boiling points of the alkenes. As the molecules get longer and heavier, the boiling points increase. Any molecule which contains double bonds like this is said to be **unsaturated**.

Alkenes are members of a homologous series, so they all show similar chemical properties. These are different from those of the alkanes, because the molecules have different structures. Some of the reactions of alkenes are as follows.

They burn with a smoky yellow flame to give carbon dioxide and water:

ethene + oxygen ⟶ carbon dioxide + water

$C_2H_4(g) + 3O_2(g) \longrightarrow 2CO_2(g) + 2H_2O(g)$

Many margarines are said to be 'high in polyunsaturates'. This means that they contain fat molecules with double bonds in them.

The double bond in alkenes makes them very reactive. They will react with bromine so that the red-brown colour of the bromine disappears.

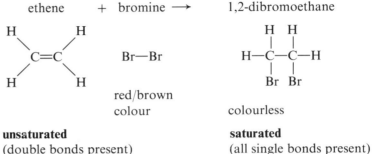

unsaturated
(double bonds present)

saturated
(all single bonds present)

This is called an **addition reaction**. The double bond opens up to allow the bromine atoms to add on to the carbon atoms. Bromine, or bromine water, is used to test for a double bond. It works with any unsaturated molecule. Even bacon will decolourise bromine water! When you read that a margarine is high in 'polyunsaturates', it simply means it has a lot of double bonds. Another similar test for a double bond is to use dilute acidified potassium manganate(VII) solution. This too, is decolourised by unsaturated molecules.

Cracking

All the fractions from distilling crude oil are useful, but there is a great demand for the smaller molecules. These are needed for petrol and to make plastics. Chemists have found a way to break the less useful, longer chains into shorter ones. It is called **catalytic cracking**, or cat-cracking for short. The larger molecules are passed over a hot catalyst and they are split into shorter ones. In the laboratory we can break the longer chains in paraffin oil into shorter ones by using the apparatus shown in the diagram.

Cracking paraffin oil

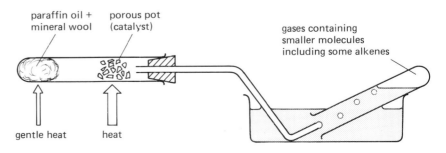

Cracking is also carried out in industry on a large scale. The oil, containing long chains of carbon atoms, is heated to 400–700 °C in the presence of a catalyst of aluminium oxide (Al_2O_3). The long chains are broken down to make smaller molecules. Alkenes are always formed as one of the products of cracking.

Cracking

| long hydrocarbon molecule | → cat-cracking | shorter alkane molecules | + | alkene |

Plenty of this from crude oil, but little demand for it.   Useful for petrol for cars.   Useful to make plastics.

Example

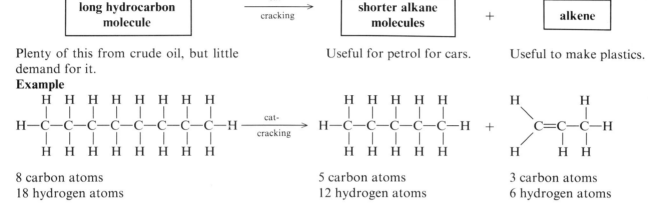

8 carbon atoms   5 carbon atoms   3 carbon atoms
18 hydrogen atoms   12 hydrogen atoms   6 hydrogen atoms

Note that both products of this reaction are shorter than the original molecule. The total number of atoms has not changed.

Testing for carbon and hydrogen in a compound

To test whether a compound contains the elements carbon or hydrogen, it is mixed with some black copper(II) oxide powder, and heated.

Testing for carbon and hydrogen in a compound

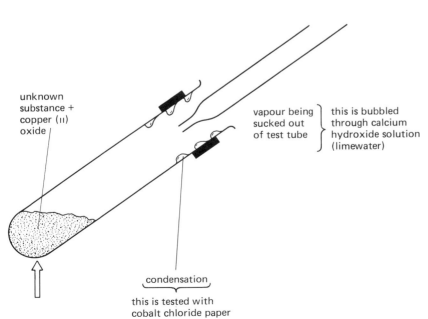

Test for carbon dioxide

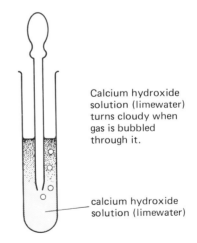

Calcium hydroxide solution (limewater) turns cloudy when gas is bubbled through it.

calcium hydroxide solution (limewater)

Test for water

cobalt chloride paper changes colour: blue → pink

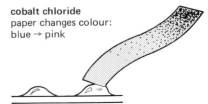

If the unknown substance contains carbon, carbon dioxide will be evolved. If the substance contains hydrogen, then water will be evolved:

| Unknown substance (X) | + | copper(II) oxide (black) | → | copper metal (pink) | + | water | + | carbon dioxide |

$$X + CuO \rightarrow Cu + H_2O + CO_2$$

The only place the hydrogen in the water could have come from is X, so X must contain hydrogen as part of a compound. Similarly the only place the carbon in the carbon dioxide could have come from is compound X, so X must also contain carbon.

The isomers of butane, C_4H_{10}

```
  H   H   H   H
  |   |   |   |
H-C - C - C - C-H
  |   |   |   |
  H   H   H   H


  H   H   H
  |   |   |
H-C - C - C-H
  |   |   |
  H       H
      |
    H-C-H
      |
      H
```

The isomers of butene, C_4H_8

```
  H       H   H
   \      |   |
    C=C - C - C-H
   /      |   |
  H       H   H


  H   H   H   H
  |   |   |   |
H-C - C = C - C-H
  |           |
  H           H


          H
          |
        H-C-H
  H     |
   \    |
    C = C
   /    |
  H   H-C-H
          |
          H
```

Isomers

The formula of butane is C_4H_{10}. It has four carbon atoms and ten hydrogen atoms. The carbons have to be joined to each other, but they do not have to be in a straight chain. There are two ways that the carbon atoms can be arranged in butane. Both of these compounds have the same molecular formula, C_4H_{10}, but their structural formulae are different. When two compounds have the same molecular formula but different structural formulae, they are called **isomers**. Butene has three isomers, each with the molecular formula C_4H_8.

Coal, oil and gas – limited resources

Britain is said to be an island of coal, surrounded by a sea full of oil and gas! Many other countries do not have these natural resources, and have to spend a lot of money importing them from abroad. These reserves are being used up quite rapidly, and will not be replaced. Britain has coal reserves to last for several hundred more years, but the oil and gas that comes from the North Sea will start to run out after about the year 2000.

The expected lifetimes of fossil fuels in Britain

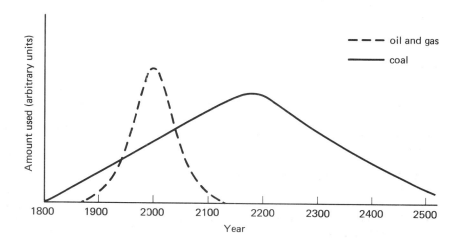

These resources are limited, and many people feel it is a waste to be burning large amounts of oil, when it is so useful to make paints, plastics, dyes, drugs, etc. Eventually other energy sources will have to be found. Some research is already going on into ways of harnessing energy from the sun, the wind or the waves. These 'new' energy sources have only been seriously studied quite recently. It still costs more to produce energy from them than from the fuels used at present.

One interesting project carried out by Manchester City Council is a factory which turns rubbish from the refuse department into crude oil. The process copies the way that oil was formed millions of years ago. All the glass and metal is removed from the rubbish, leaving plastics, paper, fabrics etc. These are then put under high pressure and temperature, so that eventually crude oil is formed.

A wind-powered generator in the Orkneys: it uses a renewable resource to produce electricity, and does not pollute the environment.

Summary

1 Carbon forms millions of compounds. The study of these is called **organic chemistry**.

2 Coal, oil and natural gas are **limited resources**. They are used as raw materials to make many organic chemicals.

3 Before crude oil becomes useful, it must be **fractionally distilled**. Each fraction produced has different uses.

4 **Alkanes** are simple hydrocarbons, e.g. methane CH_4.
Alkanes are **saturated**, and they burn with a clean blue-yellow flame.

5 **Alkenes** are **unsaturated** hydrocarbons, e.g. ethene C_2H_4. They contain two carbon atoms linked by a double bond.
All alkenes will:
- burn with a smoky flame.
- decolourise bromine water.
- decolourise acidified potassium manganate(VII) solution.

These reactions are used as a test for unsaturation.

6 In **cracking**, a substance is heated strongly with a catalyst. Cracking breaks down large hydrocarbon molecules into smaller, more useful ones.

Questions

1 ● Write an equation for the complete combustion of:
(a) ethene (C_2H_4), (b) methane (CH_4), (c) carbon (C). **R**

2 ● There are three isomers of pentane (C_5H_{12}). Draw their structural formulae. **U**

3 ● Draw the structural formulae of three isomers of butene (C_4H_8). **U**

4 ● Draw dot-cross diagrams for: (a) methane (CH_4), (b) ethene (C_2H_4). **R**

5 ● Draw a diagram to show a fractionating column. Show the positions where you would expect to tap off bitumen, paraffin, lubricating oil and petroleum gases.
What is the name given to the process where molecules containing longer chains of carbon atoms are broken down into smaller molecules? **R**

6 ● Give one example of an alkane and one example of an alkene. State one reaction shown by both types of chemical. Write an equation for each reaction. State one reaction shown only by alkenes. Write an equation for this reaction. **R**

7 ○ When paraffin oil is heated, and the gas produced is passed over hot porous pot, a gas is produced which can be collected over water. The gas burns when lighted. It also decolourises bromine water. If the liquid paraffin has the formula:

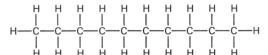

suggest two products which would be obtained on the above experiment. Give an equation to show how one of the products reacts with bromine water. **U**

8 ● Petrol is a mixture of liquid hydrocarbons.
(a) Which two elements are found in all hydrocarbons?
(b) When petrol burns, these hydrocarbons react with oxygen in the air. Name two of the gases formed in this reaction.
(c) Name one poisonous gas found in car exhaust fumes. **R**

9 ● Fossil fuels were formed millions of years ago.
(a) Give one fossil fuel that is: (i) a solid, (ii) a liquid, (iii) a gas.
(b) All fossil fuels contain carbon. Write a word equation and a symbol equation for the reaction that happens when carbon burns in a good supply of air.
(c) Why is there concern about the rate fossil fuels are being used? **R**

10 ● Use this key to answer the questions which follow it.

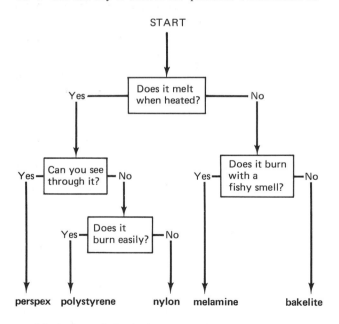

(a) A piece of plastic does not melt when heated, but does burn with a fishy smell. What is it?
(b) A piece of plastic which you cannot see through melts when heated, but does not burn easily. What is it?
(c) Which material in the key is most suitable for making the handle of a frying pan? (SEB) **H**

11 ■ Substance **A** is a crystalline solid which dissolves in water to form a solution which conducts electricity.
Substance **B** is an oily liquid which does not mix with water and does not conduct electricity.
(a) What do these tests tell you about the type of bonding (i) in **A**, (ii) in **B**?
(b) Substance **B** when warmed and shaken with bromine water removes the colour from the bromine. Explain what further information about the bonding in **B** can be deduced from this test?
(c) Some vegetable oils with the same properties as substance **B** can be reacted with hydrogen to form a greasy solid which can be used to make margarine. What type of chemical reaction takes place between the oil and hydrogen?
(d) Ethene will react in a similar way with hydrogen. Write the symbol equation for this reaction.
(e) A tub of margarine carries the label that it is 'High in polyunsaturates'. What does this mean and what advantages is the manufacturer claiming for the margarine?
(f) The label on the tub of margarine also says that the margarine contains an emulsifier. What is the purpose of the emulsifier? (MEG) **U**

12 ■ Crude oil and coal are very important, both as fuels and as sources of many useful chemicals.
(a)
(i) How has coal been formed underground?
(ii) Coal has the disadvantage of producing a lot of smoke when burned. Name a solid smokeless fuel that can be obtained from coal.
(iii) State the main use of coal in this country at the present time.
(b) Fractional distillation of crude oil can be used to produce the following fractions: petrol, fuel oil, petroleum gases, bitumen and kerosene (paraffin).
(i) Copy the diagram below and write the names of these fractions in their correct positions.

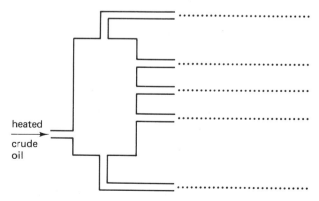

(ii) How do the relative molecular masses of the petroleum gases compare with those of the compounds present in bitumen?
(iii) State **one** important use of kerosene, and of bitumen.
(c) Some of the fractions are treated by a process called catalytic cracking to produce more useful chemicals. One product of the cracking process is ethene, C_2H_4,

an unsaturated compound. Ethene burns in air and reacts with bromine forming 1,2-dibromoethane.
(i) What happens to the molecules of a substance during cracking?
(ii) What is meant by the term 'unsaturated compound'?
(iii) Write a symbol equation for the complete combustion of ethene in oxygen.
(iv) Draw the structural formula for 1,2-dibromoethane.

(d) A major pollutant of the atmosphere is carbon monoxide. On a main road into a large city the amount of carbon monoxide in the atmosphere on the same day may vary from 10 parts per million to 200 parts per million.
(i) Explain how most of the carbon monoxide is formed.
(ii) At what time of day would you expect the largest amount of carbon monoxide?
(iii) Explain why carbon monoxide is poisonous.
(NEA) **R**

13 ■
(a) CH_4, C_2H_6, C_3H_8 and C_4H_{10} are all members of the same homologous series. They have low melting points and low boiling points and do not dissolve in water.
(i) Give the general name for this series of compounds.
(ii) Give the formula for the fifth member of the series.
(iii) State the name of the first member of the series, which is also the main constituent of natural gas.
(iv) When natural gas is burned using a bunsen burner with the air hole closed, a yellow flame is seen. A cold test-tube held in the flame is quickly blackened. Why is the test-tube blackened?
(v) When the air hole of the bunsen is opened, the flame becomes non-luminous (loses its yellow colour) as complete combustion occurs. Name the products formed.
(vi) The formula, C_4H_{10}, represents two different compounds called isomers. Draw the structural formulae of these two isomers.
(vii) State the type of chemical bonding between the atoms in these compounds.

(b) Soap can be made in the laboratory by heating castor oil with sodium hydroxide solution. When the reaction is complete, salt solution is added and, after cooling, the soap is filtered off.
If castor oil is treated with a different substance **X**, a soapless detergent is formed.
(i) Name the type of reaction occurring between the castor oil and the sodium hydroxide solution.
(ii) Explain why salt is added to the reaction mixture.
(iii) Name substance **X**.

(c) Calcium salts of soap are insoluble in water but calcium salts of soapless detergents are soluble in water. State what you would see in addition to a possible lather, when: (i) soap solution is added to hard water, (ii) soapless detergent is added to hard water.

(d) Ethanol (C_2H_5OH) is a colourless liquid which is miscible with water. It reacts with sodium forming sodium ethoxide solution and hydrogen.
(i) Explain the meaning of 'miscible with water'.
(ii) Write a symbol equation for the reaction between ethanol and sodium.

(e) Ethanol will react with a weak acid, **Y**, in the presence of concentrated sulphuric acid to produce an ester called ethyl ethanoate.
(i) Name acid **Y**.
(ii) Explain the part played by concentrated sulphuric acid in the reaction.
(NEA) **R**

14 ■ (a) The first two members of the alkane series are methane (CH_4) and ethane (C_2H_6). The first two members of the alkene series are ethene (C_2H_4) and propene (C_3H_6).
(i) Write the name and formula for the third member of the alkanes.
(ii) Write the general formula for the alkane series.
(iii) Write the name and formula for the third member of the alkenes.
(iv) Write the general formula for the alkene series.

(b) Copy out the following table and write in the structural formula for ethane and ethene. Methane is given as an example.

Methane	Ethane	Ethene
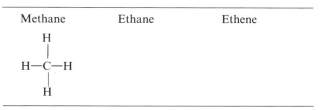		

(c) Describe one test which could be used to distinguish between samples of ethane and ethene. State the result of the test with each compound.

(d) (i) Name the reagent which is used to convert ethene to ethane.
(ii) State the conditions needed for the reaction.
(NEA) **R**

15 ■ A mixture of sucrose ($C_{12}H_{22}O_{11}$), water and yeast is placed in a conical flask and kept in a warm place for several days. Carbon dioxide is given off and a dilute solution of ethanol (C_2H_5OH) is formed in the flask.
The first stage of the process is the conversion of sucrose to a simpler sugar, glucose ($C_6H_{12}O_6$). This reaction can be represented by the equation
$$C_{12}H_{22}O_{11} + H_2O \longrightarrow 2C_6H_{12}O_6$$
The second stage is the conversion of glucose to ethanol.
(a) Name the process by which sucrose is converted to glucose.
(b) Name the process by which the glucose is converted to ethanol.
(c) Explain why boiling would not be an effective method of increasing the rate at which ethanol is formed.
(d) Write a balanced symbol equation for the conversion of glucose to ethanol.
(e) Draw a labelled diagram of an apparatus which could be used to obtain a more concentrated solution of ethanol.
(NEA) **U**

22 Everyday Organic Chemicals

Take a look around the room and at the clothes people are wearing. Many everyday objects are artificially made from organic chemicals. The bright colours of paints, plastics, clothing and many foodstuffs are due to dyes made from organic chemicals. Many of today's clothes contain polyester or nylon – two artificial fibres. Food is stored in plastic bags and containers. All these substances are called synthetic materials.

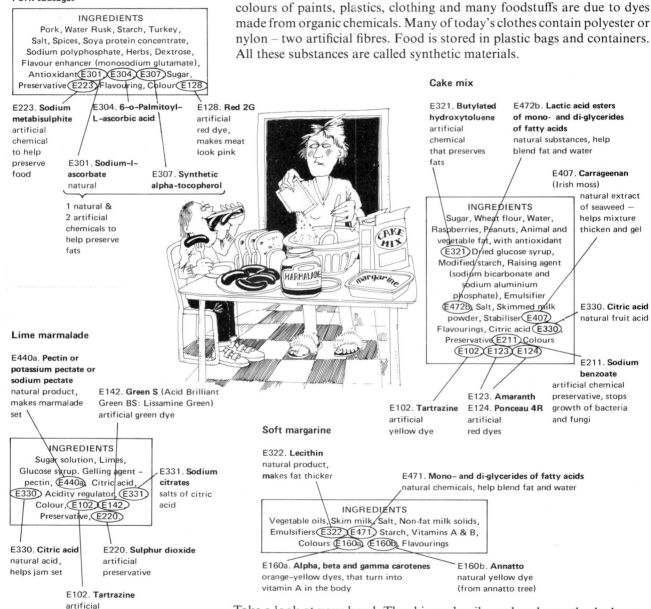

The meaning of some E-numbers

Pork sausages

INGREDIENTS
Pork, Water Rusk, Starch, Turkey, Salt, Spices, Soya protein concentrate, Sodium polyphosphate, Herbs, Dextrose, Flavour enhancer (monosodium glutamate), Antioxidant E301, E304, E307, Sugar, Preservative E223, Flavouring, Colour E128

E223. Sodium metabisulphite artificial chemical to help preserve food

E301. Sodium-l-ascorbate natural

E304. 6-o-Palmitoyl-L-ascorbic acid

E307. Synthetic alpha-tocopherol

1 natural & 2 artificial chemicals to help preserve fats

E128. Red 2G artificial red dye, makes meat look pink

Cake mix

E321. Butylated hydroxytoluene artificial chemical that preserves fats

E472b. Lactic acid esters of mono- and di-glycerides of fatty acids natural substances, help blend fat and water

E407. Carrageenan (Irish moss) natural extract of seaweed — helps mixture thicken and gel

INGREDIENTS
Sugar, Wheat flour, Water, Raspberries, Peanuts, Animal and vegetable fat, with antioxidant E321, Dried glucose syrup, Modified starch, Raising agent (sodium bicarbonate and sodium aluminium phosphate), Emulsifier E472b, Salt, Skimmed milk powder, Stabiliser E407, Flavourings, Citric acid E330, Preservative E211, Colours E102, E123, E124

E330. Citric acid natural fruit acid

E211. Sodium benzoate artificial chemical preservative, stops growth of bacteria and fungi

E102. Tartrazine artificial yellow dye

E123. Amaranth **E124. Ponceau 4R** artificial red dyes

Lime marmalade

E440a. Pectin or potassium pectate or sodium pectate natural product, makes marmalade set

E142. Green S (Acid Brilliant Green BS: Lissamine Green) artificial green dye

INGREDIENTS
Sugar solution, Limes, Glucose syrup. Gelling agent – pectin, E440a, Citric acid, E330, Acidity regulator, E331, Colour, E102, E142, Preservative, E220

E331. Sodium citrates salts of citric acid

E330. Citric acid natural acid, helps jam set

E220. Sulphur dioxide artificial preservative

E102. Tartrazine artificial yellow dye

Soft margarine

E322. Lecithin natural product, makes fat thicker

E471. Mono- and di-glycerides of fatty acids natural chemicals, help blend fat and water

INGREDIENTS
Vegetable oils, Skim milk, Salt, Non-fat milk solids, Emulsifiers E322, E471, Starch, Vitamins A & B, Colours E160a, E160b, Flavourings

E160a. Alpha, beta and gamma carotenes orange–yellow dyes, that turn into vitamin A in the body

E160b. Annatto natural yellow dye (from annatto tree)

Information about E numbers from *E for Additives: The Complete E Number Guide* by Maurice Hanssen, published by Thorsons Publishing Group Ltd, Wellingborough, Northants.

Take a look at your hand. The skin and nails, and underneath, the bones, tendons, muscles and blood, all contain millions of organic molecules. In Chapter 2, you will find a 'person' recipe. This shows the elements present in your body, that make up these molecules. All living things, both plants and animals, are made from many large and complicated organic compounds.

Foodstuffs

Many people have a 'sweet tooth'. They enjoy sweets, biscuits and cakes – all containing various **sugars**. A sugar molecule is a compound of carbon, hydrogen and oxygen. An example of a simple sugar is glucose. Athletes may take glucose tablets to give them energy. Another sugar is fructose, which is found in honey. Plants can make sugars such as these by the process of photosynthesis:

carbon dioxide + water $\xrightarrow[\text{sunlight}]{\text{photosynthesis}}$ glucose + oxygen

$CO_2(g) + 6H_2O(l) \longrightarrow C_6H_{12}O_6(aq) + 6O_2(g)$

Energy-giving foodstuffs
All of these foods are eaten to provide energy.

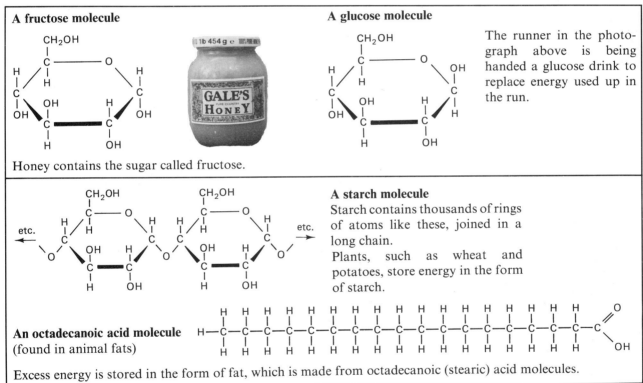

The runner in the photograph above is being handed a glucose drink to replace energy used up in the run.

Honey contains the sugar called fructose.

A starch molecule
Starch contains thousands of rings of atoms like these, joined in a long chain.
Plants, such as wheat and potatoes, store energy in the form of starch.

An octadecanoic acid molecule (found in animal fats)

Excess energy is stored in the form of fat, which is made from octadecanoic (stearic) acid molecules.

Compounds like sugars and starch are called carbohydrates. A carbohydrate is a compound of carbon, hydrogen and oxygen. The name itself will help you remember this:

	carbo	**hydr**	**ate**
Compound of:	carbon	hydrogen	oxygen

In carbohydrates, the ratio of hydrogen to oxygen atoms is always 2:1. This is the same ratio as for water.

When too many sweet things are eaten over a long time, the body stores this extra energy source as fat. Most animal fats contain octadecanoic (stearic) acid molecules. Many trees and plants also store energy in a similar form as vegetable oils.

Glucose is an example of a carbohydrate. It contains the elements carbon, hydrogen and oxygen:

Molecular formula $C_6H_{12}O_6$

12 hydrogens : 6 oxygens
 Ratio   2 : 1

These are some examples of soaps:

Soaps and detergents

Oils and fats can be broken down by boiling them with sodium hydroxide solution. A soap is formed:

animal fat + sodium hydroxide → soap + glycerol
octadecanoic acid   solution   sodium octadecanoate
(stearic acid)   (sodium stearate)

This reaction is called **saponification**. This word literally means 'soap-making'.

The molecule looks rather like a tadpole! It has a long hydrocarbon 'tail', and a negatively charged 'head'. Soap is used to help get you and your clothes clean. One way it works is to help the water 'wet' the fabric properly. Another way is that it helps loosen and remove grease and particles of dirt.

A soap molecule

sodium octadecanoate
(sodium stearate)

Molecular formula $C_{17}H_{35}COO^-Na^+$

Structural formula

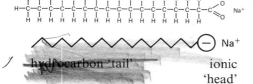

Action of soap

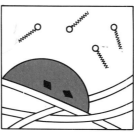 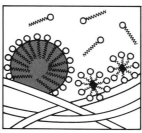 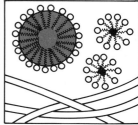

Grease and particles of dirt on fibre of material. Soap molecules in water. | 'Tails' of soap molecules bury themselves into the grease. | Grease and dirt is removed as fabric is agitated.

When you have finished washing yourself in the bath, there is always the 'scum' left behind to clean up! Scum is formed when you use soap with **hard water**. As a river flows downstream, it dissolves various chemicals. Calcium sulphate is one chemical dissolved in this way. These dissolved salts make the water 'hard'. Here is a word equation for the formation of scum:

calcium ions + octadecanoate → calcium octadecanoate
(dissolved in hard   (stearate) ions   (stearate) (scum)
water)   (in soap)

This is obviously a waste of soap – much of it goes to form scum instead of cleaning you! Soapless detergents have been developed to overcome this difficulty. They work in the same way as soap, and have a similar structure. They do not form a scum with hard water, and are often more useful.

These are examples of some soapless detergents.

A soapless detergent molecule

Molecular formula $C_{18}H_{29}SO_3^-Na^+$

Structural formula

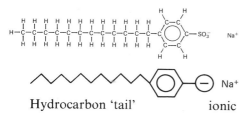

Fermentation and ethanol

The chemical reaction to make ethanol goes on in many people's homes today. They brew home-made beer and wine. In everyday language, we say that these drinks contain 'alcohol'. The chemist uses a more precise name than this. There is a homologous series containing many hundreds of different alcohols. The chemical name of the alcohol present in these drinks is **ethanol**.

Ethanol is formed when sugars, from plants or fruits, are broken down by yeast. This process is called **fermentation**:

glucose $\xrightarrow[\text{yeast}]{\text{fermentation}}$ ethanol + carbon dioxide

$C_6H_{12}O_6(aq) \longrightarrow 2C_2H_5OH(aq) + 2CO_2(aq)$

It is important that everything is kept very clean and that air is kept out of the container during fermentation. Oxygen from the air and bacteria can react with the ethanol. They turn it into ethanoic acid (vinegar). This makes the wine turn sour.

Fermentation happens slowly in the cold, but rapidly when the liquid is warmed to 25–30 °C. Yeast is also used in bread-making. It breaks down the sugars in flour, and the carbon dioxide gas produced makes the dough rise. A small amount of ethanol is also formed, but it nearly all evaporates when the bread is baked! The yeast, which is a living organism is also killed by the strong heat.

Making ethanol in the laboratory by fermentation

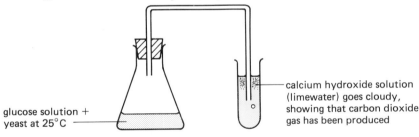

All alcoholic drinks contain a mixture of ethanol and water. To obtain fairly pure ethanol from this mixture, it has to be fractionally distilled. Pure or 'absolute' ethanol is useful as a solvent, to help dissolve various chemicals. It can also be reacted with other chemicals to help make emulsion paints. Most of the ethanol used in this way is not made by fermentation. It is formed by reacting ethene with water:

ethene + steam $\xrightarrow[\text{70 atmospheres pressure}]{\text{300 °C, phosphoric acid catalyst}}$ ethanol

$\begin{array}{c} H \\ \\ H \end{array} \!\!\! \begin{array}{c} \\ C=C \\ \end{array} \!\!\! \begin{array}{c} H \\ \\ H \end{array} + H_2O \longrightarrow$ H—C—C—OH (with H's)

Ethanol will burn easily in air. It has a hot, clean blue flame.

Many South American countries have to import all of their crude oil. Some do, however, grow plenty of sugar cane. This can be fermented to make ethanol. Distillation separates the ethanol from most of the water. Up to 20% ethanol is added to the petrol to make it go further.

An ethanol molecule

Molecular formula C_2H_6O

Structural formula H—C—C—OH (with H's on each C)

Amounts of alcohol in various drinks

Drink	Alcohol
beer	3–6%
wine	12–15%
fortified wines (e.g. sherry)	18–20%
spirits	40%

Ethanol is called a 'depressant'. This means that it depresses the body's functions.

In small quantities, ethanol supresses a person's natural inhibitions, and makes them relax. A small amount of ethanol taken in this way can be quite beneficial.

In larger quantities, ethanol depresses important functions of the body, such as speech, physical movements and linking ideas. This makes it very dangerous to drive a car, as the driver's judgement is affected.

Regular heavy drinking can lead someone to become addicted to alcohol. Such people may drink to help them cope with personal problems, but their alcoholism makes them less able to cope. The consumption of too much alcohol over a long time can permanently damage vital organs like the liver.

Synthetic molecules

Your grandparents grew up wearing clothes made from cotton or wool. They washed up in bowls made from enamelled metal. They sat on chairs stuffed with cotton or horsehair. Today we wear many **synthetic** fabrics, such as polyester or nylon. We wash up in polyethene (polythene) bowls, and sit on chairs filled with polyurethane foam.

All of these molecules are called **polymers**. A polymer is formed from lots of small molecules joined together. They often need the help of heat and a catalyst to do this. The reaction is called **polymerisation**.

Polymerisation

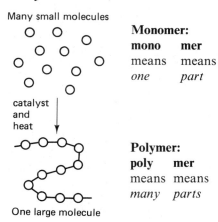

Many small molecules

catalyst and heat ↓

One large molecule

Monomer:
mono mer
means means
one part

Polymer:
poly mer
means means
many parts

Polyethene (polythene)

This is an example of a polymer, which we use to make plastic bags, buckets and bowls. The monomer used to make polyethene is ethene:

$$n\ \mathrm{CH_2{=}CH_2} \longrightarrow \left(\mathrm{CH_2{-}CH_2} \right)_n$$

ethene molecules + thousands more ethene molecules — oxygen catalyst, 200 °C → poly(ethene), chain goes on for thousands more C-atoms

This equation is often written:

n is a large number. This means the unit in brackets is repeated a large number of times.

Nylon

Nylon is a polymer that has to be made from two monomers. They have rather complicated names and structures that you don't have to remember. We will call the monomers A and B. These join together to form the nylon polymer. This reaction occurs easily, and no heat or catalyst is needed:

monomer A molecules + monomer B molecules → nylon polymer

—A—B—A—B—A—B—A—B
polymerisation
B—A—B—A—B—A—B
B—A—B → chain continues with thousands more units

Making nylon in the laboratory

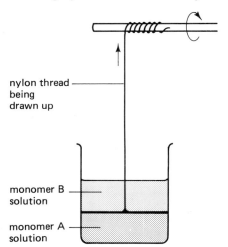

nylon thread being drawn up

monomer B solution

monomer A solution

Solvents A and B do not mix. They are **immiscible**, like oil and water. The nylon is formed as a thin sheet where the two layers meet. It can be drawn out as a thread.

Monomers used to make nylon

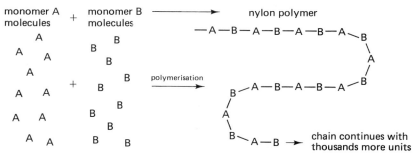

Monomer A

hexane dioyldichloride
(dissolved in 1, 1, 1–trichloroethane)

Monomer B

1, 6-diaminoethane
(dissolved in water)

Polymers and pollution

If you are out for the day enjoying a picnic and throw your apple core into a nearby bush, it doesn't matter. The apple will quickly rot away. It is said to be **biodegradable**. If you throw your plastic bottles or bags into the same bush, they may stay there for years. The plastic does not rot away like the apple. It is said to be non-biodegradable. Plastics and other polymers can be very useful in our lives. But when they are not used or disposed of carefully, they can be a nuisance.

Drugs and medicines

Nowadays, most of us have visited the doctor and been given various nasty medicines or pills to take! Our great-grandparents simply had to suffer with many of the illnesses that can now be cured by modern medicines. Many people used to die from conditions that now require only pills or simple operations to cure them.

Modern medicine has developed a great deal over the past hundred years or so. The drugs and medicines that have helped in this advance are nearly all organic molecules. Some have been discovered in herbs and plants. Others are synthetic. Many people think of a 'drug' as a substance to which you can get addicted! For the scientist, a drug is any substance that has an effect on the body. Chemists who study drugs are called **pharmacologists**.

Aspirin is an everyday drug taken by many people. It lowers your temperature, and helps relieve pain. An anaesthetic is a drug that makes you unconscious and unable to feel pain. Halothane is a commonly used anaesthetic.

When plastics are disposed of carelessly, they can cause a pollution problem.

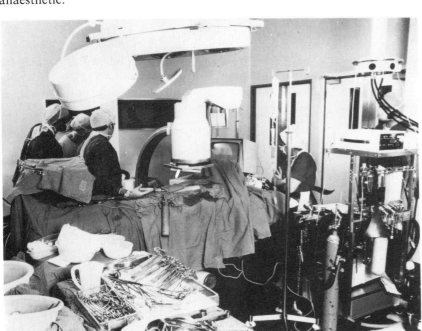

The patient being operated on wears a mask to inhale anaesthetic and air fed from equipment on the right.

An aspirin molecule
Aspirin is sodium acetylsalicylate.

A halothane molecule

Halothane is widely used as an anaesthetic.

Polymers in everyday use

Nylon is used to make fabrics, tights and ropes.

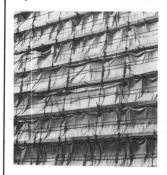 

Part of a nylon molecule:

$$-\underset{\underset{O}{\|}}{C}-NH-(CH_2)_6-NH-\underset{\underset{O}{\|}}{C}-(CH_2)_4-\underset{\underset{O}{\|}}{C}-NH \rightarrow \text{ etc.}$$

Polyethene (polythene) is a **thermosoftening** polymer. This means that when it is heated, it softens and melts. When cooled it turns solid again. It is used to cover artificial hip joints, to make them move smoothly; also to make buckets, bowls and plastic bags.

Part of a polyethene (polythene) molecule:

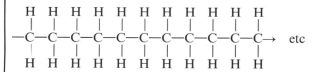

Polychloroethene (polyvinyl chloride, PVC) is used to make waterproof plastic sheets and can be moulded to make records.

Part of a PVC molecule:

PTFE (PolyTetraFluoroEthene) was first developed for use in spaceceaft. It also forms the lining of non-stick pans, e.g. Teflon.

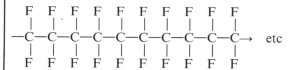

Part of a PTFE molecule:

Melamine is a **thermosetting** polymer. It decomposes if it is heated, and does not melt.

It is used to cover chipboard in cupboards and work surfaces.

Polyurethane is used to make the springy 'foam' which fills most modern furniture. It catches fire very easily, and gives off poisonous cyanide fumes. Many people die, not from the fire, but from the effect of these fumes.

22 Everyday Organic Chemistry

Summary

1. **All living things** are made from millions of organic molecules. Synthetic molecules can also be made from organic chemicals like crude oil.

2. Sugars, oils and fats are examples of **foodstuffs** used as sources of energy.

3. • **Soap** can be made by boiling a fat with sodium hydroxide solution. Soap is sodium octadecanoate (sodium stearate).

   A soap molecule: ∿∿∿∿∿─⊖

   hydrocarbon 'tail'   negatively charged 'head'
   dissolves grease   dissolves in water

   • Hard water contains dissolved salts of calcium and magnesium. It wastes soap by forming **scum**. Soapless detergents are useful in hard-water areas, as they do not form scum.

4. **Ethanol** (C_2H_6O) is made when glucose is fermented by yeast. This process is useful to brewers and bakers.

5. **Polymers** are made by joining many small monomer molecules together, e.g. polyethene (polythene), nylon.

6. Modern **drugs and medicines** are examples of useful everyday organic molecules.

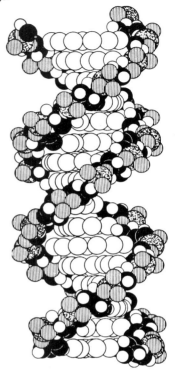

Part of a DNA molecule. DNA is one of the large organic molecules found in living things.

Questions

1. • Draw a soap molecule and give its chemical name. Explain, with the help of diagrams, how soap helps remove greasy dirt from a fabric. **R**

2. • What is hard water? Explain why hard water causes soap to be wasted. How may some of the problems caused by hard water be overcome? **R**

3. • (a) Write equations (word or symbol) to show **two** different ways of preparing ethanol. Show the reaction conditions clearly.
   (b) Why is fermentation useful to brewers and bakers?
   (c) State two uses of ethanol. **R**

4. • In which of the following reactions are large molecules broken down into smaller ones?
   (a) $6CO_2 + 6H_2O \rightarrow C_6H_{12}O_6 + 6O_2$
   (b) $C_6H_{12}O_6 \rightarrow 2C_2H_5OH + 2CO_2$
   (c) $C_{15}H_{32} \rightarrow C_{11}H_{24} + C_4H_8$
   (d) $nC_2H_4 \rightarrow -(CH_2-CH_2)_n$ (n is a large number)
   State the type of reaction happening in each of the reactions (a)–(d). **U**

5. • (a) What is a polymer?
   (b) Give an example of a polymer, giving an equation to show how it is formed.
   (c) State two uses of the polymer you have named.
   (d) Why can polymers sometimes be a nuisance when disposed of carelessly? **R**

6. ■ The following diagrams show various monomers, and the polymers that can be made from them:

	ethene	tetrafluoroethene	propene
Monomer	$H_2C=CH_2$	$F_2C=CF_2$	$H_3C-CH=CH_2$
Polymer	$-(CH_2-CH_2)_n-$ poly(ethene) (polythene)	$-(CF_2-CF_2)_n-$ polytetrafluoroethene	poly(propene)

   (a) Which of the monomer/s is/are hydrocarbons?
   (b) What would you see happening if ethene gas were bubbled through bromine water?
   (c) The molecular formula of ethene is C_2H_4. Write the molecular formula of propene.
   (d) There is a common feature in the structure of all three monomers. What is it? What name is given to compounds with this feature.
   (e) Draw the structure of poly(propene).
   (f) Give one use of polytetrafluoroethane. What unusual property has this polymer got? **U**

23 Energy

Many small children seem to have an endless supply of energy. This usually leaves their parents feeling in turn that they have very little energy! Our bodies need a constant supply of energy from the food we eat in order to work properly. Different forms of energy are all around us. Energy is constantly being changed from one form into another.

Energy all around us

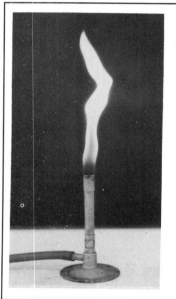

Natural gas (methane) and other fuels contain stored **chemical energy**. They are burned to produce **heat energy**.

Electrical energy is used to power this train. The electricity is used to provide movement or **kinetic energy**.

At a rock concert there is a lot of **sound energy** and **light energy**.

There is a huge amount of energy inside the atom. In a nuclear explosion, this **nuclear energy** is released.

23 Energy

Energy and changes of state

The three states of matter are solid, liquid and gas. When a solid melts to a liquid, there is a change of state. Changes of state happen between all three states of matter. Chemists are interested in finding out how much energy is involved in these changes of state. The amount of energy is measured in joules or kilojoules:

$$1000 \text{ joules} = 1 \text{ kilojoule}$$
or $1000 \text{ J} = 1 \text{ kJ}$

Changes of state

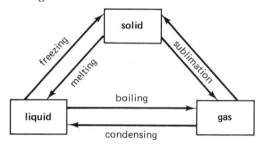

Heating water

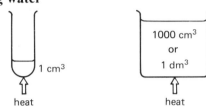

4.2 joules will raise the temperature of 1 cm³ water by 1 °C.

4200 joules or 4.2 kJ will raise the temperature of 1 litre of water by 1 °C.

To heat 1 g water by 1 °C needs 4.2 J.
To heat 100 g water by 1 °C needs (100 × 4.2) J.
To heat 100 g water by 25 °C needs (100 × 4.2 × 25) J,
$$= 10\,500 \text{ J} \quad \text{or} \quad 10.5 \text{ kJ}.$$

$$\text{energy needed to heat water} = \left[\text{mass of water in g} \times 4.2 \times \text{temperature change}\right] \text{ joules}$$

The density of water is 1.00 g cm⁻³. This means that the volume of water (in cm³) is the same number as the mass of water (in grams).

Example

How much heat energy is needed to raise the temperature of 400 cm³ water from 15 °C to 40 °C?
(4.2 J raises the temperature of 1 g water by 1 °C.)

temperature change = 40 − 15 = 25 °C

Energy needed = mass of × 4.2 × temperature
                     water   change
          =   400 × 4.2 ×   25
          = **42 000 J** or **42 kJ**

Boiling water

When water is heated until it boils, the temperature rises to 100 °C, then stays constant:

Temperature changes when water boils

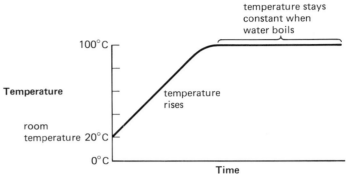

Heat energy is always involved when there is a change of state. The element in an electric kettle changes electrical energy into heat energy. The heat energy supplied to the water changes it from a liquid to a gas.

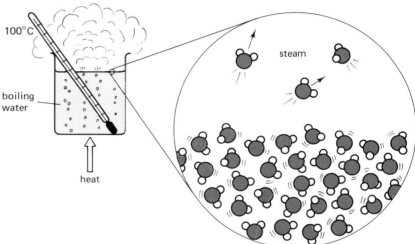

The amount of energy needed to boil away 1 mole of water can be measured in this apparatus.

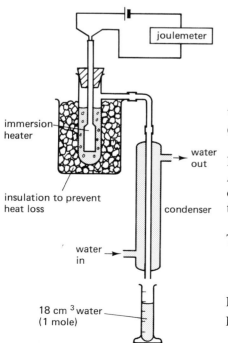

When water boils, the bonds between the molecules are broken (see Chapter 8).

Example

An immersion heater was used to boil, condense and collect 1 mole of water over a period of 15 minutes. The heater supplied 45 joules per second. Find the amount of energy needed to boil the water.

Time taken to collect 1 mole water	= 15 minutes
	= (15 × 60) seconds
	= 900 seconds
Energy supplied to water per second	= 45 joules
Energy supplied in 900 seconds	= 45 × 900
	= **40 500** J or **40.5** kJ

The energy needed to turn 1 mole of a substance at its boiling point from a liquid to a gas is called its **latent heat of vaporisation**. This is written as:

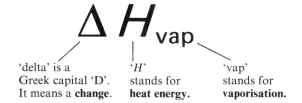

'delta' is a Greek capital 'D'. It means a **change**.

'H' stands for **heat energy**.

'vap' stands for **vaporisation**.

When steam at 100 °C is condensed to water, the process is reversed. Bonds are formed between water molecules, and energy is given out.

Example

An immersion heater supplying 20 joules per second was used to boil ethanol for a period of 500 seconds. 11.5 g ethanol was collected in this time. Find ΔH_{vap} for ethanol.
(ethanol is C_2H_6O; $M_R = 46$)

The data book value for ΔH_{vap} of ethanol is 46 kJ mol^{-1}. Comment on the difference between your answer and this value.

Time taken to collect ethanol = 500 seconds
Energy supplied by heater = 20 J second^{-1}
Energy supplied in 500 seconds = (500 × 20) joules
= **10 000 J**

11.5 g ethanol needed 10 000 J

1 g ethanol needs $\left(\dfrac{10\,000}{11.5}\right)$ J

46 g ethanol needs $\left(10\,000 \times \dfrac{46}{11.5}\right)$ J

= 40 000 J or 40 kJ

ΔH_{vap} ethanol = **40 kJ mol^{-1}**

This is less than the data book value because in the experiment not all the heat energy went into boiling the ethanol. Some was lost to the apparatus and surroundings.

Melting ice

Ice in a deep-freeze may be at −15 °C. If it is taken out of the freezer and allowed to stand in a room at, say 20 °C, the temperature of the ice will rise to 0 °C. It will remain at 0 °C until all the ice has melted. It then continues to warm up until it reaches the temperature of the room.

Fusion

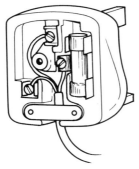

When a fuse in a plug goes, a thin piece of wire inside **melts** and breaks. This safety device then breaks the electrical circuit. In chemistry to **fuse** means to melt: 'fusion' means melting.

Temperature changes when ice melts

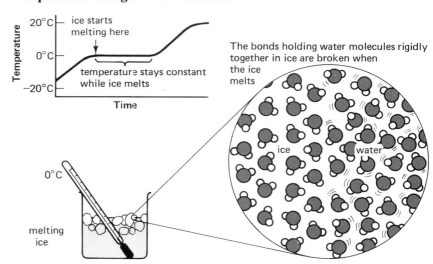

6 kJ of heat energy are needed to melt 1 mole of ice in this way. This is called the **latent heat of fusion**. It is the amount of energy needed to turn 1 mole of a substance at its melting point from a solid to a liquid. It is written ΔH_{fus}. When 1 mole of a substance at its melting point freezes from a liquid to a solid, the process is reversed. Bonds are formed in the solid and energy is given out.

Melting and boiling

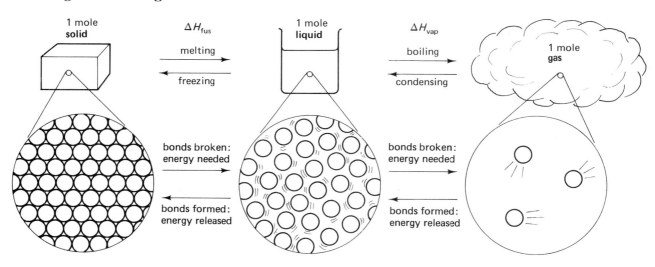

The size of the values of ΔH_{fus} and ΔH_{vap} are very important. They are a measure of the strength of the bonds in a substance.

Giant structures
- have **strong bonds** between the atoms or ions, therefore...
- they have high melting and boiling points and...
- high values for ΔH_{fus} and ΔH_{vap}.

Molecular structures
- have **weak bonds** between the molecules, therefore...
- they have low melting and boiling points, and...
- low values for ΔH_{fus} and ΔH_{vap}.

Graph of boiling points and ΔH_{vap} for various substances

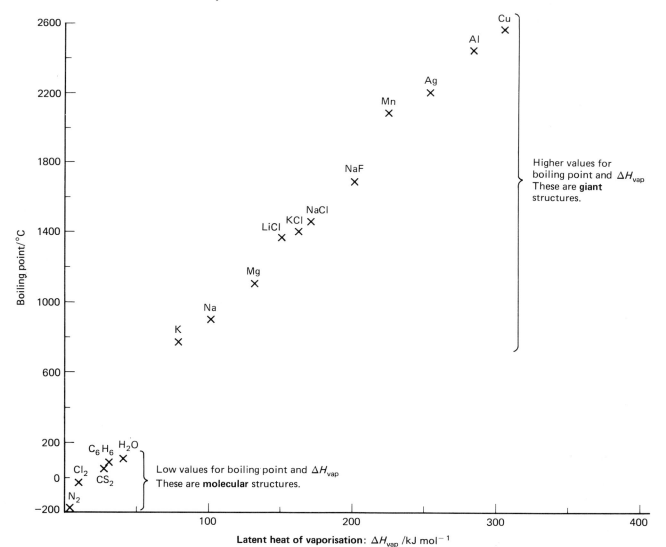

23 Energy

Energy and chemical change

An energy change often shows that a chemical reaction is happening. Sometimes heat energy is given out and chemicals get hot. In other reactions, heat energy is taken in and the chemicals get colder. Chemists find that it is useful to know about and measure these energy changes.

When dilute hydrochloric acid reacts with sodium hydroxide solution, a neutralisation reaction happens:

hydrochloric acid + sodium hydroxide ⟶ sodium chloride + water

$$HCl(aq) + NaOH(aq) \longrightarrow NaCl(aq) + H_2O(l)$$

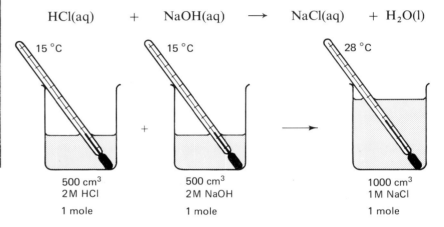

Water covers 80% of the earth's surface. It needs a relatively large amount of energy to heat it up. It also has a high value of ΔH_{vap} for a molecular liquid. This means that the world's oceans act as a giant thermostat, preventing extremes of temperature.

Temperature **rises** by (28 − 15) = 13 °C.

A reaction giving out heat energy in this way is called an **exothermic** reaction.

The amount of energy given out in a reaction like this can be found:

heat energy given out = total mass of water × 4.2 × temperature change
= 1000 × 4.2 × 13
= 54 600 J
= **55 kJ**

Note: Dilute solutions of chemicals are mostly water. This means the 4.2 value can still be used.

In this exothermic reaction, 55 kJ of heat energy are given out. This is written:

$$\Delta H = -55 \text{ kJ}$$

'delta' means a **change**   '*H*' means **heat energy**   minus sign indicates **exothermic** reaction: heat energy lost to surroundings   amount of energy given out

Neutralisation: an exothermic reaction

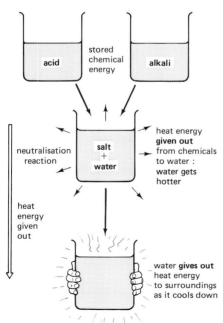

This expression is often included after an equation:

HCl(aq) + NaOH(aq) ⟶ NaCl(aq) + H$_2$O(l) $\Delta H = -55$ kJ mol^{-1}

When 1 mole of acid is neutralised by a base, the energy change is called the heat of neutralisation. This can be summed up in an **energy diagram**.

Energy diagram for a neutralisation reaction

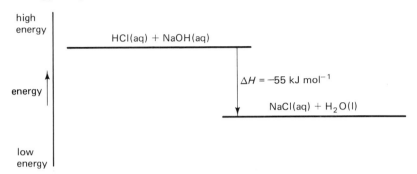

An exothermic reaction...
involves a temperature rise.
ΔH is negative: $\Delta H = -x$ kJ
The energy diagram has a downward 'step':

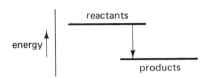

Chemicals high up on an energy diagram have a lot of stored chemical energy. In an exothermic reaction, some of this is given out as heat energy. The new substances formed have less energy, and are shown lower down on the diagram. The larger the step downwards, the more energy is given out.

When ammonium nitrate dissolves in water, this process can be written as an equation:

ammonium + water as ⟶ ammonium nitrate
nitrate   solvent   solution

NH$_4$NO$_3$(s) + aq ⟶ NH$_4$NO$_3$(aq)

An endothermic reaction...
involves a temperature fall.
ΔH is positive: $\Delta H = +y$ kJ
The energy diagram has an upward 'step':

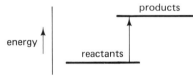

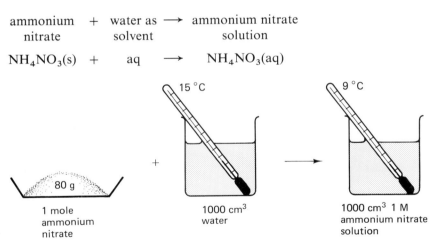

Temperature **falls** by $(15 - 9) = 6\,°C$

When a reaction takes in heat energy in this way, it is called an **endothermic** reaction.

The amount of energy taken in can be found:

heat energy taken in = mass × 4.2 × temperature
                      of water   change
                    = 1000 × 4.2 × 6
                    = 25 200 J
                    = **25 kJ**

In this endothermic reaction, 25 kJ of heat energy are taken in. This is written:

$$\Delta H = +25\,\text{kJ}$$

plus sign means endothermic reaction

Dissolving ammonium nitrate in water: an endothermic reaction

This can be written down with the equation:

$$NH_4NO_3(s) + aq \longrightarrow NH_4NO_3(aq) \quad \Delta H = +25\,\text{kJ mol}^{-1}$$

Whenever a ΔH value is written down like this, it must always have either a + or a − sign. This shows whether the reaction is endothermic or exothermic.

An energy diagram for an endothermic reaction shows an upward step:

Energy diagram for dissolving ammonium nitrate

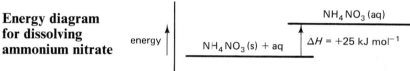

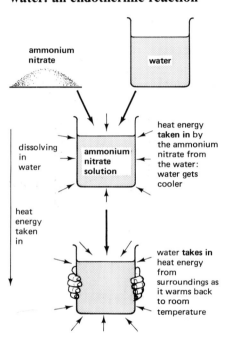

Example

When an excess of zinc powder is shaken with 50 cm³ of a 0.2 M copper(II) sulphate solution, the temperature of the mixture rises from 15 °C to 25 °C. The following reaction occurs:

$$Zn(s) + CuSO_4(aq) \longrightarrow ZnSO_4(aq) + Cu(s)$$

Find the energy change when 1 mole of copper(II) sulphate reacts in this way. Write an equation and energy diagram for the reaction. (4.2 J raise the temperature of 1 g water by 1 °C.)

Find number of moles of copper sulphate solution:

$$\text{number of moles solution} = \frac{\text{volume}}{1000} \times \text{molarity}$$

$$= \frac{50}{1000} \times 0.2$$

$$= \mathbf{0.01\ mole}$$

Find energy given out in reaction:

Energy change = mass of water × 4.2 × temperature change = 50 × 4.2 × 10

= **2100 J**

Find energy change for 1 mole:

if 0.01 mole ⟶ 2100 J

then 1 mole ⟶ $\frac{2100}{0.01}$ J

= **210 000 J or 210 kJ**

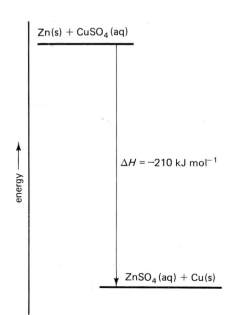

Temperature rises, so this is an exothermic reaction. ΔH must have a minus sign:

$$Zn(s) + CuSO_4(aq) \longrightarrow ZnSO_4(aq) + Cu(s) \quad \Delta H = -210\,\text{kJ mol}^{-1}$$

Chemicals as fuels

We all use various fuels every day. Many houses are kept warm in cold weather by burning wood, coal, oil or gas. Cars, lorries, trains and planes all burn various fuels. **A fuel** is any substance that burns in oxygen to produce heat energy. Another name for burning is **combustion**. Combustion reactions are always exothermic.

It is useful to know how much energy is produced by various fuels. An approximate way to measure the energy given out when various liquid fuels burn, is to use a spirit burner. This is used to heat up a known volume of water.

Measuring the heat energy produced when ethanol burns

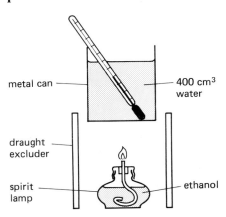

Example of results

mass of burner + ethanol before experiment	= 79.8 g
mass of burner + ethanol after experiment	= 78.3 g
mass of ethanol burned	= 1.5 g
initial temperature of water	= 15 °C
final temperature of water	= 34 °C
temperature rise	= 19 °C

M_r of ethanol C_2 H_6 O
              24 + 6 + 16
              ⎵
                46

(C = 12 H = 1 O = 16)

These results can be used to find the amount of energy given out when 1 mole of ethanol burns:

energy supplied to water = mass of water × 4.2 × temperature change
= 400 × 4.2 × 19
= 31 920 J or 31.9 kJ

1.5 g ethanol burn to give 31.9 kJ

1 g ethanol burns to give $\dfrac{31.9}{1.5}$ kJ

46 g ethanol burn to give $\dfrac{46}{1.5} \times 31.9$

= **978 kJ**

The energy given out when 1 mole of a fuel burns is called the **heat of combustion**. For ethanol, this experiment shows $\Delta H = -978$ kJ mol^{-1}.

Ethanol is C_2H_6O. Like most fuels containing carbon and hydrogen, it burns in excess air or oxygen to give carbon dioxide and water vapour:

ethanol + oxygen → carbon dioxide + water
$C_2H_6O(l)$ + $3O_2(g)$ → $2CO_2(g)$ + $3H_2O(g)$
$\Delta H = -1371$ kJ mol^{-1}

Energy diagram for the combustion of ethanol

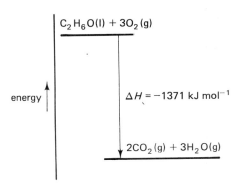

The value of ΔH from this experiment is lower than the value from tables, which is -1371 kJ. The difference is caused by some of the heat produced in the experiment being lost to the apparatus and surroundings.

The wind rotating this turbine is used to make electricity.

Examples of some fuels

Name of fuel	Formula	Equation for combustion	$\Delta H_{combustion}$ kJ mol^{-1}
Hydrogen	H_2	$H_2(g) + \tfrac{1}{2}O_2(g) \longrightarrow H_2O(g)$	-286
Carbon (coal)	C	$C(s) + O_2(g) \longrightarrow CO_2(g)$	-394
Methane (natural gas)	CH_4	$CH_4(g) + 2O_2(g) \longrightarrow CO_2(g) + 2H_2O(g)$	-890
Ethanol (methylated spirits)	C_2H_6O	$C_2H_6O(l) + 3O_2(g) \longrightarrow 2CO_2(g) + 3H_2O(g)$	-1371
Butane (camping gas)	C_4H_{10}	$C_4H_{10}(g) + 6\tfrac{1}{2}O_2(g) \longrightarrow 4CO_2(g) + 5H_2O(g)$	-2877
Octane (in petrol)	C_8H_{18}	$C_8H_{18}(l) + 12\tfrac{1}{2}O_2(g) \longrightarrow 8CO_2(g) + 9H_2O(g)$	-5512

Energy for the future

There are only limited supplies of fossil fuels such as coal, oil and natural gas. Much of the energy from these fuels is used in heating houses, in industry and in generating electricity. When eventually they run out, other ways will have to be found to provide energy.

These solar panels use the energy of the sun to make electricity.

▲ Selby (Drax) Power Station. This is one of the largest coal-burning power stations in Europe. It can produce up to 10% of the electricity needed by the whole country. The coal that is burning contains sulphur. This also burns to give sulphur dioxide gas, which is a major cause of 'acid rain'. This one power station gives off more sulphur dioxide into the air than all the industries of Sweden put together. Sweden has strict laws that control the amount of pollution pumped into the air by factories. Gases have to be 'scrubbed clean' before they are released into the atmosphere.

When two hydrogen atoms join together to make a helium atom, a large amount of energy is released. This is the way that the sun produces much of its energy. Research is going on to make this nuclear fusion work at the UKAEA Laboratory and the Joint European Torus Project at Culham, Oxford. ▶

As fossil fuels become more scarce, so the price of energy rises. It makes sense to conserve energy, and governments in many countries organise campaigns for this. Good insulation in homes, offices and factories can save millions of pounds on heating costs.

Summary

> 1 **Energy** can exist in many forms such as heat, electricity, sound, light, movement and nuclear energy.
>
> 2 Energy is measured in **joules** (J) and **kilojoules** (kJ).
> 1000 J = 1 kJ
>
> 3 Equation to find the amount of energy used in **heating water**:
> $$\text{energy} = \left[\frac{\text{mass of}}{\text{water/g}} \times 4.2 \times \frac{\text{temperature}}{\text{change}}\right] \text{joules}$$
>
> 4 ΔH_{vap} is the latent heat of vaporisation. It is the energy needed to turn 1 mole of a substance at its boiling point from a liquid to a gas.
>
> 5 ΔH_{fus} is the latent heat of fusion. It is the energy needed to turn 1 mole of a substance at its melting point from a solid to a liquid.
>
> 6 A substance with **high values** for ΔH_{vap} and ΔH_{fus} will also have high boiling and melting points. This is because there are strong bonds between the particles. The substance probably has a **giant structure**.
>
> 7 A substance with **low values** for ΔH_{vap} and ΔH_{fusp} will also have low boiling and melting points. This is because there are weak bonds between particles. The substance probably has a **molecular structure**.
>
> 8 • **Exothermic** reactions give out heat energy to the surroundings.
> • There is a temperature rise.
> • ΔH is negative.
>
> 9 • **Endothermic** reactions take in heat energy from the surroundings.
> • There is a temperature fall.
> • ΔH is positive.
>
> 10 **Energy diagrams** show changes in energy during a reaction.
>
> *Exothermic*   *Endothermic*
>
>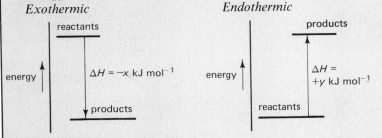
>
> 11 The **heat of combustion** of a fuel is the energy given out when 1 mole of a fuel burns in excess oxygen.

The size of the tide at La Rance in northern France is enough to generate electricity for the area.

Sweden is a very energy-conscious country and its houses have very thick layers of insulation in the walls and roof. The windows, such as these, are all either triple or quadruple glazed. In some areas, hot water from a central supply is provided to homes, which also saves on energy costs.

Questions

1 ● Part of the contents page of a book is given below. Which pages would you look up to get information about keeping down the cost of heating in your home?

D	distillation	10	H	heat energy	5
	double glazing	12		heating	5
	draught excluders	13		hydrogen	22
E	energy	2	I	insulation	14
F	fault	15	L	lagging	12
	finite supply	20		lighting	6
	fossil fuel	3	M	metre	15
	fractional distillation	18		microbes	21
	fractions	17	N	non-permeable	18
	fuel	4		non-renewable	20
G	gas	4		nuclear energy	22
	Geiger counter	20		nuclear waste	22
	geological survey	20			
	gravity	21			

(SEB) **H**

2 ● The graph shows the present supplies of energy from fossil fuels.

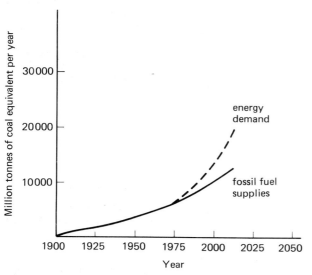

(a) What will be the difference between energy demand and fossil fuel supplies in the year 2000?
(b) In what year were fossil fuels no longer able to satisfy the energy demand?
(c) Suggest a possible value in million tonnes of coal equivalent for the supply of energy from fossil fuels in the year 2050. Give a reason for your choice.

(SEB) **H**

3 ■ Chemistry is mainly concerned with three types of energy:
  I Chemical energy.
  II Heat energy.
  III Electrical energy.
(a) One type of energy can be changed into another. When hydrogen burns in oxygen to form water, chemical energy is changed into heat. The equation for the reaction is:

$$2H_2(g) + O_2(g) \rightarrow 2H_2O(l) \quad \Delta H = -572 \text{ kJ}$$

Which has the greater amount of chemical energy, the water or the mixture of hydrogen and oxygen? Give a reason for your answer.
(b) The electrolysis of acidified water produces hydrogen and oxygen.
 (i) Copy out and write the equation for this reaction
    ___ → ___ $\Delta H =$ ___ kJ
 (ii) Copy out and complete the sentence: The change in the type of energy is from ___ to ___.
(c) Two porous electrodes are immersed in sodium hydroxide solution. A fuel, hydrogen or methane, is supplied to one electrode and oxygen to the other. This device will produce a constant current.
 (i) What is the name of this device?
 (ii) Suggest a possible use for this device.
(d) Silver(I) bromide is prepared by mixing solutions of silver(I) nitrate and potassium bromide. The cream-coloured precipitate of silver(I) bromide is filtered off, washed and spread over the filter paper. A coin is placed on this coated filter paper and a piece of burning magnesium ribbon is held above it.
  This experiment illustrates the photochemical decomposition of silver(I) bromide into its elements.
 (i) Write a word equation for decomposition of silver(I) bromide.
 (ii) Describe what you would observe at the end of the experiment when the coin is removed.
 (iii) Explain the observations you have given in (d) (ii).
 (iv) Write an ionic equation for the formation of silver(I) bromide.
 (v) Name one application of this decomposition of silver(I) bromide. (NEA) **U**

4 ■ (a) Alcohols are organic compounds which have a general formula $C_nH_{2n+1}OH$, where n is the number of carbon atoms present in one molecule. Alcohols burn completely in oxygen forming carbon dioxide and water.
  The following table gives the molar heat of combustion of a number of alcohols, i.e. the heat given out when one mole of an alcohol is completely burned in oxygen.

Alcohol	Number of carbon atoms in one molecule	Formula	Heat of combustion/ kJ mol^{-1}
methanol	1	CH_3OH	730
ethanol	2	C_2H_5OH	1370
propanol	3		2020
butanol	4	C_4H_9OH	2650
pentanol	5		

 (i) Write down the formula of propanol.
 (ii) Copy out, then balance and complete the following equation to represent the complete combustion of ethanol in oxygen.

$C_2H_5OH + \_\_O_2 \rightarrow \_\_CO_2 + \_\_H_2O; \Delta H = \_\_$ kJ

(iii) Copy out and complete the energy level diagram to show the energy changes taking place during this reaction.

chemical energy | products

(iv) Plot a graph on axes similar to those below, of the molar heat of combustion of the alcohols against the number of carbon atoms in one molecule.

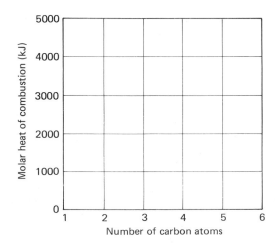

(v) Use the graph to determine the molar heat of combustion of pentanol in $kJ\,mol^{-1}$.
(vi) State the number of carbon atoms and hydrogen atoms in one molecule of the alcohol which has a molar heat of combustion of $3900\,kJ\,mol^{-1}$.
(b) Alcohols are used as fuels as one alternative to fossil fuels.
(i) State one property of alcohols which makes them useful as fuels.
(ii) Why is it important to discover sources of energy as an alternative to the use of fossil fuels? (NEA) **H**

5 ▸ Petrol is a mixture of various hydrocarbons. Here is some information about hexane, which is one of the hydrocarbons in petrol:

Name	hexane
Formula	C_6H_{14}
Relative molecular mass	86
Boiling point	69 °C
Heat of combustion	$-4200\,kJ\,mol^{-1}$

(a) What is a hydrocarbon?
(b) Hexane is useful in petrol because it is volatile and burns in an exothermic reaction. Explain the meanings of the words **volatile** and **exothermic**.
(c) Write a word equation and a symbol equation for the combustion of hexane.
(d) Draw an energy diagram for this reaction.
(e) Find the amount of energy released when 2.15 g of hexane are burned.

(f) The following are two possible arrangements of the C_6H_{14} molecule:

H H H H H H
| | | | | |
H—C—C—C—C—C—C—H
| | | | | |
H H H H H H

H H H H H
| | | | |
H—C—C—C—C—C—H
| | | | |
H H H | H
H—C—H
|
H

What are different arrangements of a molecule like this called?
Draw a third possible arrangement of atoms with the formula C_6H_{14}. **U**

6 ▸ (a) Give **two** sources of energy which do **NOT** depend directly or indirectly on solar energy.
(b) A 2.0 cm length of magnesium ribbon was added to 100 cm³ of 2.0 M hydrochloric acid. All the magnesium reacted and the temperature of the acid increased by 20 °C.
(i) If a 1.0 cm length of magnesium ribbon had been used in 100 cm³ of 2.0 M hydrochloric acid, what would the temperature rise have been?
(ii) What volume of 2.0 M hydrochloric acid would produce a temperature rise of 20 °C with 1 cm length of magnesium ribbon?
(c) (i) Calculate the quantity of energy released when 4.0 g of calcium is burnt in excess chlorine.
$$Ca(s) + Cl_2(g) \longrightarrow CaCl_2(s) \quad \Delta H = -800\,kJ\,mol^{-1}$$
(Relative atomic mass Ca = 40)
(ii) For the reaction in (c) (i), copy out and complete the following energy level diagram. Indicate clearly on the diagram the value for the heat of reaction (ΔH).

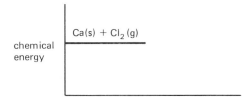

(d) Give an example of: (i) a fast reaction, one which is completed in a few seconds; (ii) a slow reaction, one which takes days or weeks. (NEA) **H**

7 ▸ (a) What is a hydrocarbon?
(b) Draw the structures of the molecules with the formulae: CH_4, C_2H_4, C_2H_6.
(c) The molecules CH_4 and C_2H_6 are the first two members of a homologous series. Name the series, and write down the formula of the third member of the series.
(d) One of the hydrocarbons present in high octane petrol is 3,3-dimethylpentane. This burns according to the following equation:
$$C_7H_{16} + 11O_2 \longrightarrow 7CO_2 + 8H_2O \quad \Delta H = -4800\,kJ$$
(i) Calculate the volume of oxygen needed for the combustion of 1000 cm³ of C_7H_{16} (all volumes measured at room temperature and pressure).
(ii) Assuming that air is one fifth oxygen, what volume of air would be required for this reaction?
(e) What mass of carbon dioxide would be produced when 5.0 g of C_7H_{16} were burned?
(Relative molecular masses: C_7H_{16} = 100, CO_2 = 44) **H**

24 Electrolysis

Apparatus for electrolysis

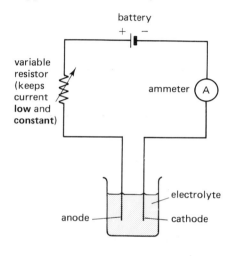

Introduction

The word electrolysis means 'splitting with electricity'. An electric current is passed through a solution of a salt in water, or through a salt that has been melted. The new substances formed give useful information about the salt.

Words and symbols used in electrolysis

Electrolyte   is the liquid that the electric current is passed through. An electrolyte may either be melted (fused) or dissolved in water.

Electrodes   These are strips of metal or carbon rods which dip into the electrolyte.

Anode   The positive electrode.

Cathode   The negative electrode.

Anions   Negative ions.

Cations   Positive ions.

—|⊢—   A battery. The shorter line is the negative terminal and the longer line is the positive terminal: —⁺|⊢⁻—

—(A)—   An ammeter.

—/\/\/\—   A variable resistor or rheostat.

What happens in electrolysis?

When lead bromide is gently heated, it melts at 370 °C. If an electric current is passed through this liquid, the lead bromide is broken down. Molten lead metal is formed at the cathode and bromine vapour at the anode. Because of the poisonous fumes, the experiment is done in a fume cupboard.

    Lead bromide is an ionic compound, i.e. $PbBr_2$ contains Pb^{2+} and Br^- and Br^- ions.

    When it melts, the ordered giant structure of ions breaks down and the ions become free to move. When the electric current is switched on, the ions start to move. They are attracted to the electrode of the opposite charge. Pb^{2+} ions move towards the cathode (negative electrode) and Br^- ions to the anode (positive electrode).

Electrolysis of lead bromide

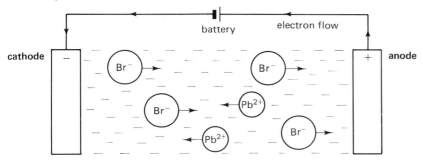

The battery acts as an 'electron pump'. Negatively charged electrons are pumped away from the anode and on to the cathode.

Lead ions Pb^{2+}	*Bromide ions* Br^- Br^-
Positive ions are called **cations**.	Negative ions are called **anions**.
Pb^{2+} ions are attracted to the **cathode**.	Br^- ions are attracted to the **anode**.
Each Pb^{2+} ion gains 2 electrons and loses its charge – it is discharged.	Each Br^- ions loses one electron and loses its charge – it is discharged.
a lead + two → a lead ion electrons atom $Pb^{2+}(l) + 2e^- \rightarrow Pb(l)$	two bromide → a bromine + two ions molecule electrons $2Br^-(l) \rightarrow Br_2(g) + 2e^-$

Most electrolysis experiments in the laboratory are done with solutions in water. Hydrochloric acid is an example of this.

Electrolysis of dilute hydrochloric acid

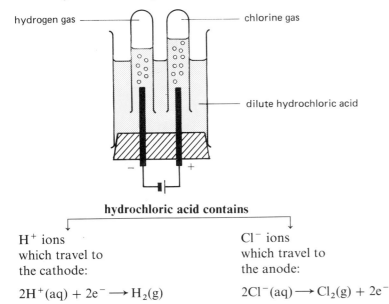

hydrochloric acid contains

H^+ ions which travel to the cathode:

$2H^+(aq) + 2e^- \rightarrow H_2(g)$

Cl^- ions which travel to the anode:

$2Cl^-(aq) \rightarrow Cl_2(g) + 2e^-$

The **electrode material** may affect the products of electrolysis. This is shown in the electrolysis of copper sulphate solution:

Electrolysis of copper(II) sulphate solution using carbon electrodes

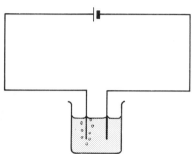

at anode: oxygen formed
at cathode: copper deposited

Copper(II) sulphate solution gets paler blue as all the copper ions in solution are deposited on the cathode.

Electrolysis of copper(II) sulphate solution using copper electrodes

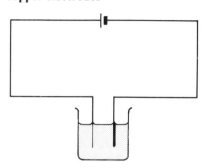

at anode: copper dissolves away
at cathode: copper deposited

Copper(II) sulphate solution stays same colour. Copper atoms dissolve off the anode into solution at the same rate they are deposited onto the cathode:

at cathode: $Cu^{2+}(aq) + 2e^- \longrightarrow Cu(s)$

at anode: $Cu(s) \longrightarrow Cu^{2+}(aq) + 2e^-$

These forks and spoons are the cathodes in a solution of a salt containing silver. A thin layer of silver is deposited on the cutlery, giving it a shiny and attractive finish.

Electrolysis of solutions of **alkali metal salts** does not give the expected products. Sodium chloride solution, for example, contains the ions Na^+ and Cl^-. Chloride ions are attracted to the anode and discharged as chlorine gas, as expected:

$2Cl^-(aq) \longrightarrow Cl_2(g) + 2e^-$

The sodium ions are attracted to the cathode, but sodium metal is too reactive to be formed from the ions and they remain in solution in the water. Water itself provides H^+ ions, and these are discharged instead:

$2H^+(aq) + 2e^- \longrightarrow H_2(g)$

Electrolysis of **water** splits it up into hydrogen and oxygen. The formula of water is H_2O, and *twice* as much hydrogen gas as oxygen is formed during electrolysis. Even pure water contains some ions:

a water molecule $\longrightarrow$ a hydrogen ion + a hydroxide ion
$H_2O(l) \longrightarrow H^+(aq) + OH^-(aq)$

These ions are discharged as follows:

at cathode: $4H^+(aq) + 4e^- \longrightarrow 2H_2(g)$

at anode: $4OH^-(aq) \longrightarrow 2H_2O(l) + O_2(g) + 4e^-$

24 Electrolysis

Measuring the amount of electricity used in electrolysis

During electrolysis experiments, chemists often need to know how much electricity is used. The amount of electricity is measured in **coulombs**. 1 coulomb (1 C) is the amount of electricity flowing when 1 ampere (1A) is passed in 1 second.

number of coulombs = amperes × seconds

This equation can be rearranged so that:

$$\text{amperes} = \frac{\text{coulombs}}{\text{seconds}} \quad \text{or} \quad \text{seconds} = \frac{\text{coulombs}}{\text{amperes}}$$

In the electrolysis of silver nitrate solution, for example, a silver cathode is weighed before and after the experiment. The current flowing and the time taken are noted.

Electrolysis of silver nitrate solution

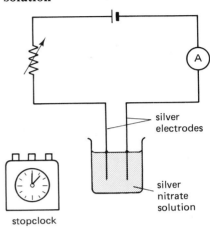

Example of results

Mass of silver cathode at start	= 15.640 g
Final mass of silver cathode	= 16.072 g
Mass of silver deposited	= **0.432 g**
Relative atomic mass of silver	= 108
Current flowing	= 0.20 A
Time	= 1930 seconds
Number of coulombs (amperes × seconds)	= 0.20 × 1930
	= **386 C**

In this experiment:

0.432 g silver was deposited by   386 C

so 1 g silver would need $\dfrac{386}{0.432}$ C

and 108 g silver would need (1 mole) $\dfrac{386}{0.432} \times 108$ C

= **96 500 C**

In this calculation, the results of an experiment to deposit a small amount of silver are used. This is multiplied up to find the amount of electricity needed to deposit 1 mole of silver atoms.

at the cathode: $Ag^+(aq)$ + e^- → $Ag(s)$
one silver ion + one electron → one silver atom

and   one mole silver atoms + one mole electrons → one mole silver atoms

One mole of electrons will deposit one mole of a 1+ ion. A mole of electrons is known as a **faraday** (symbol F).

1 faraday = 96 500 coulombs
1 F = 96 500 C

24 Electrolysis

In the electrolysis of copper(II) sulphate solution, copper metal is deposited on the cathode. Copper forms a 2+ ions, so the equation is:

$$Cu^{2+}(aq) + 2e^- \rightarrow Cu(s)$$

one copper(II) ion + two electrons → one copper atom

and one mole copper(II) ions + two moles electrons → one mole copper atoms

or two faradays

To deposit a mole of copper ions, two moles of electrons are needed:

2 faradays = 2 × 96 500 coulombs
2 F = 193 000 C

Example
In an experiment to electrolyse copper(II) sulphate solution, using copper electrodes, 0.1 A was passed through the solution for 3860 seconds. The mass of the copper cathode increased from 6.350 g to 6.478 g. Find:

(a) the amount of electricity needed to deposit 1 mole copper atoms.

(b) the charge on a copper ion.
(1 faraday = 95 500 C; Cu = 64.)

(a) mass of copper deposited = (6.478 − 6.350) = 0.128 g
Number of coulombs (amperes × seconds) = 0.1 × 3860) = 386 C
0.128 g copper was deposited by 386 C

1 g copper would be deposited by $\left[\dfrac{386}{0.128}\right]$ C

64 g copper would be deposited by (1 mole) $\left[\dfrac{386}{0.128} \times 64\right]$ C

Amount of electricity to deposit 1 mole copper atoms = **193 000 C**.

(b) number of faradays = $\dfrac{193\,000}{96\,500}$ = 2 F

Charge on copper ion is **Cu²⁺**.

One mole of:
1+ or 1− ions are discharged by 1 faraday or 96 500 C

Ag⁺ Na⁺ K⁺ H⁺ OH⁻ Cl⁻

One mole of:
2+ ions are discharged by 2 faradays or 19 300 C

Cu²⁺ Zn²⁺ Pb²⁺

One mole of:
3+ ions are discharged by 3 faradays or 289 500 C

Al³⁺

Oxidation and reduction

In Chapter 7 reduction and oxidation are explained by the loss and gain of oxygen, e.g.

copper(II) oxide + hydrogen ⟶ copper + water

$$\underset{\text{oxidation: gain of oxygen}}{\overset{\text{reduction: loss of oxygen}}{CuO(s) + H_2(g) \longrightarrow Cu(s) + H_2O(g)}}$$

Oxidation and reduction can also be explained by seeing whether electrons are lost or gained:
 oxidation: is loss of electrons
 reduction: is gain of electrons
In electrolysis, electrons are continually being lost and gained. Electrolysis therefore involves oxidation and reduction, e.g. in lead bromide electrolysis:

At cathode:

$Pb^{2+}(l) + 2e^- \longrightarrow Pb(l)$

gain of
electrons
= reduction

lead ions are reduced to lead

At anode:

$2Br^-(l) \longrightarrow Br_2(g) + 2e$

loss of
electrons
= oxidation

bromide ions are oxidised to bromine

Electrolysis in industry

Electrolysis is used in some industries to make a variety of useful materials.

Aluminium metal is extracted from aluminium oxide by electrolysis. Aluminium compounds are very common and form $7\frac{1}{2}\%$ of the earth's crust. The metal is too reactive to be formed in aqueous solution, so it is obtained from molten aluminium oxide.

Aluminium oxide (Al_2O_3) is dissolved in melted cryolite (Na_3AlF_6). This lowers the melting point of the mixture to 850 °C. The electrodes are made from carbon, in the form of graphite.

Oxygen formed at the anode reacts with the graphite and burns it away as carbon dioxide. The anodes therefore need replacing occasionally.

Electrolysis of aluminium oxide

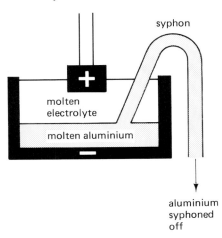

At cathode: $4Al^{3+}(l) + 12e^- \longrightarrow 4Al(l)$

At anode: $6O^{2-}(l) \longrightarrow 3O_2 + 12e^-$

24 Electrolysis

Aluminium is a very useful metal. It is strong, has a low density and, unlike iron, it does not rust. The metal is covered in a very thin layer of aluminium oxide which stops it rusting.

The frame of this greenhouse is made from aluminium. It does not rust or need painting.

The bodywork of most aeroplanes is made from aluminium. This is because of its strength and low density.

Sodium chloride is one of the cheapest and most widely available raw materials for the chemical industry. It is found in vast underground deposits.

The electrolysis of sodium chloride solution (brine) makes some very useful products: chlorine, hydrogen and sodium hydroxide solution. One way this electrolysis is carried out is in a diaphragm cell.

Electrolysis of sodium chloride solution ('diaphragm cell')

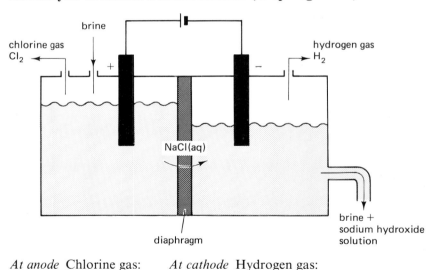

At anode Chlorine gas:

$2Cl^-(aq) \longrightarrow Cl_2(g) + 2e^-$

At cathode Hydrogen gas:

$2H^+(aq) + 2e^- \longrightarrow H_2(g)$

Chlorine is useful for

making plastics like polychloroethene (PVC)

making synthetic rubber

sterilising water and making bleach

Hydrogen is useful for

hardening vegetable oils into margarine, with a nickel catalyst

as a fuel

Sodium hydroxide is useful to

react with chlorine to make bleach

react with fats and oils to make soap

Summary

1. **Electrolysis** involves breaking down a salt by passing an electric current through it. The salt is either dissolved in water or melted.

2. - The **anode** is the + electrode.
   - The **cathode** is the − electrode.
   - **Anions** are − charged. They are attracted to the anode.
   - **Cations** are + charged. They are attracted to the cathode.

3. When ions reach an electrode, they are **discharged** by losing or gaining electrons, e.g. hydrochloric acid contains:

   $H^+(aq)$ ions and $Cl^-(aq)$ ions

   at cathode: $2H^+(aq) + 2e^- \longrightarrow H_2(g)$

   at anode: $2Cl^-(aq) \longrightarrow Cl_2(g) + 2e^-$

4. **Metals** high in the reactivity series are not discharged from aqueous solution. H^+ ions from the water are discharged instead, e.g. sodium chloride solution gives
   hydrogen at the cathode, chlorine at the anode.

5. The amount of electricity is measured in **coulombs**:
   coulombs = amperes × seconds

6. - One **faraday** = 96 500 C
   - One mole of electrons will deposit 1 mole of a 1+ ion.
   - One faraday is a mole of electrons.

7. - **Oxidation** is the loss of electrons.
   - **Reduction** is the gain of electrons.
   - In electrolysis of hydrochloric acid,
   at cathode, $H^+(aq)$ ions are reduced:
   $2H^+(aq) + 2e^- \longrightarrow H_2(g)$
   reduction = gain of electrons

   at anode, $Cl^-(aq)$ ions are oxidised:
   $2Cl^-(aq) \longrightarrow Cl_2(g) + 2e^-$
   oxidation = loss of electrons

   - Remember....**O**xidation
     Is
     Loss

     Reduction
     Is
     Gain

8. **In industry**, electrolysis is used to extract reactive metals like aluminium from their ores. It is also used to plate cutlery, etc. with silver or copper.

Chlorine is added to swimming pools to sterilize the water.

Questions

1 ■ Large quantities or rock salt are found in the United Kingdom. It is either crushed and used as it is, or purified for use as cooking salt or as a raw material to make other chemicals.
(a) State one use of crushed rock salt.
(b) Give one advantage and one disadvantage of using salt in cooking.
(c) Draw a labelled diagram of the apparatus you could use to make a sample of sodium chloride from its elements.
(d) Chlorine gas is made from the electrolysis of sodium chloride solution. Give one use of chlorine gas.
(e) Chlorine can also be used to make many other useful products. Give the names and uses of two such products made from chlorine. **R**

2 ■ (a) Copy out and complete the following table about the electrolysis of four chemicals using inert electrodes.

Electrolyte	Product at cathode (−ve electrode)	Product at anode (+ve electrode)
Molten sodium chloride		chlorine
Molten calcium bromide	calcium	
Sodium chloride solution		chlorine
Copper(II) sulphate solution		

(b) State what is meant by the terms: (i) 'electrolysis,' (ii) 'inert electrodes'.
(c) Explain why the blue colour of the copper(II) sulphate solution becomes paler during electrolysis.
(d) Explain why solid sodium chloride is a non-conductor of electricity, whereas molten sodium chloride and sodium chloride solution are good conductors of electricity. (NEA) **R**

3 ■ The following is a diagram of the apparatus and circuit needed to electrolyse the solution of copper(II) chloride shown:

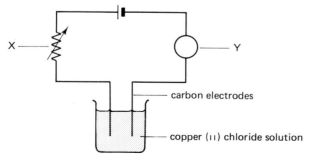

(a) What piece of apparatus should be put at Y, to show that the solution conducts electricity?
(b) What is the name of the piece of apparatus labelled X? What is it used for?
(c) Which elements are formed at: (i) the anode, (ii) the cathode?
(d) What sort of particles carry the current: (i) in the connecting wires, (ii) through the solution?
(e) What would happen if the carbon cathode were replaced by a coin? **U**

4 ■ Three different types of cell for producing electricity are described below. In each case, energy released by a chemical reaction is made available as electrical energy when the cell is used to provide a current.

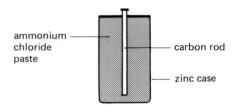

Primary cell, 1.5 volts

Primary cell (e.g. a dry cell) These cells are small and portable. They use common materials and are cheap, but the chemical reaction which produces the electricity cannot be reversed so the cell must be thrown away after use. The zinc casing of a dry cell dissolves in use, forming zinc chloride, and if batteries are kept too long, the case may leak and spill out the corrosive contents.

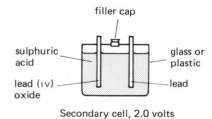

Secondary cell, 2.0 volts

Secondary cells (e.g. lead/acid accumulator) These are larger and more expensive than primary cells and very heavy. In use, both electrodes are converted to lead sulphate but this reaction can be reversed by passing an electric current through the cell (in the reverse direction to the current which is supplied by the cell when working). Thus some other source of electricity is needed to recharge the cell.

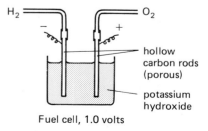

Fuel cell, 1.0 volts

Fuel cell (e.g. hydrogen/oxygen cell) These also use an irreversible reaction but in this case the 'fuel' may be continuously added to the cell while it is running, so that it can operate for very long periods. In the cell shown, the chemical change is equivalent to burning the hydrogen. Expensive catalysts are needed to make the cell work efficiently and containers are needed to store the hydrogen and oxygen.

(a) Give one advantage and one disadvantage of each type of cell.
(b) Write a word equation for the chemical change which takes place while the fuel cell is being used to supply a current.
(c) Explain what change you would expect to occur in the concentration of the acid in the lead/acid accumulator, while it is being used to supply electricity.
(d) Explain, giving reasons, which type of cell from amongst those described, would be most suitable for each of the uses described below.
  (i) The power supply for a deaf person's hearing aid,
  (ii) the power supply for a milk float,
  (iii) the power supply for the light on a buoy marking a safe passage at sea.
(e) Water from the sulphuric acid in a lead-acid battery gradually evaporates away, and from time to time the battery must be 'topped-up' with distilled water. Explain why ordinary tap water is unsuitable for this purpose. (MEG) **H**

5 ■ Aluminium is manufactured by passing electricity through a molten mixture of aluminium oxide and cryolite (a mineral containing sodium, aluminium and fluorine). The cryolite is not used up in the process. The melting point of this mixture is much lower than that of pure aluminium oxide. The cell which holds the molten mixture is lined with carbon. Molten aluminium collects at the bottom of the cell. The current is supplied through carbon rods. Oxygen formed from the aluminium oxide burns these rods away as carbon monoxide.

(a) Answer the following questions about this process.
  (i) Why is it necessary to melt the aluminium oxide?
  (ii) What are the advantages of a low melting point for the mixture in the cell?
  (iii) From the information given above, what factors are most likely to affect the cost of making aluminium?
(b) The map shows the British Isles. The grey dotted areas are called development areas, where the Government will help to pay some of the costs of starting a new industry. The black triangles show deep water ports. The arrows show the direction of the prevailing winds. The ore of aluminium is imported by sea. It is much heavier than the aluminium made from it. Aluminium refineries may produce airborne fumes and should be placed where there are no large towns downwind of the factory.

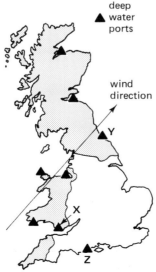

Three possible sites for aluminium refineries are shown (**X, Y, Z**). For each of these, list the advantages and disadvantages of siting a refinery at that place.
(c) Many soft drink cans are now made of aluminium and it has been suggested that used cans should be collected so that the metal can be re-cycled. Explain what factors must be considered when deciding whether the material from disposable items such as cans ought to be re-cycled. (MEG) **H**

6 ▶ Many metals react with dilute hydrochloric acid. The following table shows some of these reactions:

Name of metal	Reaction with dilute hydrochloric acid
Zinc	Hydrogen gas formed slowly
Strontium	Hydrogen gas produced very rapidly, solution gets hot
Copper	No reaction
Magnesium	Hydrogen gas formed fairly fast. Solution gets warm

(a) Describe how you would test for the presence of hydrogen gas.
(b) Put these four metals in order of reactivity, with the most reactive first.
(c) Copper(II) ions and zinc metal undergo a displacement reaction, as follows:

$$Cu^{2+}(aq) + Zn(s) \longrightarrow Cu(s) + Zn^{2+}(aq)$$

Give three observations you might make during this reaction.
(d) The reaction shown in (c) may also be carried out in **a cell**. What is a cell?
(e) Copper metal may be obtained at the cathode by the electrolysis of an aqueous solution of a copper(II) chloride. What is produced at the cathode during the electrolysis of a solution of sodium chloride? **U**

7 ▶ When copper(II) chloride solution is electrolysed using carbon electrodes, the following equation shows the overall change that takes place:

$$CuCl_2(aq) \longrightarrow Cu(s) + Cl_2(g)$$

(a) What would be formed at the cathode? Write an ion–electron equation for this reaction.
(b) What would be formed at the anode? Write an ion–electron equation for this reaction.
(c) Describe a test for the substance produced at the anode.
(d) During an experiment to electrolyse some copper(II) chloride solution in this way, a current of 0.5 A was passed for 4825 seconds.
  Calculate: (i) the mass of copper, (ii) the volume of chlorine gas formed.
  (Cu = 64; 1 mole of a gas occupies 24 000 cm³ at room temperature and pressure; the charge on 1 mole of electrons is 96 500 coulombs)
(e) Write ion–electron equations for the reactions at both electrodes if the carbon rods were replaced by copper strips.
(f) State two experimental conditions that will help copper to be properly deposited. **U**

25 Electricity from Chemical Reactions

The first sign that many chemical reactions are happening is that they give out heat energy. For some reactions, the apparatus and chemicals can be set up in such a way that most of this energy can be turned into electricity. The batteries we use in radios, torches, cars, etc. all make use of this. They contain chemicals which react together and produce an electric current.

A simple cell

When a chemical reaction is made to produce electrical energy, a **cell** has been formed. There are many different cells and only a few are mentioned here.

The reaction between zinc and copper

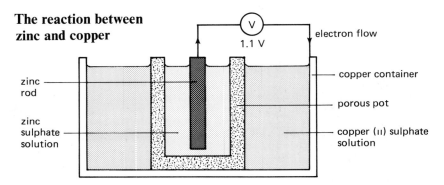

When this cell is set up as shown, a small electrical current flows round the external wire. The following processes happen:

1 Atoms in the zinc rod give up electrons which pass round the external wire as an electric current. Zinc ions are formed in solution:

$$Zn(s) \longrightarrow Zn^{2+}(aq) + 2e^-$$

zinc atoms on rod — Zinc ions dissolve into solution... — ...losing electrons which pass round the wire.

2 Zinc ions and copper ions are attracted towards the copper pot.

3 Copper ions in solution gain electrons and form a deposit of copper metal:

$$Cu^{2+}(aq) + 2e^- \longrightarrow Cu(s)$$

Copper ions in solution... — ...gain electrons from the copper pot, and... — ...copper metal is deposited.

In this experiment, copper and zinc are used. It is possible to use many such pairs of metals, and obtain an electric current.

Examples of cells

Metal 1	Metal 2	Potential difference /volts
Magnesium	Zinc	1.62
Magnesium	Lead	2.25
Magnesium	Copper	2.72
Magnesium	Silver	3.18

25 Electricity from Chemical Reactions

Energy from cells

The **dry battery** contains various chemicals that react together to make electrical energy.

A dry battery

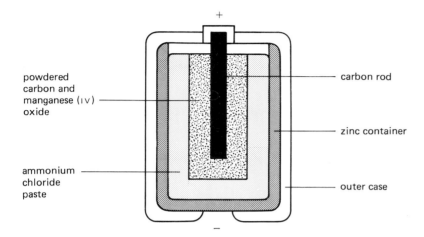

This vehicle is powered by a series of batteries. As petrol becomes more expensive and supplies of crude oil run out, perhaps there will be more electric-powered vehicles on the road. Electric vehicles are quiet and pollution-free.

Summary

1 A **cell** produces electrical energy from chemical energy.

2 In a cell, when two substances react together, an **electric current** is made to pass round an external circuit.

3 Dry **batteries** and vehicles batteries are useful types of cell.

26 Reversible Reactions

When magnesium ribbon is burned in air, it gives out a brilliant white light and leaves a white ash of magnesium oxide.

$$\text{magnesium} + \text{oxygen} \longrightarrow \text{magnesium oxide}$$

$$2Mg(s) + O_2(g) \longrightarrow 2MgO(s)$$

It is very hard to turn magnesium oxide back into magnesium and oxygen again. This is a **one-way-only** reaction.

Many reactions can go **both ways** – they can be easily reversed. This chapter looks at some examples of reversible reactions.

The burning magnesium in this distress flare gives out a bright light. When magnesium is burned in air, the reaction cannot easily be reversed.

An example of a reversible reaction

When iodine and chlorine react together, they form a brown liquid called iodine monochloride.

$$\text{iodine} + \text{chlorine} \longrightarrow \text{iodine monochloride}$$

$$I_2(s) + Cl_2(g) \longrightarrow 2ICl(l)$$

This brown liquid can be reacted with more chlorine.

Reacting iodine monochloride with chlorine

The brown iodine monochloride liquid reacts with chlorine to form yellow crystals of iodine trichloride:

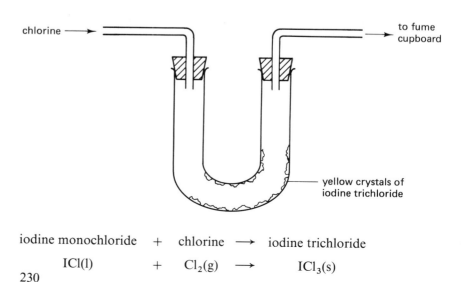

$$\text{iodine monochloride} + \text{chlorine} \longrightarrow \text{iodine trichloride}$$

$$ICl(l) + Cl_2(g) \longrightarrow ICl_3(s)$$

Adding and removing chlorine have caused this reaction to be **reversed**. A reversible reaction is shown with the sign ⇌ in place of the usual arrow:

ICl(l) + Cl$_2$(g) ⇌ ICl$_3$(s)

Chemicals on the left of the equation are called **reactants**.

Chemicals on the right of the equation are called **products**.

The ⇌ sign in any equation shows that the reaction is reversible.

The reaction

ICl(l) + Cl$_2$(g) ⟶ ICl$_3$(s)

is called the forward reaction.

The reaction

ICl(l) + Cl$_2$(g) ⟵ ICl$_3$(s)

is called the back reaction.

When forward and back reactions are happening at the same rate, a state of 'balance' is reached.

The effect of adding chlorine

ICl(l) + Cl$_2$(g) ⇌ ICl$_3$(s)

Adding Cl$_2$ makes more ICl$_3$.

The rate of any reaction is increased by increasing the concentration of the reactants. In this reaction, increasing the concentration of chlorine increases the rate of the forward reaction.

The effect of removing chlorine

ICl(l) + Cl$_2$(g) ⇌ ICl$_3$(s)

Removing chlorine makes more ICl.

When the concentration of chlorine is lowered, this decreases the rate of the forward reaction. The back reaction continues at the same rate, however, forming more ICl and Cl$_2$.

Removing chlorine from iodine trichloride

When the U-tube is turned upside-down, dense chlorine fumes pour out. Brown liquid ICl forms again:

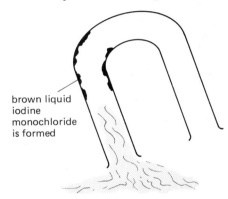

iodine ⟶ iodine + chlorine
trichloride monochloride

ICl$_3$(s) ⟶ ICl(l) + Cl$_2$(g)

Another example of a reversible reaction

When a dilute acid is added to yellow potassium chromate(VI) solution it turns to orange potassium dichromate(VI). Adding alkali reverses the reaction:

potassium chromate(VI) + sulphuric acid ⇌ potassium dichromate(VI) + potassium sulphate + water

$2K_2CrO_4(aq)$ + $H_2SO_4(aq)$ ⇌ $K_2Cr_2O_7(aq)$ + $K_2SO_4(aq)$ + $H_2O(l)$
yellow   orange

$\xrightarrow{\text{adding dilute acid}}$

$\xleftarrow{\text{adding alkali}}$

Adding dilute acid increases the acid concentration. This increases the rate of the forward reaction and makes more orange dichromate(VI).

Adding dilute alkali lowers the sulphuric acid concentration by neutralising it. This decreases the rate of the forward reaction. The back reaction still continues at the same rate removing orange dichromate(VI) and making yellow chromate(VI).

The effect of temperature and pressure

Many reversible reactions are affected by changes of temperature and pressure. In the Haber process for making ammonia, the following reaction occurs:

nitrogen + hydrogen ⇌ ammonia

$N_2(g) + 3H_2(g) \rightleftharpoons 2NH_3(g) \quad \Delta H = -92\,kJ$

The forward reaction is exothermic and, for 1 mole of nitrogen used, it gives out 92 kJ of heat energy. Another way of writing this would be:

$N_2(g) + 3H_2(g) \rightleftharpoons 2NH_3(g) + 92\,kJ$

Ammonia plant in Ontario, Canada. The method used to manufacture ammonia is based on the Haber process.

It is as if heat is a product of the forward reaction. In the back reaction, when 92 kJ of heat energy are added to 2 moles of ammonia, then it splits up into nitrogen and hydrogen.

Adding heat energy to this reaction by increasing the temperature favours the back reaction. Lowering the temperature favours the forward reaction. To get a good yield of ammonia, low temperatures are needed. In practice, the rate of reaction is too slow if the temperature is lowered too much. A compromise has to be reached, and the reaction is carried out between 350 and 500 °C.

For endothermic reactions the effect is the opposite.

Reversible reactions involving gases may also be affected by **pressure**. In the following reaction:

$$\text{hydrogen} + \text{iodine} \rightleftharpoons \text{hydrogen iodide}$$
$$H_2(g) + I_2(g) \rightleftharpoons 2HI(g)$$

There are 2 moles of gas on the left of the equation and 2 moles on the right. There is no change in volume either side of the equation. For this reaction, changing the pressure does not affect the reaction.

In this reaction, again:

$$\underbrace{N_2(g) + 3H_2(g)}_{\text{4 moles}} \rightleftharpoons \underbrace{2NH_3(g)}_{\text{2 moles}}$$

$$\xrightarrow{\text{increased pressure}}$$

In the forward reaction, 4 moles of gases shrink to 2 moles.
In the back reaction 2 moles of gas expands to 4 moles.

Increasing the pressure helps the forward reaction and opposes the back reaction. Increased pressure makes more ammonia.

Dynamic equilibrium

When reactions are reversible, a dynamic equilibrium is set up.
 The word **dynamic** means 'moving'. Two processes are going on at the same time – the forward and the back reactions.
 Equilibrium means 'a state of balance'. The concentration of all the substances stay the same at equilibrium. This is because forward and back reactions are happening at the same rate.

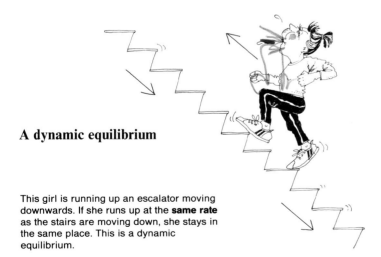

A dynamic equilibrium

This girl is running up an escalator moving downwards. If she runs up at the **same rate** as the stairs are moving down, she stays in the same place. This is a dynamic equilibrium.

Summary

1 When a reaction can go both ways, it is **reversible**.

2 In the following reaction:

$$A + B \rightleftharpoons C + D$$

- The rate of the **forward reaction** can be increased by
  adding more A and/or B
  removing C and/or D

- the rate of the **back reaction** can be increased by
  adding more C and/or D
  removing A and/or B

3 **Temperature** can affect endothermic or exothermic reactions.

- In exothermic reactions:

$$A + B \rightleftharpoons C + D \quad \Delta H = -x\,kJ$$

  increased temperature makes more A and B.
  decreased temperature makes more C and D.

- In endothermic reactions:

$$A + B \rightleftharpoons C + D \quad \Delta H = +x\,kJ$$

  increased temperature makes more C and D.
  decreased temperature makes more A and B.

4 **Pressure** can affect reactions involving gases, when there is a change in volume either side of the equation, e.g:

$$\underbrace{2A(g) + B(g)}_{3 \text{ moles}} \rightleftharpoons \underbrace{C(g)}_{1 \text{ mole}}$$

$$\xrightarrow{\text{increased pressure}}$$

In this reaction, increasing the pressure favours the forward reaction.

5 In a dynamic equilibrium:

- **dynamic** means moving. Two reactions are going on at the same time – the forward and back reactions.

- **equilibrium** means 'a state of balance'. The concentrations of products and reactants stay constant, because the forward and back reactions are happening at the same rate.

Questions

1 ■ When bismuth(III) chloride is added to water, a reaction occurs and a white precipitate forms:
$$BiCl_3(aq) + H_2O(l) \rightleftharpoons BiOCl(s) + 2HCl(aq)$$
(a) Explain the meaning of the sign $\rightleftharpoons$.
(b) Suggest one way by which the amount of the white precipitate in the equilibrium mixture could be decreased.
(c) Why does the method you have suggested decrease the amount of precipitate?
(d) What would be the effect on the amount of precipitate if sodium hydroxide solution is added to the equilibrium mixture? Explain your answer. (NEA) **U**

2 ▶ In the Haber process to make ammonia the following reaction takes place:
$$N_2(g) + 3H_2(g) \rightleftharpoons 2NH_3(g) \quad \Delta H = -92 \text{ kJ mol}^{-1}$$
The following graph shows how the conditions under which the reaction is carried out affect the yield of ammonia produced.

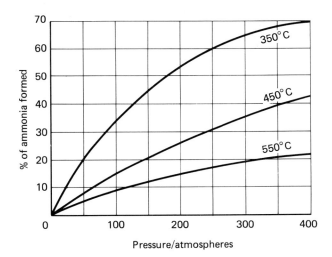

(a) How is the yield of amonia affected by an increase in:
  (i) temperature, (ii) pressure?
(b) Use the graph to predict the percentage yield of ammonia at 500 °C and 250 atmospheres.
(c) A catalyst of finely divided iron is used in this process.
  (i) What is a catalyst?
  (ii) Why is the iron finely divided? **H**

3 ▶ Sodium carbonate (Na_2CO_3) is manufactured on a large scale by heating sodium hydrogencarbonate ($NaHCO_3$). Carbon dioxide and water are also formed.
(a) Write an equation for this reaction.
(b) Hydrogencarbonate ions react with water to form the following equilibrium:
$$HCO_3^-(aq) + H_2O(l) \rightleftharpoons CO_3^{2-}(aq) + H_3O^+(aq)$$
Copy out this equation, and write under each of the four species: 'A' for any acid and 'B' for any base.
(c) What is the effect on the reaction shown in (b) of adding a dilute acid? **U**

4 ▶ Ammonia gas can be prepared by heating a mixture of ammonium chloride and calcium hydroxide using the following apparatus:

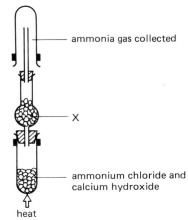

(a) What substance would you use at X to dry the ammonia?
(b) Ammonia reacts with water as it dissolves in it. Write out and complete the following equation for this reaction:
$$NH_3(g) + H_2O(l) \rightleftharpoons$$
Under each species, write 'A' for any acid and 'B' for any base present.
(c) Ammonia neutralises dilute sulphuric acid as follows:
$$2NH_3(g) + H_2SO_4(aq) \rightarrow (NH_4)_2SO_4(aq)$$
Calculate the exact volume of ammonia gas (measured at room temperature and pressure) needed to neutralise 25 cm³ 0.1 M sulphuric acid.
(1 mole of a gas occupies 24 000 cm³ at room temperature and pressure) **H**

27 Sulphur and Sulphuric Acid

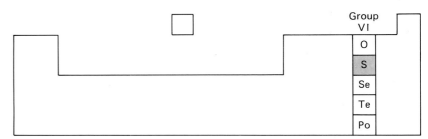

Sulphur is usually found in areas where the earth's crust is quite thin, like Rotorua in New Zealand.

Sulphur is a non-metal found in Group VI of the periodic table. Large amounts of sulphur are found in certain volcanic regions of the world. Areas where there is volcanic activity often have some very unpleasant smells, due to some of the gases formed. Sulphur dioxide, formed when sulphur burns, has a sharp choking smell, and hydrogen sulphide smells of bad eggs.

Allotropes of sulphur

Sulphur is a molecular solid. The forces between sulphur molecules are quite weak, so sulphur has the fairly low melting point of 119°C.

A sulphur molecule

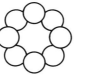 

A sulphur molecule contains eight atoms joined together in a ring.

Written S_8 ← This means each sulphur molecule contains eight sulphur atoms joined together.

Sulphur can exist as two physical forms or **allotropes**. The molecules in each allotrope are packed together differently. This causes each form to have different crystals shapes. The name of each allotrope comes from the shape of the crystal it forms. The two forms are called **rhombic** sulphur and **monoclinic** sulphur.

Making rhombic sulphur	Making monoclinic sulphur
This can only be made at temperatures below 96 °C.	This can only be made at temperatures between 96 °C and 119 °C.
1. Dissolve sulphur in a solvent like xylene to make a saturated solution. (Sulphur does not dissolve in water.)	1. Sulphur is gently heated until it just melts.
2. Excess sulphur is filtered off.	2. Liquid sulphur is poured into a filter paper cone and allowed to cool.
3. Solution is left to evaporate.	3. Cone-shaped piece of sulphur is broken open when it has just solidified.
Diamond shaped crystals of rhombic sulphur (or α-sulphur) are left.	Needle-shaped crystals of monoclinic sulphur (or β-sulphur) are left.
Rhombic sulphur is only stable below 96 °C.	Monoclinic sulphur is only stable between 96 °C and 119 °C.
Density 2.07 g cm^{-3}	Density 1.96 g cm^{-3}

The allotropes of sulphur have different densities. This is because the S_8 molecules are packed together more tightly in rhombic sulphur than in monoclinic.

Heating liquid sulphur

Sulphur goes through some unusual changes as it is being heated:

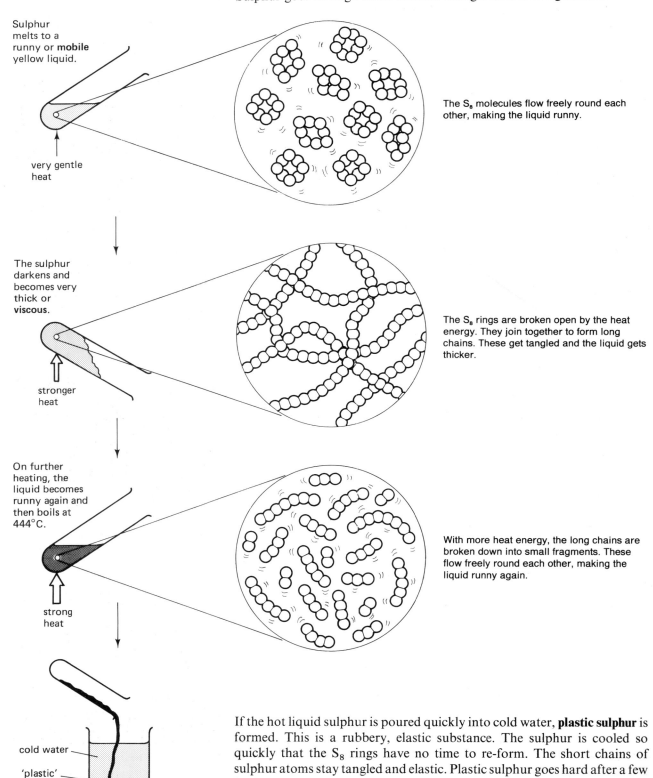

Sulphur melts to a runny or **mobile** yellow liquid.

very gentle heat

The S_8 molecules flow freely round each other, making the liquid runny.

The sulphur darkens and becomes very thick or **viscous**.

stronger heat

The S_8 rings are broken open by the heat energy. They join together to form long chains. These get tangled and the liquid gets thicker.

On further heating, the liquid becomes runny again and then boils at 444°C.

strong heat

With more heat energy, the long chains are broken down into small fragments. These flow freely round each other, making the liquid runny again.

cold water
'plastic' sulphur

If the hot liquid sulphur is poured quickly into cold water, **plastic sulphur** is formed. This is a rubbery, elastic substance. The sulphur is cooled so quickly that the S_8 rings have no time to re-form. The short chains of sulphur atoms stay tangled and elastic. Plastic sulphur goes hard after a few hours, as S_8 rings slowly re-form.

Burning sulphur

The two sulphur allotropes have different physical properties, but they both react chemically in the same way. Both forms of sulphur, for example, burn easily in air:

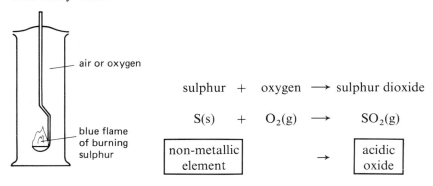

This tree has been damaged by acid rain. Many of the fossil fuels like coal and oil contain sulphur as an impurity. When the fuel burns, sulphur dioxide is released into the atmosphere. This is water soluble and makes rainwater quite acidic.

It is thought that Europe's acid rain is largely caused by sulphur dioxide from industrial areas in Britain and Germany.

When sulphur dioxide dissolves in water, it produces an acid solution of pH 1.

Making sulphuric acid

Millions of tonnes of sulphuric acid are made every year, all over the world. It is made by the **Contact process**. This has the following stages:

1 Sulphur is burned in air to make sulphur dioxide:

$S(s) + O_2(g) \rightarrow SO_2(g)$

2 Sulphur dioxide and more air are reacted together. They are passed through a catalyst of vanadium(V) oxide. (V_2O_5). This increases the rate of reaction:

$2SO_2(g) + O_2(g) \underset{}{\overset{450°C}{\rightleftharpoons}} 2SO_3(g)$

sulphur   oxygen   sulphur
dioxide   from air   trioxide

The amount of sulphur trioxide can be increased by using an excess of air, which increases the rate of the forward reaction.

3 The sulphur trioxide is dissolved into 98% sulphuric acid, together with a controlled amount of water. These react together to make sulphuric acid:

sulphur trioxide + water → sulphuric acid

$SO_3(g) + H_2O(l) \rightarrow H_2SO_4(l)$

Since all three of these reactions are exothermic, the whole process produces heat energy. This can be used to make electricity or for other nearby factories. The fact that energy is produced rather than needed means that sulphuric acid can be produced very cheaply. It is very useful in making fertilisers, plastics, paints and detergents.

Sulphur dioxide is added to many foodstuffs to preserve them.

Plant for producing sulphuric acid by the Contact process.

Sulphuric acid in the laboratory

Concentrated sulphuric acid is a dense, very dangerous liquid. It has a strong 'liking' or affinity for water. It removes the water from skin and flesh, leaving only charcoal behind!

Sulphuric acid can also be used to dry gases, as it absorbs any water vapour they contain. It cannot be used to dry alkaline gases such as ammonia, as it reacts to form salts.

Drying gases with concentrated sulphuric acid

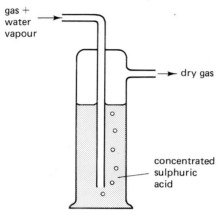

Dilute sulphuric acid is a useful laboratory acid. It reacts with many metals, bases and carbonates, e.g:

sulphuric acid + magnesium → magnesium sulphate + hydrogen

$H_2SO_4(aq) + Mg(s) \rightarrow MgSO_4(aq) + H_2(g)$

sulphuric acid + copper(II) oxide → copper(II) sulphate + water

$H_2SO_4(aq) + CuO(s) \rightarrow CuSO_4(aq) + H_2O(l)$

In each reaction a salt called a sulphate is produced (see Chapter 14).

Summary

1. **Sulphur** is a non-metal in Group VI of the periodic table. It occurs naturally.

2. Sulphur forms two **allotropes**.
   - **Rhombic** (α) sulphur is formed as diamond-shaped crystals below 96 °C.
   - **Monoclinic** (β) sulphur forms needle-shaped crystals between 96 °C and 119 °C.

3. **Solid sulphur** exists as **molecules** of eight sulphur atoms in a ring. This is written S_8.

4. When **liquid sulphur** is heated it undergoes several changes, as the S_8 rings are broken down.

5. **Plastic sulphur** is formed when hot liquid sulphur is suddenly cooled in cold water.

6. Sulphur **burns in air** to produce the acid gas sulphur dioxide. This causes acid rain.

7. Sulphuric acid is made from sulphur by the **Contact process:**
   (a) $S(s) + O_2(g) \rightarrow SO_2(g)$
   (b) $2SO_2(g) + O_2(g) \underset{}{\overset{V_2O_5/450°C}{\rightleftharpoons}} 2SO_3(g)$
   (c) $SO_3(g) + H_2O(l) \rightarrow H_2SO_4(l)$

8. - **Concentrated** acid has a strong affinity for water.
   - **Dilute** sulphuric acid reacts with metals, bases and carbonates to make salts called **sulphates**.

Questions

1 ● When sulphur is heated in a test tube, the *yellow crystals* melt to form a *golden-yellow mobile liquid* which changes at 180 °C into a *dark brown, very viscous liquid*. More heating to about 400 °C produces a *brown, less viscous liquid*.
(a) What will happen if sulphur is heated in air?
(b) What is the molecular structure of sulphur in the yellow crystals?
(c) If the brown liquid at 400 °C is cooled rapidly to room temperature, which form of sulphur is produced?
(d) Explain why the molten sulphur becomes viscous.
(NEA) **R**

2 ● The pie charts below show the uses of sulphuric acid and sodium hydroxide in industry.

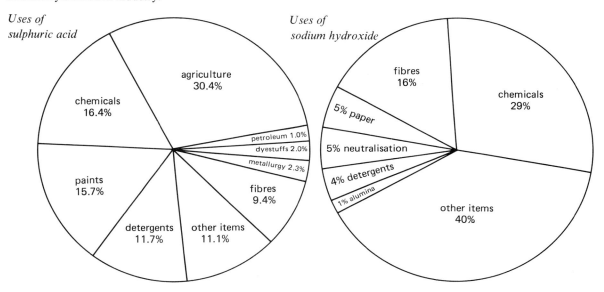

(a) What are the largest uses of (i) sulphuric acid, and (ii) sodium hydroxide, other than 'other items'?
(b) Which substance, sulphuric acid or sodium hydroxide, has the larger percentage of its output used in the making of detergents?
(c) Which uses of (i) sulphuric acid, and (ii) sodium hydroxide take 1% of each chemical?
(d) Give one of the uses of sulphuric acid which requires more than 5% of sulphuric acid production but is not a use of sodium hydroxide. (SEB) **H**

3 ■ Sulphuric acid is made on a large scale by the Contact process, in which sulphur dioxide and oxygen from the air react to make sulphur trioxide:
$$2SO_2(g) + O_2(g) \rightleftharpoons 2SO_3(g) \quad \Delta H = -94 \, kJ$$
The sulphur trioxide is then converted into sulphuric acid.
(a) Suggest one way of making sulphur dioxide.
(b) What does the sign '$\rightleftharpoons$' mean in the equation?
(c) What does '$\Delta H = -94 \, kJ$' mean in the equation?
(d) the reaction shown is carried out in the presence of a catalyst of vanadium(v) oxide. What does a catalyst do?
(e) Give one use for sulphuric acid.
(f) Sulphur dioxide in the air can cause 'acid rain'. Name one process that releases sulphur dioxide into the air.
R

28 Ammonia, Fertilisers and Food

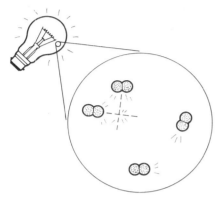

Molecules of nitrogen gas, N_2.

Nitrogen gas is used inside light bulbs. This is because it is very inert and does not react with the white-hot metal filament.

Every day, you breathe in and out many thousands of litres of nitrogen gas. 78% of the air is nitrogen. It is a gas that is very unreactive or inert.

Nitrogen gas is used inside light bulbs. This is because it is very inert and does not react with the white hot metal filament.

Nitrogen is an essential element for plants and animals. It is an important part of the **proteins** that are found in all living things. Although there is so much nitrogen gas in the air, plants and animals cannot absorb it directly. The nitrogen has to be changed into water-soluble compounds, like nitrates. This is called 'fixing' nitrogen. Plants usually take in nitrogen through their roots, in the form of nitrates dissolved in water. Some nitrates exist naturally in the soil, but if crops are continuously harvested from the same place, the soil becomes less fertile. The nitrogen compounds need to be replaced. This happens at a slow rate. Farmers often add synthetic fertilisers containing nitrogen compounds, to speed up the process.

Replacing nitrogen compounds in the soil

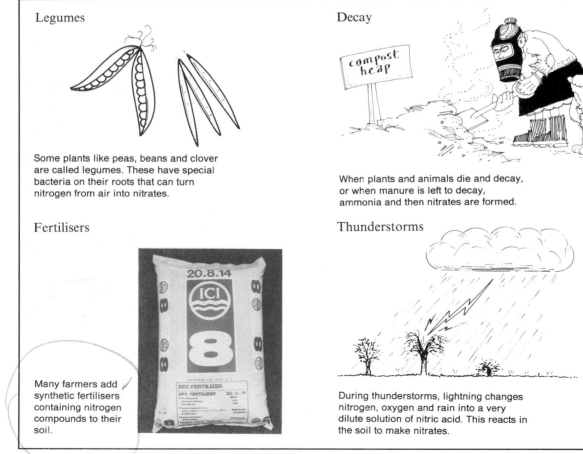

Legumes

Some plants like peas, beans and clover are called legumes. These have special bacteria on their roots that can turn nitrogen from air into nitrates.

Fertilisers

Many farmers add synthetic fertilisers containing nitrogen compounds to their soil.

Decay

When plants and animals die and decay, or when manure is left to decay, ammonia and then nitrates are formed.

Thunderstorms

During thunderstorms, lightning changes nitrogen, oxygen and rain into a very dilute solution of nitric acid. This reacts in the soil to make nitrates.

The way that nitrogen and its compounds are added to the soil and removed from it is summed up in the nitrogen cycle.

The nitrogen cycle

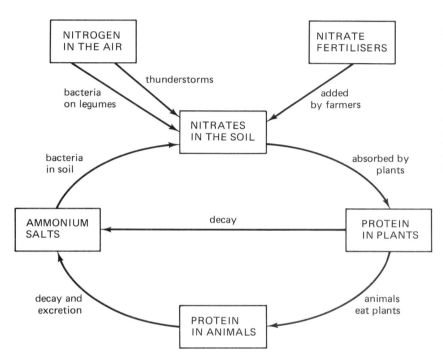

Compound fertilisers

Plants need many elements for healthy growth.
Nitrogen produces growth in green leaves and shoots. **Phosphorus** compounds produce healthy root systems. **Potassium** compounds help produce fruit. Fertilisers containing all three of these elements (and sometimes other elements too) are called compound fertilisers. The labels on such fertilisers often show the amount of 'NPK' which are the symbols of the elements nitrogen, phosphorus and potassium.

Nitrogen from the air is made into ammonia, NH_3, on a very large scale in the Haber process. The ammonia is then used to make fertilisers.

The Haber process

In the Haber process, nitrogen and hydrogen gases are reacted together to make ammonia. Nitrogen is obtained from the air and hydrogen from steam and methane.

The nitrogen and hydrogen in the right proportions are heated together under pressure and passed over an iron catalyst.

nitrogen + hydrogen $\rightleftharpoons$ ammonia

$N_2(g) + 3H_2(g) \rightleftharpoons 2NH_3(g)$

The equation shows that each nitrogen molecule reacts with three hydrogen molecules to make two molecules of ammonia. The high pressures of between 80 and 200 atmospheres help the nitrogen and hydrogen combine in this way. Keeping the pressure high is very expensive and as better catalysts are made, the pressure can be lowered.

The temperature is kept between 350 °C and 500 °C. A higher temperature would increase the rate of reaction and produce ammonia faster. Too high a temperature makes the ammonia break down into nitrogen and hydrogen again.

Fritz Haber (1868–1934) invented the process used all over the world to make ammonia from nitrogen and hydrogen. He was awarded a Nobel Prize in 1918 for his work. He also devised and manufactured poison gases for World War I, such as chlorine, phosgene and mustard gas. He described the use of such gases as 'a higher form of killing'.

Making ammonia in the laboratory

Ammonia gas is made by heating an ammonium salt with an alkali. Water vapour is removed by passing the gas formed through lumps of calcium oxide. Since ammonia is lighter than air, it can be collected in an upturned jar.

Making ammonia in the laboratory

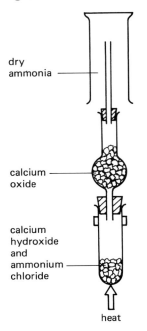

calcium + ammonium → calcium + **ammonia** + water
hydroxide   chloride   chloride

$Ca(OH)_2(s) + 2NH_4Cl(s) \rightarrow CaCl_2(s) + \mathbf{2NH_3(g)} + 2H_2O(g)$

Properties of ammonia

Physical properties
Ammonia is a colourless gas, that is less dense than air. It has a powerful smell and is very soluble in water.

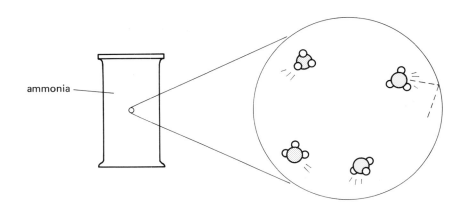

Chemical properties
Reaction with water (fountain experiment)

Ammonia is very soluble in water. About 1200 cm³ of ammonia will dissolve into each 1 cm³ water. Because of this, water is sucked up into a flask of ammonia in the 'fountain' experiment.

ammonia + water ⟶ ammonia
 gas   solution

$NH_3(g) + aq \rightarrow NH_3(aq)$

Ammonia is a stable gas

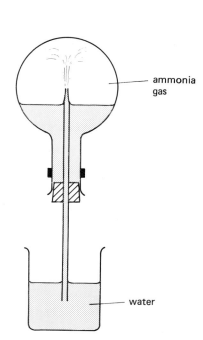

pH:

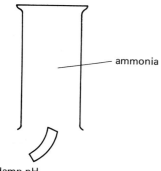

Ammonia dissolves into water to give an alkaline solution of pH 9–10.

Some of the ammonia molecules in solution react with the water to form ions:

ammonia + water ⇌ ammonium ions + hydroxide ions

$NH_3(aq) + H_2O(l) \rightleftharpoons NH_4^+(aq) + OH^-(aq)$

↑ these ions make the solution alkaline

Neutralisation:

Since ammonia is an alkali, it will **neutralise** acids to make ammonium salts, e.g:

ammonia + sulphuric acid → ammonium sulphate

$2NH_3(g) + H_2SO_4(aq) \rightarrow (NH_4)_2SO_4(aq)$

ammonia + hydrogen chloride → ammonium chloride

$NH_3(g) + HCl(g) \rightarrow NH_4Cl(s)$

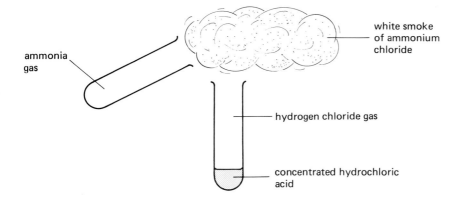

This neutralisation reaction is used as a test for ammonia.

Nitric acid

Nitric acid is made from ammonia as follows.

1. A mixture of ammonia and air are heated to about 850 °C and passed through a catalyst gauze made of platinum and rhodium – two transition metals:

ammonia + oxygen ⇌ nitrogen + water
          (from air) monoxide

$4NH_3(g) + 5O_2(g) \rightleftharpoons 4NO(g) + 6H_2O(g)$

Nitrate fertiliser being spread on grassland:

Nitric acid and ammonia neutralise each other to make ammonium nitrate:

ammonia + nitric → ammonium
solution   acid   nitrate

$NH_3(aq) + HNO_3(aq) \rightarrow NH_4NO_3(aq)$

About 3 million tonnes of ammonium nitrate fertilisers are used in the world every year.

2. The nitrogen monoxide is reacted with air to give nitrogen dioxide:

nitrogen + oxygen → nitrogen
monoxide (from air) dioxide

$2NO(g) + O_2(g) \rightarrow 2NO_2(g)$

3. Nitrogen dioxide and air are dissolved into water to make nitric acid:

nitrogen + water + oxygen → nitric acid
dioxide   (from air)

$4NO_2(g) + 2H_2O(l) + O_2(g) \rightarrow 4HNO_3(aq)$

In the laboratory, dilute nitric acid is very useful. It shows most of the properties of an acid, e.g. it forms an acidic solution in water and reacts with bases and carbonates to make salts called **nitrates**, e.g:

nitric acid + copper(II) oxide → copper(II) nitrate + water

$2HNO_3(aq) + CuO(s) \rightarrow Cu(NO_3)_2(aq) + H_2O(l)$

Acid + Base → Salt + Water

Most acids react with metals to give a salt and hydrogen Nitric acid is unusual in that it reacts with most metals to give nitrogen oxides instead of hydrogen:

copper + dilute nitric → copper(II) nitrate + water + nitrogen
            acid   monoxide

$3Cu(s) + 8HNO_3(aq) \rightarrow 3Cu(NO_3)_2(aq) + 4H_2O(l) + 2NO(g)$

Copper nitrate is what policemen get paid for working overtime in the evenings. (from Professor Brainstorm's Dictionary).

Fertilisers, food and pesticides

The population of the world is increasing at an alarming rate. Every minute 240 children are born into the world, all of whom need feeding. Yet in some poor countries where the population is increasing the fastest, many people die of hunger, especially young children, the sick and the old.

Chemists can help a great deal in increasing crop yields, although the problem is not simply one of growing more food. Often food is available in a country, but people who are poor cannot afford to buy it.

By using improved varieties of seeds and better irrigation, crop yields can be increased. The use of fertilisers also improves crop yields. These are expensive, however, and using too much fertiliser can pollute rivers and drinking water supplies. Pesticides, too, are useful in killing the animals and insects that destroy many crops. The use of pesticides needs to be carefully controlled, as some of them are very poisonous.

Paraquat: a nitrogen-containing weedkiller

The control of weeds is essential for the growth of crops. Paraquat is a very effective and useful weedkiller. It is widely used in agriculture and by home gardeners.

A paraquat molecule

Many Western countries can afford the fertilisers and farming methods to produce more grain than they need. This is stored in large quantities in special buildings.

One disadvantage of paraquat is that it is very poisonous. Small children have died after drinking paraquat that had been stored in orange squash bottles left in garden sheds.

Wealth and food are not equally distributed in the world. Poverty, corruption, and the continued failure of the rains have caused the malnutrition of this Ethiopian mother and child.

To allow more soil nutrients to these fruit trees, a weedkiller containing paraquat is used to kill grass under them.

Summary

1. **Nitrogen** in the air is unreactive and cannot be taken in by plants and animals. All plants and animals need nitrogen for proteins.

2. Nitrogen reaches **the soil** as nitrates through the action of thunderstorms and nitrogen-'fixing' bacteria.

3. Continuous harvesting of crops means that farmers need to add extra nitrogen to the soil, often in the form of **nitrate fertilisers**.

4. Ammonia is made on a large scale by the **Haber process**:

   - nitrogen + hydrogen ⇌ ammonia
     (from air) (from methane)

     $N_2(g) + 3H_2(g) \rightleftharpoons 2NH_3(g)$

   - Conditions: 350–500 °C
     80–200 atmospheres pressure
     iron catalyst

5. Ammonia is made in the **laboratory** by the following reaction:

   $Ca(OH)_2(s) + 2NH_4Cl(s) \rightarrow CaCl_2(s) + 2NH_3(g) + 2H_2O(g)$

6. Ammonia has the following properties:
   - colourless
   - pungent smell
   - very soluble in water, giving an alkaline solution
   - neutralises acids to make ammonium salts, e.g:

   $NH_3(g) + HCl(g) \rightarrow NH_4Cl(s)$

7. Ammonia is used to make **nitric acid** in the following series of reactions:

   $4NH_3(g) + 5O_2(g) \xrightleftharpoons[\text{catalyst; 850°C}]{\text{platinum/rhodium}} 4NO(g) + 6H_2O(g)$

   $2NO(g) + O_2(g) \rightarrow 2NO_2(g)$

   $4NO_2(g) + 2H_2O(l) + O_2(g) \rightarrow 4HNO_3(aq)$

8. **Ammonium nitrate**, made from ammonia and nitric acid, is a very widely used **fertiliser**.

Questions

1. The map right shows an area of land on the edge of a small town surrounded by farm land. Local people have complained that the life in the river is affected by water pollution. The river authority discovered a high level of nitrate in the river at point **X**.

   (a) List **three** possible sources of nitrate pollution in the area shown on the map. For each of them, say how the level of nitrate pollution would be expected to vary with the seasons of the year, and explain why the variation occurs.

   (b) What effects might be caused in the river by nitrate pollution and how would they affect plant and animal life in the water?

   (c) Write a plan for an investigation that could be done to find what the source of the nitrate pollution was (you do not need to describe any chemical tests for nitrates).

   (MEG) **H**

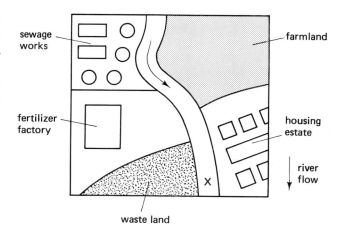

28 Ammonia, Fertilisers and Food 249

2 ● Some man-made chemicals, when added to the soil, help produce greater yields of crops.
 (a) What name is given to such chemicals?
 (b) Ammonia is used to make many of these chemicals. Which two elements are present in ammonia?
 (c) What is the formula of ammonia?
 (d) Ammonia can neutralise nitric acid as follows:

   ammonia + nitric acid ⟶ ammonium nitrate

   Ammonium nitrate is widely used to help crops grow. State one advantage and one disadvantage of using ammonium nitrate.
 (e) Pesticides are chemicals used to kill animals and insects that destroy crops. State one advantage and one disadvantage of using pesticides. **R**

3 ■ The following diagram shows part of the nitrogen cycle:

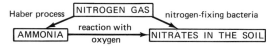

 (a) What is the formula of: (i) nitrogen, (ii) ammonia?
 (b) Where is the nitrogen obtained that is used in the Haber process?
 (c) Ammonium nitrate (NH_4NO_3) is widely used as a fertiliser. Calculate the percentage of nitrogen in this compound.
  (H = 1   N = 14   O = 16)
 (d) Why are nitrogen-containing fertilisers added to land that is used to grow crops?
 (e) In agricultural areas where nitrogen fertilisers are widely used, the fertilisers can get washed into rivers. What sort of problems can this cause? **R**

4 ■ (a) Nitrogen is an element essential for the development of plants and animals. The percentage of nitrogen in the atmosphere remains constant by the operation of the nitrogen cycle in nature.
  (i) Name the type of compound containing nitrogen which is present in all plants and animals.
  (ii) Most plants take in nitrogen in a combined form. State the atmospheric conditions necessary for nitrogen from the air to be converted directly to nitrogen compounds.
  (iii) Some plants are able to use nitrogen directly from the atmosphere. Give **one** example of such a plant.
  (iv) Describe two natural processes by which nitrogen in plants is eventually returned to the soil.
 (b) Ammonia is prepared in the laboratory by the action of heat on a mixture of an ammonium compound and an alkali. The dry gas is collected by upward delivery.
  (i) Name a suitable ammonium compound.
  (ii) Name a suitable alkali.
  (iii) Name **two** other products of the reaction.
  (iv) Write a symbol equation for the reaction.
  (v) Which one of the following is used to dry ammonia?
   A calcium carbonate   B anhydrous calcium chloride
   C calcium oxide   D anhydrous copper(II) sulphate
   E concentrated sulphuric acid
  (iv) State two properties of ammonia which determine the method of collection.
  (vii) Explain why dry ammonia has no effect on dry indicator paper but a solution of ammonia has a pH value greater than 7.
 (c) When concentrated nitric acid is added to a solution containing iron(II) ions, Fe^{2+}, a brown gas **X** is given off and a solution containing iron(III) ions, Fe^{3+}, is formed.
  (i) State, giving a reason for your answer, the type of reaction taking place when iron(II) ions are converted to iron(III) ions.
  (ii) Write an ion-electron equation for the conversion of iron(II) ions to iron(III) ions.
  (iii) Give the name or formula of gas **X**.   (NEA) **R**

5 ■(a) (i) Write a word equation and a symbol equation for the laboratory preparation of ammonia from an ammonium salt and an alkali.
  (ii) Name a chemical which is used to dry ammonia in this preparation.
  (iii) Give **two** large-scale uses of ammonia.
 (b) (i) Give the formulae of the ions present in an aqueous solution of ammonia.
  (ii) How would you show that only a small proportion of the dissolved ammonia has reacted with the water to form ions?
  (iii) Aqueous ammonia is added to a solution of zinc chloride. A white precipitate and a colourless solution are formed. Name these products.
   (NEA) **R**

6 ■ Describe how ammonia is manufactured by the Haber process. Describe how temperature, pressure and the use of a catalyst help make the process economical.   **R**

7 ■ Plants need compounds containing nitrogen in order to grow healthily. These compounds are absorbed through the plant roots from soil water. They enter the soil both by natural processes and by the intervention of people. This century it has become possible to manufacture ammonia on a large scale by the Haber process. The ammonia produced is used to make compounds which are used as fertilizers.
 (a) Why can nitrogen gas in the air in soil **not** be used by most plants?
 (b) Name one natural process which produces nitrogen compounds that can enter the soil in a form that can be used by plants?
 (c) Explain why natural sources of nitrogen compounds are not sufficient for modern agriculture.
 (d) Copy out and complete the table to show what natural raw materials are used as a source of the reacting chemicals used in the production of ammonia in the Haber process.

Reacting substances	Natural source (raw material)
Hydrogen	
Nitrogen	

 (e) In the Haber process, the nitrogen and hydrogen are reacted at 400 °C. Why do you think the reaction is carried out at high temperature instead of ordinary temperature?
 (f) Ammonia is usually converted into a solid chemical such as ammonium nitrate for use as a fertilizer. Write the word equation for the reaction which is used to make ammonium nitrate from ammonia.
 (g) The formula of ammonium nitrate is NH_4NO_3. The relative atomic masses of the elements present are:
  N = 14   H = 1   O = 16.
  Calculate the % by mass of nitrogen in ammonium nitrate.   (MEG) **U**

29 Radioactivity

Marie Curie (1867–1934) was the first person to win two Nobel prizes. They were for her work in discovering many of the first known radioactive elements. Some of the harmful effects of radioactivity were not then known about, and she may have died from these.

Radioactivity is all around us. Our bodies give off radiation, and so do the walls of our houses and our television screens. Many rocks, especially granite, contain radioactive materials, and so does the air we breathe. People have always lived with these small amounts of radioactivity inside and all around them. Yet the existence of radioactivity has only been known for the last 100 years.

What is radioactivity?

When a small child builds up a pile of bricks, the pile will grow until it becomes unstable. It easily falls down then, and becomes stable again:

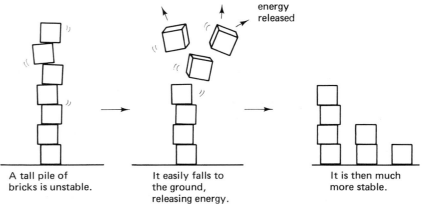

Some atoms behave in exactly the same way. The nucleus of some atoms is very unstable. The atom very easily gives out particles from the nucleus, sometimes with the release of energy. Eventually a smaller and more stable nucleus is formed:

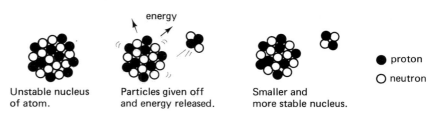

This release of particles and energy from an atom is called **radiation**. Elements that break down in this way are said to be **radioactive**. Elements 83–105 are all radioactive. The nucleus of these atoms is so large that it is unstable and breaks down. Some smaller atoms can also be radioactive when they have an unstable nucleus.

Atomic structure

The two main parts of the atom are the inner nucleus and the outer electrons. The chemical properties of an element are caused by the way its **electrons** are arranged. Radioactivity comes from the **nucleus**.

A carbon atom

× electrons
● protons
○ neutrons

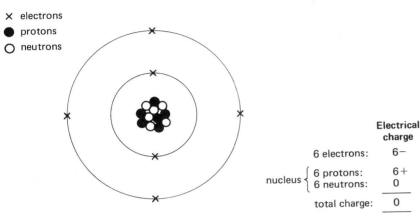

	Electrical charge
6 electrons:	6−
nucleus { 6 protons:	6+
6 neutrons:	0
total charge:	0

This nucleus is not drawn to scale — it is much smaller than this.

The carbon atom in this example has an **atomic number** of 6. The atomic number is the number of protons in the nucleus. Elements in the periodic table are arranged in order of their atomic numbers. It is the number of protons that decides which element is present. Any atom with 6 protons in the nucleus is carbon. If there were 7 protons the element would be nitrogen – element number 7. If there were 5 protons, it would be boron – element number 5.

If someone could find a cheap way to knock 3 protons out of a lead atom (element number 82) they would be able to make gold (element number 79)!

Electrons weigh very little compared to protons and neutrons. The mass of an atom is concentrated in the nucleus. The carbon atom in the example has a mass number of 12. The mass number is the number of protons and neutrons in the nucleus of an atom. This carbon atom can be written as follows:

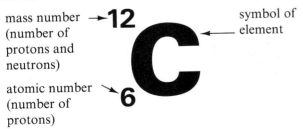

mass number (number of protons and neutrons) → 12
symbol of element
atomic number (number of protons) → 6

This is the most common form of carbon atom, and it is sometimes called 'carbon-12'. Relative atomic masses are measured on the **carbon-12 scale**. The masses of all other atoms are compared with the mass of a carbon-12 atom. Carbon-12 atoms are not radioactive.

Another form of carbon atom called carbon-14 is radioactive.

A carbon-14 atom

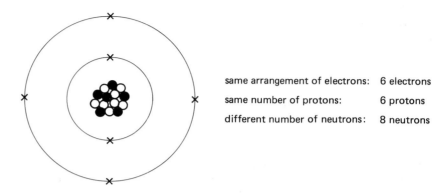

same arrangement of electrons: 6 electrons
same number of protons: 6 protons
different number of neutrons: 8 neutrons

This atom is still carbon as it has 6 protons in the nucleus. The difference is in the two extra neutrons. These make the atom heavier than carbon-12. The different forms of carbon atom are called **isotopes**. Isotopes of elements contain the same number of protons, but different numbers of neutrons. They have the same atomic number but different mass numbers. Many radioactive atoms have much larger numbers of protons and neutrons than this.

Isotopes of uranium

isotope	$^{233}_{92}U$	$^{234}_{92}U$	$^{235}_{92}U$	$^{238}_{92}U$
number of protons	92	92	92	92
number of neutrons	141	142	143	146

Note: The number of neutrons in an isotope can be found by subtracting the atomic number from the mass number.

Radioactive decay

There are two main ways in which radioactive atoms can break down. These are called alpha (α) decay and beta (β) decay.

Alpha (α) decay

An alpha (α) particle
mass number = 4
(2 protons and 2 neutrons)

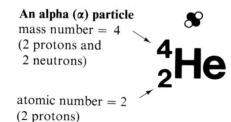

atomic number = 2
(2 protons)

When an atom breaks down by alpha decay, it gives off an alpha particle. This contains two protons and two neutrons. Since element number 2, helium, contains two protons, an alpha particle has the symbol $^{4}_{2}He$.

When an atom loses an alpha particle, the nucleus gets smaller and lighter:

an atom of $\rightarrow$ an atom of + an alpha
uranium-238   thorium-234   particle

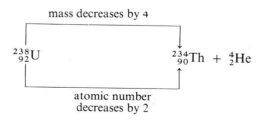

mass decreases by 4

$^{238}_{92}U \quad\quad ^{234}_{90}Th + ^{4}_{2}He$

atomic number decreases by 2

Alpha particles are fairly heavy and can travel through only a few centimetres of air before being stopped.

Beta (β) decay

Atoms that break down by beta decay give off a **beta particle**. A beta particle is an electron.

In beta decay, a neutron in the nucleus turns into a proton and an electron:

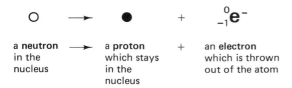

The electron formed is not 'at home' in the nucleus and is expelled from the atom as a beta particle. The atom remaining has one less neutron and one extra proton, e.g.

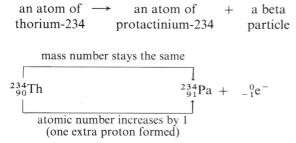

A beta (β) particle
Mass number = 0 (very little mass)

Atomic number is written as −1, to show the charge on the electron.

$_{-1}^{0}e^{-}$ stands for electron

Beta-particles are very light and can travel through several metres of air before being stopped. Some radioactive elements also give off **gamma rays** (γ-rays) when they break down. These high-energy rays can travel several kilometres through the air and are only stopped by thick layers of lead.

This scientist has to handle radioactive substances by remote control, looking through thick layers of protective lead glass.

Measuring radioactive decay: half lives

The level of radioactivity anywhere is measured by a device called a Geiger counter. This is sensitive to radioactivity. The number of 'counts' given off by a radioactive substance, say, every minute, can be measured and plotted on a graph. This is called a decay curve.

Half-life of various isotopes

Name	Symbol	Half-life
carbon-14	$^{14}_{6}C$	5600 years
potassium-40	$^{40}_{19}K$	1300 million years
iodine-131	$^{131}_{53}I$	8 days
uranium-238	$^{238}_{92}U$	4500 million years
plutonium-242	$^{242}_{94}Pu$	400 000 years

A decay curve

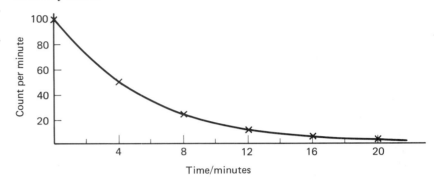

Each isotope decays at its own rate. It cannot be made to decay faster by heating or adding a catalyst. The **half-life** is the time taken for half the number of radioactive particles in a sample to break down. In this time, the count rate will be halved.

From the curve shown in the graph:

count:	100 ⟶ 50	50 ⟶ 25	25 ⟶ 12.5
time taken:	4 mins	4 mins	4 mins

The half-life of this substance is therefore 4 minutes.

Nuclear power stations like this one at Oldbury make electricity from radioactive materials. Nuclear power stations do not pollute the air like coal- and oil-burning power stations. At the end of the process, however, they always leave radioactive nuclear 'waste'. At present it is stored in cooled underground tanks or sealed in containers and dumped at sea. Because of the long half-life of some of the isotopes, they will still be dangerously radioactive after more than a million years.

Radioactivity in everyday life

Some radioactive processes release large amounts of energy. When uranium-235 is bombarded with neutrons, the neutrons split the atom up with the release of a large amount of energy. It also sets off a chain reaction:

1 neutron + a uranium-235 ⟶ a strontium-90 + a xenon-143 + **3** neutrons + energy
　　　　　　　　atom　　　　　　　　atom　　　　　　atom

$^{1}_{0}n$ + $^{235}_{92}U$ ⟶ $^{90}_{38}Sr$ + $^{143}_{54}Xe$ + $3^{1}_{0}n$

Each of the 3 neutrons formed can themselves split another uranium-235 atom.

If this process is not controlled, a nuclear explosion will take place. In a nuclear power station, the same or similar processes occur. The reaction is carefully controlled and the heat energy produced is used to make electricity. The same process can be used to cause terrible destruction or to make useful energy.

Nuclear power stations in the United Kingdom are run to very high safety standards, and release only very small amounts of radioactive materials into the environment. Some people are very concerned about the use of nuclear energy. They feel that radiation released into the environment and the dangers involved in any accident are more important than the supply of cheap electrical energy.

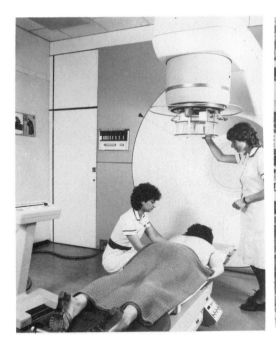

Cancer cells can be destroyed by radiation. This patient is being treated by gamma ray radiation coming from cobalt–60.

In 1986, a failure of machinery and human error at this nuclear power station at Chernobyl in the Soviet Union, led to the release of a dangerous amount of radioactive gas into the air which spread to many European countries.

Summary

1. Radiation comes from the **nucleus** of an atom. Radioactive elements have an unstable nucleus, which breaks down into smaller, more stable particles, with the release of energy.

2. **Isotopes** of elements contain the same number of protons, but different numbers of neutrons, e.g:

    chlorine-35 chlorine-37
    $^{35}_{17}Cl$ $^{37}_{17}Cl$
    17 protons   17 protons
    18 neutrons 20 neutrons

3. **Alpha decay** involves the loss of 2 protons and 2 neutrons from the nucleus, e.g:

    $^{242}_{94}Pu \longrightarrow \,^{238}_{92}U + \,^{4}_{2}He$
    an α-particle

4. **Beta decay** involves the loss of an electron. A neutron in the nucleus turns into a proton which remains and an electron which is expelled, e.g:

    $^{14}_{6}C \longrightarrow \,^{14}_{7}N + \,^{0}_{-1}e$
    a β-particle

5. **Gamma rays** are high-energy rays, given out in radioactive decay.

6. The **half life** of a radioactive isotope is the time taken for the count of a sample to be halved.

7. The **energy** from radioactive decay can be used to make electricity in nuclear power stations, or in the explosion of nuclear weapons.

Questions

1 • Uranium-235 is used in nuclear reactors to produce heat. The heat is removed from the reactor at Dounreay in Scotland using molten sodium.
  (a) Uranium-235 is used in reactors rather than the isotope uranium-238. Copy out and complete the table below.

Isotope	Number of protons	Number of electrons	Number of neutrons	Atomic mass
Uranium-235	92		143	235
Uranium-238		92		

  (b) Give the name used for reactions that produce heat, and the units used to measure the quantity.
  (c) The heat produced in the reactor is carried away by molten sodium. Give TWO advantages that sodium has over water as a coolant. (SEREB) **U**

2 • Radioactive elements can be used to provide energy in nuclear power stations.
  (a) Name a naturally occurring radioactive metal used in power stations.
  (b) State an advantage of making electricity from nuclear fuel.
  (c) State one danger from using radioactive chemicals in power stations. What precaution is taken to avoid this danger?
  (d) Plutonium is a man-made radioactive metal, used in nuclear power stations. As well as being very poisonous, plutonium has a **half-life** of 32 500 years. Why does such a long half-life make plutonium dangerous? **R**

3 ■ Radioactive iodine is used in medicine to find out about and treat disorders of the thyroid gland. The isotope used has a mass number of 131 and an atomic number of 53.
  (a) In an atom of this isotope, state the number of: (i) protons, (ii) neutrons, (iii) electrons.
  (b) A non-radioactive isotope of iodine has a mass number of 127. How is an atom of this isotope different from an atom of iodine-131?
  (c) The following table shows how the radioactive count of a sample of iodine-131 changed over a number of days:

Time/days	0	8	16	24	32	40
Count/day^{-1}	10 000	5000	2500	1250	625	313

  (i) Plot a graph of the count per day (vertical axis) against time (horizontal axis).
  (ii) Use your graph to find the half-life of iodine-131.
  (iii) Why does this value for the half-life make iodine-131 suitable for use on patients in medicine? **H**

4 ■ (a) Copy out and complete the following table.

Particle	Mass number	Atomic number	Number of: protons	neutrons	electrons
Boron atom, B	11		5		
Magnesium ion, Mg^{2+}	24	12			
Oxide ion, O^{2-}	16	8			

  (b) There are two isotopes of hydrogen, ^1H and ^2H. Each of these isotopes forms water when burned in oxygen. Copy out and complete the following table. (Relative atomic mass of oxygen = 16.)

Isotope	Mass number	Number of: protons	neutrons	Relative molecular mass of water formed
^1H	1			
^2H	2			

One of these forms of water is used as a coolant in nuclear power stations. This may result in it becoming radioactive. What problem does this cause?
  (c) Draw a diagram which shows the electron arrangement in a molecule of silicon tetrachloride, $SiCl_4$. Only the outer energy level electrons need be shown for each atom. (NEA) **H**

5 ▶ The element gallium is in Group III of the periodic table and exists as two isotopes $^{69}_{31}Ga$ and $^{71}_{31}Ga$.
  (a) Copy out and complete the following table.

	$^{69}_{31}Ga$	$^{71}_{31}Ga$
Number of protons Number of neutrons Number of electrons		

  (b) State the number of electrons in the outer energy level of a gallium atom.
  (c) Write the formula for an ion of gallium.
  (d) Write the formula for: (i) gallium chloride, (ii) gallium sulphate.
  (e) A sample of gallum contains 60% of atoms of $^{69}_{31}Ga$ and 40% of atoms of $^{71}_{31}Ga$. Which one of the following is the relative atomic mass of this sample of gallium?
  69.2   69.8   70.2   70.8 (NEA) **H**

Answers to Questions involving Calculations

Chapter 4 (p.26)
12 (b) (i) 0.2 mole; (ii) 0.1 mole; (iii) 2.4 litres.
14 (b) 1 g N_2 = 860 cm^3, 1 g Ne = 1200 cm^3. (c) C_3H_8

Chapter 6 (p.43)
5 (a) (i) 16.5 g; (ii) 28.0 g. (b) B = 40°C, B to C = 6.6 g.
9 (b) Expt. 1 = 4.5 g, Expt. 2 = 26.5 g.

Chapter 9 (p.74)
3 (c) (i) 41 cm^3; (ii) 82 cm^3.
6 (b) 0.1 g. (c) (i) 60 cm^3

Chapter 12

Mole Calculations I (p.105)

	(a)	(b)	(c)	(d)	(e)	(f)	(g)	(h)
1	108 g	24 g	120 g	233 g	14 g	0.4 g	0.24 g	1.4 g
2	3 moles	2 moles	3 moles	1.5 moles	0.5 mole	0.25 mole	0.05 mole	0.05 mole
3	44 g	60 g	16 g	36.5 g	58.8 g	102 g	30 g	64 g
4	138 g	98 g	63 g	53.5 g	164 g	80 g	74 g	342 g

Mole Calculations II (p.108)

	(a)	(b)	(c)	(d)	(e)	(f)	(g)	(h)
5	10 g	11.76 g	0.4 g	1.1 g	3.2 g	72 g	12.3 g	5.28 g
6	0.5 mole	0.5 mole	0.025 mole	0.125 mole	0.1 mole	0.05 mole	0.25 mole	0.16 mole

Mole Calculations III (p.110)

	(a)	(b)	(c)	(d)	(e)	(f)	(g)	(h)
7	CO	CaF_2	NF_2	CH_4	$MgSO_4$	(i) CH_2O (ii) $C_2H_4O_2$	C_6H_6	$C_6H_{12}O_6$

Mole Calculations IV (p.113)

	(a)	(b)	(c)	(d)	(e)	(f)	(g)	(h)
8	0.01 mole	0.005 mole	0.025 mole	0.25 mole	0.25 mole	0.001 mole	0.0065 mole	2 moles
9	2400 cm^3	48 dm^3	12 dm^3	600 cm^3	6 dm^3	144 cm^3	108 cm^3	120 dm^3

Mole Calculations V (p.117)

	(a)	(b)	(c)	(d)	(e)	(f)	(g)	(h)
10	0.5 mole	4 moles	0.05 mole	0.02 mole	2 moles	0.0001 mole	0.0001 mole	10 moles
11	2.0 M	0.8 M	0.8 M	0.4 M	0.1 M	2.0 M	0.01 M	0.04 M
12	0.25 M	0.25 M	0.65 M	0.5 M	0.1 M	0.5 M	0.05 M	0.2 M

Chapter 12 (p.121)
1 (a) 18 g. (b) 32 g. (c) 111 g. (d) 64 g. (e) 53.5 g.
2 (a) $PbBr_2$.
3 (a) 0.004 mole. (b) (i) 0.008 mole; (ii) 80 cm^3.
  (c) (i) 0.004 mole; (ii) 0.26 g.
4 (b) (ii) 1 mole; (iii) 0.05 mole; (iv) 0.05 mole; (v) 2.2 g; (vi) 1200 cm^3.

Chapter 13 (p.130)
2 (b) (i) CuO = 0.8 g; Cu = 0.64 g; O = 0.16 g; (ii) 0.01 mole;
  (iii) 0.01 mole; (iv) 80.
3 (a) 1.4 g. (b) 300 cm^3. (c) 100 cm^3. (d) 1.6 g. (e) 50 cm^3.
  (f) 12.5 cm^3. (g) 1.47 g. (h) 750 cm^3.
4 (a) 40 g. (b) 85 g. (c) 21.25 g.
5 (a) H_2SO_4 = 0.025 mole, NaCl = 0.05 mole,
    Na_2SO_4 = 0.025 mole, HCl = 0.05 mole.
  (b) Zn = 0.002 mole, HNO_3 = 0.004 mole,
    H_2 = 0.002 mole
    $Zn(NO_3)_2$ = 0.002 mole.
  (c) Na_2CO_3 = 0.005 mole, HCl = 0.01 mole,
    NaCl = 0.01 mole,
    H_2O = 0.005 mole, CO_2 = 0.005 mole.

(d) Cu = 0.0025 mole, AgNO₃ = 0.005 mole,
Ag = 0.005 mole, Cu(NO₃)₂ = 0.0025 mole.
(e) NH₃ = 0.002 mole, N₂ = 0.001 mole, H₂ = 0.003 mole.
(f) PbO₂ = 0.006 mole, H₂ = 0.012 mole, Pb = 0.006 mole,
H₂O = 0.012 mole
(g) I₂ = 0.002 mole, Cl₂ = 0.002 mole, ICl = 0.004 mole.
(h) NaHCO₃ = 0.01 mole, Na₂CO₃ = 0.005 mole,
H₂O = 0.005 mole, CO₂ = 0.005 mole.
6 (c) 0.0025 mole. (d) 0.005 mole.

Chapter 14 (p.145)
5 (b) 49.2 g.
7 (b) (i) 44; (ii) 106; (iii) 88 g.

Chapter 19 (p.180)
6 (e) 160. (f) 56 tonnes.

Chapter 20 (p.185)
3 (c) 2 moles CuO : 1 mole C, 80 g CuO : 12 g C,
8.0 g CuO : 1.2 g C.

Chapter 23 (p.216)
4 (a) (v) 3250 kJ mol⁻¹; (vi) 6.
5 (e) 105 kJ.
6 (b) (i) 10°C; (ii) 50 cm³. (c) (i) 80 kJ.
7 (d) (i) 11 000 cm³ (or 11 dm³);
(ii) 55 000 cm³ (or 55 dm³). (e) 15.4 g.

Chapter 24 (p.226)
7 (d) (i) 0.8 g; (ii) 300 cm³.

Chapter 26 (p.235)
4 (c) 120 cm³.

Chapter 28 (p.248)
3 (c) 35%.
7 (g) 35%.

Chapter 29 (p.257)
3 (c) (ii) 8 days.
5 (e) 69.8.

Hazard Warning Symbols

Any dangerous chemical has to show the hazards associated with it, and an international system of warning symbols is used. They include the following.

 Harmful

 Flammable

 Corrosive

 Toxic

 Explosive

 Oxidising

 Radioactive

The Periodic Table of the Elements

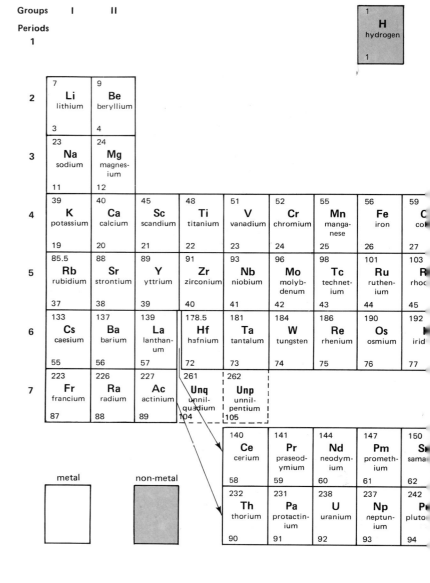

Atomic number	Element	Symbol	Relative atomic mass, A_r
1	hydrogen	H	1
2	helium	He	4
3	lithium	Li	7
4	beryllium	Be	9
5	boron	B	11
6	carbon	C	12
7	nitrogen	N	14
8	oxygen	O	16
9	fluorine	F	19
10	neon	Ne	20
11	sodium	Na	23.3
12	magnesium	Mg	24
13	aluminium	Al	27
14	silicon	Si	28
15	phosphorus	P	31
16	sulphur	S	32
17	chlorine	Cl	35.5
18	argon	Ar	40
19	potassium	K	39
20	calcium	Ca	40
21	scandium	Sc	45
22	titanium	Ti	48
23	vanadium	V	51
24	chromium	Cr	52
25	manganese	Mn	55
26	iron	Fe	56

The elements in order of atomic number

The Periodic Table

	III	IV	V	VI	VII	VIII
						4 **He** helium 2
	11 **B** boron 5	12 **C** carbon 6	14 **N** nitrogen 7	16 **O** oxygen 8	19 **F** fluorine 9	20 **Ne** neon 10
	27 **Al** aluminium 13	28 **Si** silicon 14	31 **P** phosphorus 15	32 **S** sulphur 16	35.5 **Cl** chlorine 17	40 **Ar** argon 18
64 **Cu** copper 29	65 **Zn** zinc 30	70 **Ga** gallium 31	73 **Ge** germanium 32	75 **As** arsenic 33	79 **Se** selenium 34	80 **Br** bromine 35	84 **Kr** krypton 36
108 **Ag** silver 47	112 **Cd** cadmium 48	115 **In** indium 49	119 **Sn** tin 50	122 **Sb** antimony 51	128 **Te** tellurium 52	127 **I** iodine 53	131 **Xe** xenon 54
197 **Au** gold 79	201 **Hg** mercury 80	204 **Tl** thallium 81	207 **Pb** lead 82	209 **Bi** bismuth 83	210 **Po** polonium 84	210 **At** astatine 85	222 **Rn** radon 86

157 **Gd** gadolinium 64	159 **Tb** terbium 65	162.5 **Dy** dysprosium 66	165 **Ho** holmium 67	167 **Er** erbium 68	169 **Tm** thulium 69	173 **Yb** ytterbium 70	175 **Lu** lutetium 71
247 **Cm** curium 96	247 **Bk** berkelium 97	251 **Cf** californium 98	254 **Es** einsteinium 99	253 **Fm** fermium 100	256 **Md** mendelevium 101	254 **No** nobelium 102	257 **Lw** lawrencium 103

Atomic number	Element	Symbol	Relative atomic mass, A_r
27	cobalt	Co	59
28	nickel	Ni	59
29	copper	Cu	64
30	zinc	Zn	65
31	gallium	Ga	70
32	germanium	Ge	73
33	arsenic	As	75
34	selenium	Se	79
35	bromine	Br	80
36	krypton	Kr	84
37	rubidium	Rb	85
38	strontium	Sr	88
39	yttrium	Y	89
40	zirconium	Zr	91
41	niobium	Nb	93
42	molybdenum	Mo	96
43	technetium	Tc	99
44	ruthenium	Ru	101
45	rhodium	Rh	103
46	palladium	Pd	106
47	silver	Ag	108
48	cadmium	Cd	112
49	indium	In	115
50	tin	Sn	119
51	antimony	Sb	122
52	tellurium	Te	128
53	iodine	I	127
54	xenon	Xe	131
55	caesium	Cs	133
56	barium	Ba	137
57	lanthanum	La	139
58	cerium	Ce	140
59	praseodymium	Pr	141
60	neodymium	Nd	144
61	promethium	Pm	147
62	samarium	Sm	150
63	europium	Eu	152
64	gadolinium	Gd	157
65	terbium	Tb	159
66	dysprosium	Dy	163
67	holmium	Ho	165
68	erbium	Er	167
69	thulium	Tm	169
70	ytterbium	Yb	173
71	lutetium	Lu	175
72	hafnium	Hf	178
73	tantalum	Ta	181
74	tungsten	W	184
75	rhenium	Re	186
76	osmium	Os	190
77	iridium	Ir	192
78	platinum	Pt	195
79	gold	Au	197
80	mercury	Hg	201
81	thallium	Tl	204
82	lead	Pb	207
83	bismuth	Bi	209
84	polonium	Po	210
85	astatine	At	210
86	radon	Rn	222
87	francium	Fr	223
88	radium	Ra	226
89	actinium	Ac	227
90	thorium	Th	232
91	protoactinium	Pa	231
92	uranium	U	238
93	neptunium	Np	237
94	plutonium	Pu	242
95	americium	Am	243
96	curium	Cm	247
97	berkelium	Bk	247
98	californium	Cf	251
99	einsteinium	Es	254
100	fermium	Fm	253
101	mendelevium	Md	256
102	nobelium	No	254
103	lawrencium	Lr	257
104	unnilquadium	Unq	261
105	unnilpentium	Unp	263

Properties of the Elements in Alphabetical Order

Element	Symbol	Atomic number	Relative atomic mass, A_r	Melting point /°C	Boiling point /°C	Density /g cm^{-3} (solids & liquids)	Density /g dm^{-3} (gases)
actinium	Ac	89	227	1197	3327	10.1	
aluminium	Al	13	27	659	2447	2.7	
antimony	Sb	51	122	630	1637	6.7	
argon	Ar	18	40	−189	−186		1.66
arsenic	As	33	75	sublimes at 613		5.7	
astatine	At	85	210	—	—	—	
barium	Ba	56	137	710	1637	3.5	
beryllium	Be	4	9	1283	2487	1.9	
bismuth	Bi	83	209	272	1559	9.8	
boron	B	5	11	2027	3927	2.5	
bromine	Br	35	80	−7	58	3.1	
cadmium	Cd	48	112	321	765	8.7	
caesium	Cs	55	133	29	685	1.9	
calcium	Ca	20	40	850	1492	1.6	
carbon (diamond)	C	6	12	3550	4830	3.5	
chlorine	Cl	17	35.5	−101	−34		2.99
chromium	Cr	24	52	1903	2642	7.2	
cobalt	Co	27	59	1495	2877	8.9	
copper	Cu	29	64	1083	2582	8.9	
fluorine	F	9	19	−220	−188		1.58
francium	Fr	87	223	27	677	—	
gallium	Ga	31	70	30	2237	5.9	
germanium	Ge	32	73	937	2827	5.4	
gold	Au	79	197	1063	2707	19.3	
hafnium	Hf	72	178	2222	5227	13.3	
helium	He	2	4	−270	−269		0.17
hydrogen	H	1	1	−259	−253		0.08
indium	In	49	115	156	2047	7.3	
iodine	I	53	127	114	183	4.9	
iridium	Ir	77	192	2454	4127	22.4	
iron	Fe	26	56	1539	2887	7.9	
krypton	Kr	36	84	−157	−153		3.46
lanthanum	La	57	139	920	3367	6.2	
lead	Pb	82	207	328	1751	11.3	
lithium	Li	3	7	181	1331	0.5	
magnesium	Mg	12	24	650	1117	1.74	
manganese	Mn	25	55	1244	2041	7.4	
mercury	Hg	80	201	−39	357	13.5	
molybdenum	Mo	42	96	2617	4827	10.2	

Element	Symbol	Atomic number	Relative atomic mass, A_r	Melting point /°C	Boiling point /°C	Density /g cm^{-3} (solids & liquids)	Density /g dm^{-3} (gases)
neon	Ne	10	20	−248	−246		0.84
nickel	Ni	28	59	1455	2837	8.9	
niobium	Nb	41	93	2497	4927	8.6	
nitrogen	N	7	14	−210	−196		1.17
osmium	Os	76	190	2727	4227	22.6	
oxygen	O	8	16	−219	−183		1.33
palladium	Pd	46	106	1550	3127	12.0	
phosphorus (white)	P	15	31	44	281	1.82	
platinum	Pt	78	195	1770	3827	21.5	
polonium	Po	84	210	254	962	9.3	
potassium	K	19	39	63	766	0.86	
radium	Ra	88	226	700	1527	5.0	
radon	Rn	86	222	−71	−62		8.9
rhenium	Re	75	186	3180	5627	21.0	
rhodium	Rh	45	103	1966	3727	12.4	
rubidium	Rb	37	85	39	701	1.5	
ruthenium	Ru	44	101	2427	3727	12.4	
scandium	Sc	21	45	1400	2477	3.0	
selenium	Sc	34	79	217	685	4.8	
silicon	Si	14	28	1410	2677	2.3	
silver	Ag	47	108	961	2127	10.5	
sodium	Na	11	23.3	98	890	0.97	
strontium	Sr	38	88	770	1367	2.6	
sulphur	S	16	32	119	445	2.1	
tantalum	Ta	73	181	2997	5427	16.6	
technetium	Tc	43	99	2127	4627	11.5	
tellurium	Te	52	128	450	987	6.2	
thallium	Tl	81	204	304	1467	11.8	
tin	Sn	50	119	232	2687	7.3	
titanium	Ti	22	48	1677	3277	4.5	
tungsten	W	74	184	3377	5527	19.3	
vanadium	V	23	51	1917	3377	6.1	
xenon	Xe	54	131	−112	−108		5.5
yttrium	Y	39	89	1500	3227	4.4	
zinc	Zn	30	65	419	908	7.1	
zirconium	Zr	40	91	1852	4377	6.5	

Chemical Words

Some of the chemical words used in this book are explained here.

An **acid** is a compound that reacts with a base to form a salt. Solutions of acids in water have a pH of 1–6.

An **alkali** is a water soluble base. Alkalis neutralise acids and have a pH of 8–14.

Allotropes are different solid physical forms of the same element.

Alpha decay occurs when a radioactive atom loses an alpha particle. An alpha (α) particle is the nucleus of a helium atom. Written ^4_2He.

Anhydrous means 'without water'. Anhydrous salts are those with no water of crystallisation.

Anions are negatively charged ions. In electrolysis, they move to the anode.

An **anode** is a positively charged electrode.

Atoms are the smallest particles that can be obtained by chemical means.

The **atomic number** of an element is the number of protons in the nucleus. Elements in the periodic table are arranged in order of their atomic numbers.

Avogadro's number is the number of particles in one mole of a substance. It is 6.023×10^{23}.

A **base** is a compound that neutralises an acid to make a salt.

Beta decay occurs when a radioactive atom loses a beta (β) particle. A beta particle is an electron. Written $^{\ \ 0}_{-1}e$.

Brownian movement is the random movement of small particles, e.g. smoke, as they are bombarded by the air molecules around them.

A **catalyst** is a substance that changes the rate of a chemical reaction. It is unchanged chemically or in mass at the end of the reaction.

A **cathode** is a negatively charged electrode.

Cations are positively charged ions. In electrolysis they move to the cathode.

A **cell** turns most of the energy from a chemical reaction into an electric current. Batteries are one type of cell.

The **chemical properties** of a substance are the ways in which it reacts chemically with other substances.

A **chemical reaction** is a process that forms one or more new elements or compounds.

Chromatography involves the separation of a mixture of substances. A solution containing a mixture of dyes could be separated by how strongly they are absorbed onto paper compared to how well they dissolve in the solvent used.

Combustion is the chemical name for burning. It happens when a substance reacts very quickly with oxygen.

A **compound** is formed when two or more elements are chemically joined together.

Coulombs measure the amount of electrical charge used in an experiment. Coulombs = amps × seconds.

A **covalent** bond is formed when atoms share a pair of electrons.

Cracking involves breaking down hydrocarbon molecules. One of the products is always unsaturated.

Density is the mass of a given volume of a substance. For solids and liquids the mass of $1 cm^3$ is usually given ($g\, cm^{-3}$) and for gases the mass of one litre ($g\, dm^{-3}$).

Diffusion is the rapid random movement of particles in a liquid or gas.

Displacement is a chemical reaction in which a more reactive substance takes the place of or 'displaces' a less reactive one.

Distillation can be either 'simple' or 'fractional'. **Simple distillation** is a one-step process where a solution is boiled, the solvent turns to a gas and is condensed. **Fractional distillation** involves vaporising and condensing a mixture of liquids a number of times. They are separated out because of their different boiling points.

Dynamic equilibrium happens when two opposite reactions are happening at the same time and at the same rate. It is shown in an equation by the symbol $\rightleftharpoons$.

Electrolysis is the breaking down of a compound containing ions into its elements by use of an electric current.

Electrons are negatively charged particles that surround all atoms. An electric current is a flow of electrons.

Electronic configuration shows the arrangement of electrons in shells around an atom.

An **element** is a substance made from only one sort of atom, that cannot be broken down into simpler particles by chemical means.

Empirical formula is the simplest ratio of atoms in a compound.

Endothermic reactions take in heat energy. There is a fall in temperature and ΔH is $+x\, kJ$.

Enzymes are biological catalysts.

Equations show in either words or symbols the reactants and products of a chemical reaction.

Exothermic reactions give out heat energy. There is a temperature rise and ΔH is $-x\, kJ$.

A **Faraday** is the amount of electrical charge needed to discharge one mole of a singly charged ion. 1 Faraday = 96 500 coulombs.

Fermentation happens when yeast breaks down a sugar into ethanol and carbon dioxide.

A **formula** of an element or compound shows which elements are present and in what proportion.

Fossil fuels are those produced many millions of years ago from the decaying remains of plants or animals. Examples of fossil fuels are coal, oil and natural gas.

A **fuel** is a substance that burns in air or oxygen, giving out heat energy.

A **giant structure** is an arrangement of atoms or ions that is repeated over and over again throughout the whole of the substance.

Half life is the time taken for half the atoms in a sample of a radioactive chemical to break down.

A **homologous series** is a 'family' of organic chemicals with members of the family having similar structures, properties and general formula.

Hydrated means 'containing water'. Hydrated salts contain water of crystallisation.

Hydrocarbons are compounds of hydrogen and carbon.

Hydrolysis is the breaking down of a compound by reacting it with water. A catalyst is sometimes used as well.

Indicators are compounds that change colour at a particular pH value.

Ions are atoms or groups of atoms with an electrical charge.

Isomers have the same molecular formula, but with atoms arranged in a different structure.

Isotopes are atoms of the same element but containing different numbers of neutrons. They have the same atomic number but different mass numbers, e.g. $^{12}_{6}C$ and $^{14}_{6}C$.

Latent heat of fusion is the energy needed to turn one mole of a substance, at its melting point, from a solid to a liquid (ΔH_{fus}).

Latent heat of vaporisation is the energy needed to turn one mole of a substance, at its boiling point, from a liquid to a gas. (ΔH_{vap}).

A **macromolecule** is a giant structure of atoms held together by covalent bonds, e.g. diamond, silica.

Mass number is the number of protons + neutrons in an atom. It is shown above the symbol of the element: $^{12}_{6}C$ has a mass number of 12.

Molarity is the number of moles of a substance dissolved in one litre of a solution, e.g. a 1.5 M (molar) solution contains 1.5 moles of solute dissolved in each litre of solution.

A **mole** is the amount of substance that chemists often use to measure chemicals in. One mole of an element is its relative atomic mass in grams, e.g. C = 12, so one mole of carbon atoms weighs 12 g.

Molecules are groups of atoms held together by covalent bonds. Molecules may be elements (e.g. H_2) or compounds (e.g. H_2O). They may be small (e.g. NH_3) or large (e.g. poly(ethene)).

A **mixture** contains two or more substances that can be easily separated by physical means, such as boiling, filtration etc.

A **nanometre** (nm) is a very small unit of measurement, used to describe the size of atoms. One nanometre is a metre divided ten, nine times over (1×10^{-9} m).

Neutralisation occurs when an acid and a base react together to produce a salt.

Neutrons are particles in the nucleus of an atom. They have a mass but no electrical charge.

The **nucleus** of an atom is its small central core, made of protons and neutrons.

Organic chemistry is the study of the compounds that carbon forms with other elements.

Oxidation happens when a substance gains oxygen in a chemical reaction. Oxidation is loss of electrons.

An **oxidising agent** is one that brings about oxidation. Oxidising agents often contain a lot of oxygen, e.g. $KMnO_4$.

The **periodic table** sets out the chemical elements in order of their atomic numbers. Rows going across the table are called periods, and columns going down are called groups.

pH is a number that shows how acid or alkaline solution is. The pH scale goes from 1 to 14. pH 1 is very acidic, pH 7 is neutral and pH 14 is very alkaline.

The **physical properties** of a substance are things that can be measured or observed about it, such as colour, density, boiling point etc.

A **polymer** is a large molecule formed by reacting many small molecules together. Poly(ethene) is a polymer made by reacting many ethene molecules together.

A **precipitate** is an insoluble substance formed during a chemical reaction in solution.

Protons are positively charged particles found in the nucleus of atoms.

A **radical** is an ion made from a group of several atoms e.g. CO_3^{2-}; SO_4^{2-}; NH_4^+.

Radioactive atoms have an unstable nucleus. When this breaks down, the atom gives off radiation in the form of α and/or β particles.

The **reactivity series** lists elements in order of how reactive they are. A more reactive element will displace a less reactive one from a solution of its salt.

A **reducing agent** is one that brings about reduction. Reactive metals are good reducing agents, e.g. zinc.

Reduction happens when a substance loses oxygen in a chemical reaction. Reduction is a gain of electrons.

Relative atomic mass (A_r) of an element is a number that compares the mass of each atom with all the others. Relative atomic mass is measured on the carbon-12 scale, where all atoms are compared to the mass of an atom of carbon-12, which is taken to be 12.000 000.

Relative molecular mass (M_r) is the sum of the relative atomic masses of each of the atoms in one mole of a substance.

A **salt** is formed when an acid and base neutralise each other. Salts always contain two ions – one from the acid and one from the base, e.g. sodium chloride contains sodium ions from an alkali such as sodium hydroxide and chloride ions from an acid such as hydrochloric acid.

Saturated molecules are organic compounds, where each carbon atom is bonded to its maximum of four other atoms. Saturated compounds always contain single covalent bonds.

A **saturated solution** contains the maximum amount possible of solute dissolved in a solution at that temperature.

Solubility measures how well a substance dissolves in a particular solvent at a given temperature. It is measured in grams of solute per 100 g water.

A **solute** is the substance that has been dissolved to make a solution.

A **solution** is formed when a solid, liquid or gas is dissolved into a solvent. Aqueous solutions are formed when the solvent used is water.

A **solvent** is any liquid that dissolves substances into itself.

State symbols show whether a substance shown in a equation is a solid (s), liquid (l), gas (g) or is in aqueous solution (aq).

Sublimation happens when a solid turns straight into a gas, or a gas turns straight into a solid, without the liquid state in between.

A **symbol** is one or two letters that are used to represent each element, e.g. the symbol for carbon is C, and for iron Fe.

Unsaturated molecules are organic compounds, where each carbon atom is bonded to only two or three other atoms. Unsaturated compounds always contain double or even triple covalent bonds.

Water of crystallisation is water that is loosely bonded into crystals of some salts, e.g. $CuSO_4 \cdot 5H_2O$.

X-ray diffraction of substances is a way of finding out the arrangement of atoms. When X-rays are shone onto the substance, a pattern of dots is formed from which the structure can be deduced.

Index

For items with more than one page number, bold type indicates main reference.

A
acid rain 239
acid strength 135
acids 133
addition reaction 190
aerosol sprays 25
air pollution 24
airships 173
alcoholic drinks 199
alkali metals 150
alkalis 136
allotropes, carbon 183
allotropes, sulphur 237
aluminium
   production 223
   structure 94
   uses 224
ammonia 136, 232, 243–**244**
ammonium chloride **169**, 245
anaemia 178
anhydrous crystals 38
anions 218
anode 218
argon 24, 80, **172**
aspirin 201
atomic number **78**, 251
atoms 4
Avogadro's number 102

B
balancing equations 127
barium 155
bases 137
batteries 229
beryllium 155
beta decay 253
biodegradable plastics 201
blast furnace 177
bleach 170
boiling 58
bromine 164, **166**
bromine diffusion 55
Brownian movement 56
butane 188
butene 189

C
caesium 150
calcium 155, **158**
   carbonate **155**, 158
   hydroxide **136**, 156, 158
   hydroxide solution
      (limewater) **23**, 158
   oxide **156**, 158
   phosphate 155
   sulphate 159
cancer treatment 255
carbohydrates 197
carbon 182
   dioxide 22
   monoxide 25
carbon-12 scale 251
catalysts **71**, 176
cathode 218
cations 218
cells 228
changes of state **58**, 205
chemical
   'families' 148
   energy 204
   properties 19
   reaction 9, **14**
Chernobyl 255
chlorine 165
chromatography 8
chrome plating 179
chromium 174
citric acid 133
coal 184
cobalt 174
combustion 29
   heat of 213
compounds 9
concentration, effect on rates 68
condensing 60
Contact process 239
copper 174
copper(II)
   chloride, preparation 142
   oxide, formula 109
   sulphate, electrolysis **220**, 222
   sulphate, preparation 140
coulombs 221
covalent bonds 88
cracking 190
crystal shapes 57
Curie, Marie 250

D
decay curves 254
decomposition 20
density
   definition 35
   of transition metals 175
detergents 198
diamond 183
diffusion
   in gases 53
   in liquids 56
displacement **49**, 167
dissolving 59
distillation, fractional **7**, 18, 187
distillation, simple **6**–7
distress flares 230
DNA molecule 203
drilling bit 183
dry batteries 229
dynamic equilibrium 233

E
E-numbers 196
effervescence 22
electric
   current 94
   kettle 206
   powered vehicles 229
electrical energy 204
electrodes 218
electrolysis 218
electrolyte 218
electronic configuration 79
electrons **76**, 79
electrostatic attraction of ions 83
element 4
empirical formula 110
endothermic reactions 211–**212**
energy 204
energy diagram 211
enzymes 71
equations 15, **122**
equations, balancing 127
equilibrium 233
ethane 188
ethanoic acid 133
ethanol 199
   combustion of 213
ethene **189**, 199
evaporation 58
exhaust fumes 73
exothermic reactions 210

F
Faradays 221
fats 197
fertilisers **242**, 247
fluoride toothpastes 170

fluorine 164
food preservatives 239
formula 13
   from reacting masses 108
   of ionic compounds 86
fossil fuels 186
'fountain' experiment 244
fractional distillation 7, 18, 187
fractionating column 7, **187**
freezing 60
fructose 197
fuels **213**, 214
fusion (melting) 208
fusion energy 214

G
gamma rays 253
gas masks 165
gases 53
   effect of temperature 112
germanium 182
giant structure **28**, 57, 92
glass 154
glucose 197
grain mountain 247
graphite 183

H
Haber process 232, **243**
Haber, Fritz 243
hair colour 176
hair conditioner 138
half life 254
halogens 164
halothane 201
hardness in water **159**–160, 198
heat energy 204
heat of combustion 213
'heavy' metals 174
helium 172
helium atom, structure 76
Hodgkin, Dorothy 57
homologous series 189
hydrated crystals 38
hydrocarbons 187
hydrochloric acid 133, **168**
hydrogen 31
   chloride 167, **168**
   ions 135
   peroxide **20**, 71
hydroxide ions 137

I
ice 35
immiscible liquids 200
indicators 132

ink 6
insulation of homes 215
iodine 164, **166**
iodine trichloride 230
ionic compounds 81
ions, table of 86
ions with several charges 84
iron 174
   and sulphur mixture 6
   extraction 177
   in blood 178
iron(II) chloride 176
iron(III) bromide 167
isomers 192
isotopes 252

J
jewels, colour 176

K
kinetic energy 204
krypton 172

L
large molecules 91
latent heat
   of fusion 208
   of vaporisation 207
lead 182
   bromide, electrolysis 219
   sulphate, preparation 143
   in petrol 184
'lead' in pencils 183
legumes 242
light bulbs 80, **173**
limestone 155
limewater test 23
liquids 56
lithium 150
   chloride 153
litmus 132
litres 111

M
magnesium 155
   chloride 155, **157**
   oxide 108, **156**
   sulphate, preparation 139
malnutrition 247
manganese 174
marble 155
margarine
   from oils 33
   polyunsaturated 190

melamine 202
melting **58**, 59
metal oxides 29
   reaction with hydrogen 48
metallic bonds 94
metals
   physical properties 28
   reaction with acids 46
   reaction with oxygen 44
   reaction with water 45
   structure 94
methane 188
methyl orange 132
mixture 6
molarity 114
molecular formula 110
molecule **14**, 54
molecules
   large 91
   small 90
moles
   and structure 103, **118**
   in solution 114
   of atoms 104
   of gases 111
   of molecules 106
monoclinic sulphur 237
monomer 200

N
nanometres 77
'native' copper 174
neon 172
neutrons 76
nickel 174
nitric acid 133, **246**
nitrogen 19
   cycle 243
   fertiliser 246
   fixing 242
   monoxide 246
noble gases 172
non-metals 29
non-stick surfaces 170
NPK fertilisers 243
nuclear energy 204
nuclear fusion 214
nucleus of atom 76
nuclear power stations 255
nylon **200**, 202

O
oiled sea birds 187
organic chemistry 186
oxidation 33, **223**
oxides 29
oxygen 20
ozone layer 25

P

paraquat 247
pencil 'lead' 183
periodic table 146–7
'person' recipe 5
pesticides 247
pH 132
pharmacology 201
phenolphthalein 132
photography 170
physical property 6, **19**
Pietà 155
plastic sulphur 238
pollution
    of air 24
    of water 40
poly(ethene) **200**, 202
    molecule 91
polymers 200
polyurethane 202
portable gas cookers 189
potassium 150
    chloride 153
    chromate(VI) 232
    dichromate(VI) 232
    hydroxide 152
    oxide 152
precipitation **23**, 143
pressure – effect on rates 69
product 16
propane 188
propene 189
proteins 242
protons 76
PTFE 202
PVC 202

Q

quartz watch 92

R

radicals 85
radioactivity 250
radon 172
rates of reaction 64
reactant 16
reactivity series 47, **51**
reduction 33, **223**
relative atomic mass 100

relative molecular mass 105
reversible reactions 230
rhombic sulphur 237
rock salt 6
Rotorua 236
rubidium 150

S

salt mines 150
salting roads 154
salts 138
saturated
    molecules 189
    solution 36
saturation – test for 139
scandium 174
scum 160, **198**
sea water 150
seaweed 164
sewage treatment 39
shampoo 138
silicon 182
    chips 184
    dioxide structure 92
silver
    bromide 170
    plating 220
size of atoms 77
slag 177
small molecules 90
smoke cell 54
soap 198
soapless detergents 198
sodium 150
    chloride **153**, 167, 224
    hydroxide **136**, 152
    nitrate, preparation 141
    oxide 152
solar panels 214
soldering 184
solids 57
solubility
    definition 36
    of various compounds 142
solution 36
starch 197
state symbol 16
states of matter 52

steel 178
stonework erosion 24
street lamps 154
strontium 155
sublimation 8, **59**
sugars 197
sulphur 236
    and iron mixture 6
    dioxide 239
    trioxide 239
sulphuric acid 133, **239**, 240
surface area **71**, 72
swimming pools 170
symbol 12

T

tarnishing 44
'Teflon' 170
temperature – effect on rates 67
thunderstorms 242
tidal power 215
tin 182
titanium 174
transition metals 174

U

universal indicator 132
unsaturated molecules 189

V

vanadium 174
vinegar 133

W

water 34
    of crystallisation 38
    pollution 40
    tests for 38
    treatment 39
wind-powered generator **193**, 214
wind turbine 214

X

xenon 172
X-ray diffraction 57